Marie-José Gransard teaches a course, 'Venice in Literature', in Cannaregio and conducts tours of the city. She has worked with Hilary Spurling on her biography of Matisse and with Anthony Holden for his biography of Lorenzo Da Ponte. She divides her time between Venice and London.

Venice

A LITERARY GUIDE FOR TRAVELLERS

Marie-José Gransard

I.B. TAURIS

LONDON · NEW YORK

Published in 2016 by
I.B.Tauris & Co. Ltd
London • New York
www.ibtauris.com

ISBN: 978 1 78076 983 7
eISBN: 978 0 85772 914 9

A full CIP record for this book is available from the British Library
A full CIP record is available from the Library of Congress

Library of Congress Catalog Card Number: available

Typeset by JCS Publishing Services Ltd, www.jcs-publishing.co.uk
Printed and bound in Sweden by ScandBook AB

For Noam, Theo and Sascha

Contents

ILLUSTRATIONS

Unless stated otherwise, all photos are by the author, Lucio Marco Zorzi and Noam Sala Budgen.

Preface

Soon after my arrival in Venice 11 years ago, I was invited to give a series of cultural seminars in Italian for adult Venetians; I chose to cover visitors who had left a literary legacy about the city. This book is the result of my research. I embarked on the task with enthusiasm, changing countries of origin each year to avoid repetition. We first looked at English writers and artists, followed by Germans, Spaniards and so on. When we had covered most nationalities, but not all writers by any means, I moved to the largely neglected field of women writers and artists in Venice, including this time native Venetians and others from Europe and the United States. The demi-monde of Venice is a part of this, of course, but I have been led naturally to the theme for my future teaching programme, which will cover the Venetian women who left very different marks on the city and spent their lives involved in manual work, such as the lace-makers, pearl-stringers and milliners. All this is also occasionally recorded in various writings.

I took my students out of the classroom, partly to satisfy my own curiosity about the city, but also to share my exploration with them. Although they had spent their whole lives in Venice, most of them had never been given the opportunity to enter mythical and beautiful palazzi and historic buildings. Many still stay in their own part of the city (*sestiere*) and rarely venture very far beyond it. Discovering the places where writers and artists lived, stayed and worked was a part of the fun, and in a small city like Venice one could make progress in a very short time. Having arranged to visit these private and public places, we talked about the writers' lives and circumstances in Venice and read extracts from their writings.

This proved popular with the students and we were allowed access to magical places, thanks to the extraordinary hospitality and generosity of their current guardians or owners.

This guide is not intended to be a standard guide to Venice and its sights. Most people reading it will have access to at least one of the legion of specialist guides of the city. I am attempting to show Venice to my reader through the chosen writer or artist's eyes, and to indicate, where I can, the places and buildings associated with each one. The layout of Venice has not changed very much in the last five hundred years, and so it is still possible to find many places as the writers found them. One of the main differences will probably be that up to the end of the nineteenth century most people (particularly the wealthy) would have travelled from place to place on the water, generally in a gondola, sometimes privately owned or rented, and would have approached a palace or a house from the waterside (*porta d'acqua*). Nowadays most houses and palaces are approached from the less prominent and sometimes hidden service door on the street side.

In spite of years of research in the libraries, walking around, listening and inquiring, I know that I have only scratched the surface. New facts, new stories and new writers appear constantly. One contact leads with serendipity to another. This guide does not therefore claim to give an exhaustive view of writers in Venice. My selection is personal and includes lesser-known writers, in the hope that my readers will share some of the excitement of discovery. As well as professional writers, I have included artists, musicians and ambassadors, as so many wrote evocatively about the city and it would be so difficult to omit them. Their names are in bold in the text to highlight their written legacy or the part they have played in the story of Venice.

Key to Map (Overleaf)

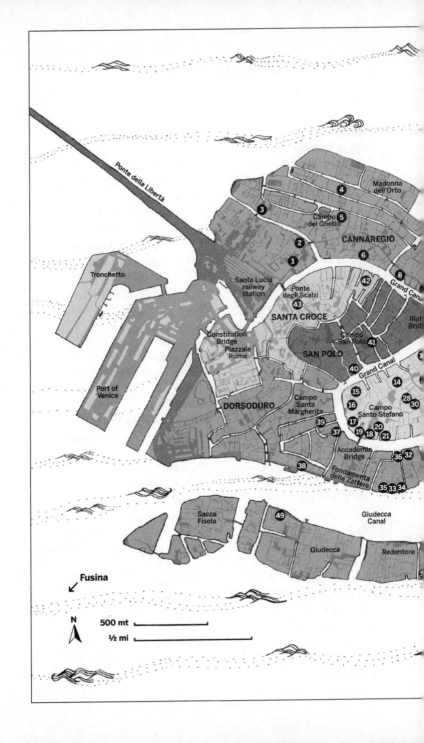

Illustration: Francesca Saccani – Graphic design: Anna Saccani

ACKNOWLEDGEMENTS

This has necessarily been a work of collaboration, as I have received guidance, assistance and suggestions from many quarters. My research has been carried out mainly in libraries: in London the British Library; in Venice the Archives, the Marciana, the Querini Stampalia, the Correr Museum, Ateneo Veneto and Fondazione Cini. All have been most accommodating, and staff at the Marciana kindly allowed me to photograph their bust of Petrarch. I have consulted David Budgen (who also provided the translation of Pushkin), Vincenzo Patanè, John Venning, Edward Williams, Marco Zentiluomo and Lucio Marco Zorzi for their expert knowledge. I would like to thank them all, as well as Pamela Morgan for having checked my work, and especially Jenifer Ball, who has for more than a year stood by to correct, translate and help me to shape what was originally in six languages. To Lucio Marco Zorzi and Mariagrazia Dammicco I owe in great part my knowledge of the city and its stories. My son Sebastian has encouraged me throughout and given me much professional advice. The cover photograph was taken by my grandson Noam. The map was commissioned from graphic artists Anna and Francesca Saccani.

I am also very grateful to the Venetians who have become my students, friends and colleagues, and to others, too many to name, who in the last ten years have generously allowed me to take my students into their houses, palaces, foundations, museums, gardens, hotels, bars and offices.

1

INTRODUCTION

There is nothing new to be said about her.

(Henry James, *Italian Hours*)

From the very beginning Venice has been a magnet, a crossroads for all kinds of travellers, owing to its geographical situation, its wealth and power, its aesthetic appeal and its magical scenery. Travellers and visitors became increasingly drawn by its tragic decline in the nineteenth century.

It was often the first stop in a long journey south through Italy. Travellers would also plan to include Padua, Vicenza, Florence, Rome and Naples, and continue to Sicily. Throughout the centuries a constant stream of people has moved through or stayed in Venice. Before the twentieth century, visitors did not come to shop, feed pigeons and stare at the Basilica or climb the Campanile. They came in much smaller numbers, and for many reasons. Trade brought Turks, Germans, Slavs and Greeks. Venice was the most popular and best organised point of departure for the long and hazardous journey by sea for Crusaders to Jerusalem and it was a refuge for those whose religion was threatened: Knights Templar, Knights of Malta, Armenian Mechitarists, Franciscans, Benedictines, Jesuits, Jews and Gesuati. For centuries the Venetian Republic was seen as a haven for them, a place to settle in peace, away from persecution.

The Republic of Venice was known as La Serenissima – 'the Most Serene' – and foreigners had always been impressed by its reputation for tolerance, hospitality and generosity. According to one sixteenth-century writer, Francesco Sansovino, the city's name came from the Latin *veni etiam*, 'come back again' or 'return to this beautiful place'.

The city certainly knew then and knows now how to entertain. Religious festivities for Ascension Day (Festa della Sensa), for example, were always followed by an impressive meal given also to pilgrims, and intended to enhance the city's reputation. On these occasions the head of the Republic, the doge, offered trays of sweetmeats as well as wines in great quantities. Venetian regattas, pageantry, processions, bull runs, musical and theatrical entertainments became famous worldwide. The wealth displayed profoundly impressed Henri III of France, whose table napkin at the Doge's banquet was made of sugar. A fourteenth-century visitor recorded seeing toys made of gold and people eating with a strange implement called a *forchetta* (fork).

The Serenissima was widely considered, rightly or wrongly, to be a model of democracy: 'Many historians agree that it generally provided better government than elsewhere,' wrote Elizabeth Horodowich in her 2009 *Brief History of Venice*.

Venice provided a haven for those deprived of free expression in the rest of Europe. The first publishing houses were founded in Venice in the fourteenth and fifteenth centuries, providing an outlet for a remarkable range of classical works and drawing contemporary writers to the city to be published. The concept of Venice as a sanctuary allowing personal freedom persisted to the twentieth century. Many Russians fleeing censorship, the threat of imprisonment, execution or the gulag after the 1917 revolution gathered in the city, particularly favouring the island of the Lido. The poet Alexander Pushkin dreamed in the nineteenth century of this escape, but he was never to fulfil it because for political reasons he was never allowed to leave tsarist Russia.

Venice prided itself on being in the vanguard in many areas, not all of them benign: its dress code (envied for its elegance, opulence and innovation everywhere in Europe), the first ghetto, the first quarantine hospitals, the first hospital for tuberculosis sufferers, the first biological warfare protection, the first bank, lottery, newspaper, travel guidebook (by Francesco Sansovino), the first industrial revolution, first opera house open to the paying public, the first European theatre, the first coffee house, and, as we have seen, the first table fork. Venetians claim even to have invented playing cards. This extraordinarily innovative city attracted a stream of writers and artists, including Albrecht Dürer, Verrocchio, Leonardo da Vinci, Jacopo Sansovino, Palladio and Canova. Some visitors remained in the city for long periods as ambassadors – Dante, Petrarch, Sir Henry Wotton, the Duke of Montealegre and Quevedo – or as consuls (Joseph Smith) or as mere embassy secretaries (Rousseau, Nicolas Amelot de La Houssaye). Although as foreigners they were confined to some areas of the city and were not allowed to deal directly with Venetian patricians, they reported in their writings the generally pleasant Venetian way of life.

In the nineteenth century, many young men, particularly from England and Germany, were sent by their wealthy and powerful families on a Grand Tour to complete their cultural education, or on shopping missions (Walpole, Goethe, Ruskin). Others came for love, like Lady Mary Wortley Montagu, George Sand and Alfred de Musset. Thomas Coryat and Charles de Brosses were attracted by Venice's famous courtesans. Visitors to Venice naturally took in museums, churches and palaces, a trip up the Brenta River, a stop at Padua, Vicenza or Treviso, Baedeker later clutched dutifully in hand, and Ruskin's *The Stones of Venice*. Some like Byron and Shelley ventured further and went to Este, others as far as Trieste on the Adriatic, like the German poet Rilke.

Venice represented the ultimate city for those who sought its past fame, beauty, power and wealth nostalgically. Mark Twain called it the 'Venice of poetry and romance'. For a long time it was, with Paris and London, one of the largest and most powerful cities in Europe, a major centre for music and entertainment. It offered variety and excitement, coloured by the less salubrious reputation it had enjoyed since the fifteenth century. In the eighteenth century those who came looking for liberty found also libertinage, as it had become a city of earthly pleasures, with gambling, alluring amorous adventures, endless festivities and carnivals. This was another concept of paradise altogether, a *centro dei piaseri* (centre of pleasure) according to Giorgio Baffo, a seventeenth-century licentious Venetian poet. Lady Mary Wortley Montagu described it more candidly as 'a sink of vice'. It was arguably Europe's most popular playground for the privileged and adventurous.

This changed abruptly in 1797 when, after the French Revolution, the French army led by Bonaparte took the city and the last doge was deposed. The French were succeeded by an Austrian occupation, which was to last until 1866. The fallen city then gained popularity for different reasons, inspiring a deluge of writing, in praise of or bewailing its faded beauty and tragic fate. Romantic poets and writers saw the fall of the Venetian Republic as a catastrophic event, putting an end to the city's glorious past. It had become a melancholic yet fascinating fallen giant, continuing to inspire Romantic poets, scholars, historians, painters and artists. On his deathbed, the 25-year-old Keats, who had not managed to go further than Rome, was reported to have exclaimed: 'To Venice!' Proust and Goethe knew all about it before setting foot in the city, and Edgar Allan Poe set his short story 'The Appointment' in a fantasy Venice which he knew mainly through Byron's writings.

The 'myth' did not work its magic on everyone, however; the city had its detractors. Futurist poet and writer Marinetti professed to hate the place so much that he planned his own vision of the city with motorways and factories, speeding towards the future. Other detractors included D. H. Lawrence and more recently the French philosopher Régis Debray, who wrote a mostly critical pamphlet *Against Venice* (*Contre Venise*) in an attempt to clear away the clichés. But today, for many, Venice remains a cultural centre to which enlightened visitors come for theatre, concerts, exhibitions, art and film festivals, marathons, cooking competitions, boat races and the Carnival, and to experience this strange aquatic city, so unlike anywhere else in the world.

Some have been attracted and others repulsed by the image of Venice as a dangerous location full of mystery and darkness. Dante, one of the first recorded visitors, approaching the city through the lagoon, was struck by the humid, foggy, melancholic, almost hellish scenery. Many centuries later, Dickens described his arrival in a spectral scene which dissolved into the fog like a Turner painting. The tradition of the Gothic novel and horror story was inspired partly by the treatment of prisoners dying slowly in the infamous Venetian prisons, public executions, torture, the power and excesses of the Inquisition, the gloomy deteriorating palaces with their decadent relics of the ancient aristocracy. Nineteenth- and twentieth-century literature has a long list of writers, including Michael Dibdin and Donna Leon, who have used the city as a background for tales of mystery, fear, danger and death, not to mention the more than 500 films which have been shot there, of which Nicholas Roeg's *Don't Look Now* and Luchino Visconti's *Death in Venice* remain unforgettable.

It can now take less than half a day to travel from London to Venice. Once the railway line reached the city in 1846 it became possible to enjoy a glorious arrival by train. Before then, getting to Venice could take months, encountering difficult and dangerous conditions. The approach by boat through Fusina was slow and unpleasant, cold and dangerous, particularly at night and in the depth of winter. Incredibly, the English seventeenth-century traveller Thomas Coryat walked from his native Somerset in the south-west of England all the way to Venice.

Many who did arrive safe and sound were not immediately allowed in, but were held in *lazzaretti* (quarantine centres) for as long as two months, as happened to French writer Rousseau. George Sand and Musset were both ill on arrival. Even at the end of the nineteenth century, the journey was taxing, as described in Thomas Mann's *Death in Venice*. His protagonist Aschenbach unusually travels by train to Trieste, and then makes an uncomfortable boat journey, followed by a disturbing gondola trip to the Lido. When they had finally recovered, Venice captured the imagination of most visitors.

This literary guide will look at more than 100 writers, including artists, musicians and painters who left a written testimony. The choice is personal and inevitably not comprehensive, but it seemed important to include not only English and American writers, but also French, Russian, Spanish, German and Italian. And what about the Venetians? Mary McCarthy in her 1956 study *Venice Observed* decided rather unfairly: 'There aren't any Venetian writers apart from Goldoni.' She might have mentioned Casanova, who knew how to tell a good story, and a number of others. I have included some lesser-known Venetians, chroniclers such as Marino Sanudo and Francesco Sansovino. But on the whole they are greatly outnumbered by the outsiders who have written essays, memoirs, diaries, letters, poems and novels dedicated to this extraordinary place which continues to fascinate and inspire. The writings of ambassadors have also been included, as their correspondence and dispatches are both entertaining and informative. This book will perhaps encourage the reader to make his or her own discoveries.

The deluge of writing on Venetian subjects continues: according to a local bookshop, an average of 500 new books appears every year on the subject. Let Friedrich Nietzsche perhaps have the last word for the moment: 'A hundred deep solitudes create together the image of Venice – this is her magic. An image for the men of the future.'

FAITH, ART AND POLITICS

Indeed it seems as if the whole world flocks there and that human beings have concentrated all their force for trading.

(Pietro Casola, 1494)

From the Middle Ages and throughout the Renaissance, Venice was sought out by visitors, pilgrims waiting for onward transport to the Holy Land, or others attracted by the ultimate trading city. Merchants may not have been very diligent reporters on life in the Serenissima, but many others did keep written records of their visit. Some pilgrims left testimonies, like Ignatius Loyola, as did the French, English and Spanish ambassadors and their secretaries, including Rousseau. Foreign scholars such as Rawdon Brown, and artists and painters like Dürer, Velázquez and Turner, invited to the city to work or to study, also left impressions, generally in letters.

During the long wait to embark for the Holy Land, pilgrims had plenty of time to explore the hundreds of churches and religious institutions, not for the artworks or great buildings, but rather to see the precious relics, which were a great attraction. After the sack of Constantinople by Venice in 1204, there was an abundance of relics. The historian Ana Munk describes in her 2006 article, 'The Art of Relic Cults in Trecento Venice', how profitable to the city was 'the steady revenue generated by holy pilgrimages to Venice'. Churches like San Salvatore and San Cassiano were rich in relics which can still be seen today. Munk cites a visiting chancellor from the fifteenth-century court of Francesco Sforza in Milan whose 'experience of the church interior revolved mainly around a performing object, a bleeding cross he saw in the middle of the church'.

Almost forgotten and now hardly visited, many of these are still *in situ*, like the body of Santa Lucia in San Geremia, her face covered by a metal mask to hide the signs of deterioration. In his intriguing 2010 guide *Secret Venice* the French publisher Thomas Jongley and his local collaborators offer an impressive list of relics, many still housed in the Treasury of the Basilica, including 'the arm with which St George is said to have held the lance that killed the dragon, a lock of Virgin's hair, [. . .] a phial of Christ's blood'.

Seventeenth-century travellers like **François Maximilien Misson** (1650–1722) were more sceptical about the profusion of relics in the city. A French Protestant who fled France for his own safety after the revocation of the Edict of Nantes in 1685, Misson joined the many Huguenots who took refuge in England. Appointed as tutor to a young English nobleman, he accompanied his charge to Italy in 1687–8 and wrote his *New Journey to Italy* (*Nouveau voyage d'Italie*) of 1691 in the form of 41 letters. Letters 16 to 18 and 25 are dedicated to Venice. In these the fictitious recipient of the letters is supposed to have requested information about the city. The book was popular with travellers, and it is particularly informative on Venetian relics.

A staunch Protestant, Misson is disparaging about the actual value or authenticity of the relics he encounters, but he seems to be obsessed, as he proceeds to list them: 'At San Moisè they keep diverse relics which consist of legs, arms and jaws [. . .] When I find something better, perhaps the foreskin of the Philistine, the verruca of St Francis, the Trojan Horse's shoe, (because everything is good enough to be a relic), I will tell you.' Among the relics he saw in the Basilica, he mentions pieces of the True Cross, bones, the Virgin's hair and milk, and Moses' stone in the Zen Chapel. He writes in Letter 25: 'When we visited the Treasury, they had not told us anything about St Mark's thumb, nor that the saint had mutilated himself to avoid being made a priest: but the legend states that this important event took place.' Misson also strongly recommends spending Carnival in Venice and Holy Week in Rome.

In the Middle Ages, Venice was often a starting point for pilgrims planning a trip to the Holy Land. Travel by sea was more comfortable and safer than overland, but cost 30 to 40 ducats – a small fortune at the time. Venice's popularity lay not only in its convenient location, but also in its reputation as a sacred place, a gate of heaven. As Francesco Sansovino put it, it was 'revered by everyone as a sacred thing on earth to be worshipped, were this possible'. The city had even been visited by saints, including **Francis of Assisi** (1182–1226), there in 1220 or 1224, according to the legend. The story goes that, returning from the Holy Land during the Fifth Crusade, and staying on the small Venetian island known now as San Francesco del Deserto, St Francis planted his pilgrim's staff in the neighbouring marshes. It grew miraculously into a pine (or perhaps cypress) tree, in which birds began to sing. As he started praying, the birds carried on singing, and, distracted, he asked them to stop, whereupon they dutifully obeyed. On the spot where this miracle happened, a Franciscan monastery was founded; it is still occupied by Franciscan monks and can be visited or used for retreat.

Another future saint arrived in Venice for the same reason a couple of centuries later. Born in Azpeitia in the Spanish Basque country, **Ignatius Loyola** (1491–1556) had started a military career, which he abandoned in 1521 after being seriously injured. This led to his conversion and to a life of prayer and asceticism. Having made a vow of poverty, he decided at the age of 30 to dedicate himself to philosophy and theology, studying in Alcalá and Paris. Approaching Venice by boat in 1524, the future founder of the Order of Jesuits was miraculously allowed in without any formalities: 'When they arrived in Venice, the guards went to inspect their boat and he was the only one allowed in.' His contemporary memoirist continues to recount that once in Venice, where 'the entire world flocks', he wondered at the 'inestimable value of goods in shops and markets'.

Like so many, Ignatius was on his way to the Holy Land, but had no money and had to survive by begging and sleeping rough under the arcades of Procuratie Vecchie, and possibly near the Punta della Dogana, close to the present seminary. He probably visited many churches, packed with relics. His journey to Palestine was, we may suppose, supported by Doge Andrea Gritti, who received him personally. He embarked on the *Negrona* in Venice and arrived via Cyprus at Jaffa on 25 July 1524, fortified by several apparitions of God and the prospect of seeing Jerusalem. Leaving Palestine on 3 October, he arrived by boat in Puglia in the south of Italy and walked back to Venice, where he arrived in January 1525. During the next few years he continued his studies in Paris and Spain, and then returned to Venice in 1536 to prepare a second pilgrimage. This time he stayed near what is now Molino Stucky on Giudecca at San Biagio Hospital (Ospedale degli Incurabili di San Biagio), an institution which traditionally housed pilgrims heading for Palestine. His living conditions had improved. As he wrote to Jaime Cazador, 'I have been living mainly in Venice for a month and a half, and my health has enormously improved [. . .] I feel I could not find more favourable conditions of life anywhere else in this country.'

However, continuing hostilities with Turkey prevented him from making this second pilgrimage. Instead he was ordained on 24 June in Venice and later went to Rome, where in 1539 he founded the Society of Jesus, which he had conceived in Venice in 1537. He died in Rome in 1556. The time he spent in Venice, as well as the journey to the Holy Land, were recorded in *A Pilgrim's Journey: Autobiography of St Ignatius de Loyola* (1586), written by his travelling companion and confessor Luis Gonçalves de Camara, and in many letters. In spite of the 'various miracles' which saved Ignatius' life on numerous occasions, the road to the Holy Land was paved with danger, and the vivid account describes plague, hunger, theft, attacks and threats from the Turks.

His legacy to Venice, thanks to his friendship with the prior of the Trinità Convent, was the founding of a Jesuit College in 1550 near Santa Maria della Salute. Ignatius is described elsewhere as 'a smallish Spaniard, a little lame (he had undergone an amputation), with lively eyes'. A more conventional representation can be found in at least three church paintings in Venice, including *The Deposition of Christ with Saints* by Augustine Ugolini in San Geremia.

Because of the Jesuits' allegiance to Pope Paul V, they became unwelcome in the Serenissima, which was in conflict with Rome, and were expelled between 1606 and 1657. Not until 1715 were the Jesuits, now supported by the powerful Manin family, able to build their impressively extravagant rococo church, Gesuiti, at Fondamente Nove. The extraordinarily exuberant decoration does not appeal to everyone, including Ruskin, and William Dean Howells later described it as 'indescribably table-clothy'. A statue of Loyola still occupies part of the altar.

Also noteworthy is **Pietro Casola** (1427–1507), a noble churchman from Milan who preceded Ignatius Loyola in Venice, embarking on his pilgrimage to Jerusalem in 1494. *Canon Pietro Casola's Pilgrimage to Jerusalem in the Year 1494* gave invaluable information on the dangers and vicissitudes encountered by these brave pilgrims, as well as detailed descriptions of the half-finished Doge's Palace and Venetian dress, particularly that of the ladies, of which he clearly disapproved:

> These Venetian women, especially the pretty ones, try as much as possible in public to show their chests – I mean the breasts and shoulders – so much so, that several times when I saw them I marvelled that their clothes did not fall off their backs [. . .] these Venetian women, both high and low, have pleasure in being seen and looked at; they are not afraid of the flies biting them [. . .] Perhaps this custom pleases others; it does not please me.

In fifteenth- and sixteenth-century Venice, many painters and artists braved the arduous journey to see Venetian art and sometimes even to work in the city. That was the case of German painter **Albrecht Dürer** (1471–1528). He is likely to have first arrived in 1494 from Nuremberg and lodged in the Fondaco dei Tedeschi near the Rialto, the centre for German traders. He would probably have spent time with painters such as Bellini, Vivarini and Mantegna.

It is documented that Dürer was in Venice between 1505 and 1507. He was by then a recognised and celebrated painter, his engravings already famous throughout Europe. On the night of 27 January 1505 a terrible fire had destroyed the Fondaco dei Tedeschi by the Rialto Bridge, and the decision was taken to rebuild it and have its external walls decorated by Titian and Giorgione. As it was impossible to stay in the damaged Fondaco, Dürer took lodgings nearby in the parish of San Bartolomeo, in an inn run by Peter Pender.

Dürer was in the city to paint an altarpiece, *La Festa del Rosario*, for the German community church of San Bartolomeo. He completed the project in four months. The altarpiece was moved out of Venice in 1606 and can now be seen in the Prague National Gallery. Although content with his work, Dürer was not happy with his relationship with Venetian painters, 'let me tell you that the painters here are very hostile to me', with the exception of Giovanni Bellini, who, according to Dürer, was 'still the best painter'. Bellini had completed a similar altarpiece in the Church of San Zaccaria. Perhaps the influence of Bellini can be seen in the presence of an angel musician at the Madonna's feet in Dürer's own altarpiece. The Venetian influence is suggested by Dürer's two portraits of women, now in Berlin and Vienna. These show similarities to portraits attributed to Bellini, originally in the famous collection of Andrea Vendramin, and are very similar to Giorgione's portrait of Laura. During his time in Venice, Dürer also completed *Christ among the Doctors*, at the same time that Cima di Conegliano was working on the same subject. Dürer did not spend all his time at his easel. He made the most of life, even taking dancing lessons – 'in Venice I became a gentleman.'

It can be assumed that, as Venetian painters were great admirers of his realistic approach, Dürer in turn had some influence on their depiction of religious scenes, which introduced background landscape and imitated his use of drapery. Some art historians note that, when he left the city, Dürer was using a greater range of colours, and his paintings were more suffused with light, suggesting the lasting influence of Titian or Giorgione.

His stay is well documented by the ten letters he wrote to his friend and patron Willibald Pirckheimer, in a mixture of Venetian and German dialect, as well as in Latin. In a letter sent on 7 February 1506, he wrote:

> I wish you were here in V. There are so many pleasant people here among the Italians in whose company I am more and more, and who ought without exception to appeal to you: they are studious, good, intelligent, lutenists and flute players, informed about painting, and so many high-minded and truly virtuous people, and who treat me with honour and respect. But there are also many who to my mind are the most untrustworthy, dishonest and thieving in the world [. . .] among the Italians I have many good friends who warn me not to eat or drink with their painters. Many of the latter are my enemies and copy my works in the churches [. . .] And then they criticise and say that because they are not in the old style they are therefore no good.

He also reported on the progress of his work, and on the various purchases he had been entrusted to make, buying rare books, carpets, pearls and precious stones. These letters show a great preoccupation with the cost of living in Venice, describing minutely all his financial dealings.

A little later, in 1541, the Arezzo-born **Giorgio Vasari** (1511–74) also visited Venice for the first time. He was already a well-known painter and architect, as well as the pupil and friend of 'the divine' Michelangelo, and arrived in Venice with some Michelangelo cartoons which he sold to the Spanish ambassador, Diego de Mendoza, for the handsome sum of 200 gold ducats. In spite of important commissions from the Pope and Duke Cosimo de' Medici to remodel and decorate palaces in Florence, he found the time to write what is generally considered the first art history, *The Lives of the Most Excellent Painters, Sculptors and Architects*, published in 1550. A second revised and enlarged edition followed in 1568. Its lasting success (Vasari's work is still read and used widely today) is due to the fact that he did not just give biographical and artistic facts (which were not always accurate) but was a good storyteller and gossip. His accounts were personal, since he also was well acquainted with artists such as Titian. It was Titian's friend, the poet Pietro Aretino, who invited Vasari and introduced him to his wide cultural and artistic connections, enabling him to see paintings by Titian, Giulio Romano and Correggio. Vasari was to return to the city for a short period in 1563, when he started revising *The Lives* and included Venetian painters such as Giorgione: 'Giorgione da Castelfranco, Venetian painter, who surpassed by far the Bellinis, whom the Venetians held in such esteem', adding, 'a man of the most humble origins, he was, however, nothing but gentle and well-mannered all his life. He was brought up in Venice, continuously took delight in affairs of the heart, and was so greatly pleased by the sound of the lute that, in his time, he played and sang divinely.'

Thanks to Vasari's description we know how Giorgione contributed to the frescoed decoration, now largely vanished, of the rebuilt Fondaco dei Tedeschi. He also mentions Giorgione's tragic death:

He fell in love with a lady, and they both took great pleasure from their love affair. It happened that in the year 1511 she was infected with the plague, but without knowing this Giorgione kept on visiting her as usual and caught the plague himself, so that before long, at the age of thirty-four, he passed on to another life, to the enormous sorrow of his many friends, who loved him for his talents, and to the detriment of the world, who lost them.

About Michelangelo's brief stay in Venice Vasari wrote: 'he arrived in Venice, where he wanted to meet and become acquainted with many gentlemen, he, who always had so little imagination [. . .] left Giudecca, where he had lodgings, and where, it is said, he drew at Doge Gritti's invitation for the city the Rialto Bridge, a design rich in ornament and invention.' Michelangelo's competition entry for the bridge was rejected, but his presence is recorded on Giudecca by the naming of Calle Michelangelo, the narrow street where he stayed.

Art historians still find Vasari's descriptions of paintings invaluable, especially since some of these works have disappeared, like those lost in the great fire which destroyed the Doge's Palace in 1571. Many more vanished or were stolen at the fall of the Republic. Vasari's descriptions were not restricted to the artists and cultural life in the city, as we see in this critical depiction of Piazza San Marco:

> In the year 1529 there were butchers' stalls between the two columns of the Piazza, with a number of small wooden booths, used for the vilest of purposes, and a shame as well as deformity to the place, offending the dignity of the Palace and the Piazza, while they could not but disgust all strangers who made their entry into Venice, by the side of San Giorgio.

Vasari had been corresponding since the early 1530s with Pietro Aretino. The banker Francesco Leoni offered him hospitality during his stay in the city, which had been planned specifically to paint the sets for a production of a play, *La Talanta*, commissioned by the Compagnia della Calza, with a text specially written by Aretino. The young gentlemen who belonged to this company organised entertainments for the Carnival festivities, with dinners, balls, regattas, tournaments and open-air theatrical performances. Local painters, such as Titian, had already contributed to these *apparati*, temporary installations in Piazza San Marco, or, in the case of *La Talanta*, in an unfinished building in the Cannaregio district. Vasari brought with him three assistant painters, and everything was completed in two months for the Carnival in February 1542. The production was a great success and commissions duly followed for Vasari, one an important decorative cycle for a church in Santo Spirito in Isola (the island where foreign ambassadors were welcomed before formally entering Venice). Vasari was also asked to paint the ceiling of Palazzo Corner-Spinelli, the family's home on the Grand Canal. After nine successful months in the city, he seriously considered staying for good. However, for some reason he left, abandoning the Santo Spirito project, which was then taken over by Titian. According to the chronicler Marino Sanudo, 'Vasari lived in Venice for thirteen months to paint a ceiling for Giovanni Cornaro [. . .] Sansovino, who was in charge of the building of Santo Spirito, had Vasari draw some cartoons for three large paintings for the ceiling [. . .] but after Vasari left Venice, the three paintings were commissioned to Titian, who completed them beautifully.'

Apart from a few drawings, nothing remains of the *apparato* which Vasari designed for *La Talanta*, as sets were normally destroyed after the last performance. However, we know that Aretino's friends, Titian and Jacopo Sansovino, were very complimentary about his contribution, acknowledged by Arentino in his play: 'I have been told verbally and in writing that a Signor Giorgio d'Arezzo, about 35 years old, has made a set and an *apparato* which have been admired by Sansovino and Titian, both great men.' (Vasari was in fact 32). The design was generally considered to be a great novelty in size and originality.

The friendship between Aretino and Titian is recorded in *The Lives*: 'it brought great honour and service to the said Titian, with the result that his brush gained fame abroad.' Vasari's book mentioned other Venetian painters like Antonio and Domenico Veneziano, Carpaccio, the Bellinis, Palma il Vecchio, Lorenzo Lotto and Jacopo Robusti Tintoretto, 'such a mighty brain!' However, Vasari was not always admired in the city, which is perhaps why he left, and was later criticised for factual inaccuracy.

One part of the ceiling painted by Vasari for Palazzo Corner-Spinelli, *La Fede*, has returned to Venice, and is now at Palazzo Grimani, a lavishly restored palace near Santa Maria Formosa, and there are plans to reconstitute the whole ceiling.

In *The Lives* Vasari had reported that El Greco, the Greek painter **Doménikos Theotokópoulos** (1541–1614), 'a Greek by birth and a disciple of Titian whom he so nearly imitated, that his paintings were mistaken for those of his master', had spent some time in Venice (from December 1566 to August 1568), after which he left for Rome for two years before coming back to Venice. There is limited documentary evidence of El Greco's two visits to Venice, apart from Vasari's report, which mentions that he visited the studios of Tintoretto, Jacopo Bassano and Titian. All his life he spoke a mixture of Castilian Spanish, Italian and Venetian dialect, as he was born in Venetian-controlled Crete (then called Candia by the Venetians) and his brother Manussos was an important official in the Venetian administrative government of Crete. El Greco went to work in Titian's studio, which had a radical influence on his painting. In a letter to Philip II of Spain on 2 December 1567, Titian refers to him as 'that most valiant young man, my disciple'. He was also strongly influenced by Tintoretto.

Half a century later, **Diego Velázquez** (1599–1660) followed him to Venice. More suited to court life, he was a protégé of Philip IV of Spain, who probably sent him to Venice in 1629. He stayed at the Spanish Embassy, the home of Don Cristóbal de Benavente y Benavides. His father-in-law, the painter Francisco Pacheco, reports in his 1649 *Art of Painting*:

> Following the King's orders he left Madrid with Marqués de Espinola, embarking in Barcelona on San Lorenzo day of the year 1629. He stopped in Venice and went to stay at the Spanish ambassador's house, who treated him well and had him sitting at his table; and because of the wars of the time, when he went out in the city he was protected by guards.

Indeed, because of the troubled political relationship between the Venetian state and Spain (it was very soon after the Bedmar Plot, described later), Spaniards were unpopular and treated very suspiciously. Velázquez's visit was assumed to be for espionage. In fact, the artist had come to look at Venetian painting, but was also on a mission to purchase paintings and statues for the King, and to have casts made from some of the best sculptures. It is known from a 1634 document that he bought a *Danaë* by Titian, a *Susanna* by Luca Cambiaso and a painting by Bassano. On his second trip to Italy in 1649, Velázquez brought with him Juan de Pareja, his servant, model and assistant. On this visit to Venice he arrived on 21 April and stayed again at the Spanish Embassy, living as a guest of the ambassador, Marquis de la Fuente. The 50-year-old painter was now famous. He had disembarked in Genoa and travelled also to Emilia, Naples and eventually to Rome, where he was to paint his famous portrait of Pope Innocent X, which the Pope found 'all too lifelike'. Asked about his taste in painting, Velázquez is supposed to have said that he preferred Titian to Raphael: 'There are good and excellent painters in Venice, but Titian is the best with a paintbrush.' In 1660 the Venetian poet Mario Boschini described Velázquez's taste in painting (in Dr Donaldson's translation):

> The master stiffly bowed his figure tall
> And said, 'For Raphael to speak the truth
> I always was plain spoken from my youth
> I cannot say I like his work at all.'
> [. . .] 'I saw in Venice
> The true test of the good and beautiful,
> First in my judgment ever stands that school,
> And Titian first of all Italian men is.'

Velázquez was so happy and distracted by a putative love affair in Venice that even the Spanish King's letters ordering him to return to Madrid were obeyed only after a year and a half. He returned with his haul of quality works, including a *Venus and Adonis* by Veronese, a *Purification* by Tintoretto and the preliminary drawing by Tintoretto of his *Paradiso* for the Doge's Palace. Then he left, 'as there was nothing else to buy'. All these works are now in the Prado in Madrid.

Velázquez's time in Venice is documented by the embassy dispatches in the Madrid and Venice Archives, by Francisco Pacheco's biography and by correspondence (Rubens and Velázquez exchanged letters) and poetry (*Carta del navegar*), and also by *An Account of the Most Eminent Spanish Painters* (1739) by Palomino Vasco.

From the foundation of the Venetian state around the tenth century, local scholars, writers and historians have provided extremely detailed guides, chronicles and historical and cultural information on their beloved city. Foreign artists met fellow painters, but they also found a congenial cultural life in a city hosting some of the most respected poets and scholars of their time. One of these was **Pietro Bembo** (1470–1547), who had been born into a patrician family; his father was a senator and diplomat, and a great collector. Bembo left the Serenissima to be educated in Florence, Messina and Padua. He was promised a brilliant career in politics and the Church in Venice, but chose first a life of scholarship at the court of Ferrara, where he fell in love with Lucrezia Borgia, and later in Rome, where he became first secretary to Pope Leo X. Pietro Bembo, considered the strongest intellectual of his day and the greatest Renaissance mind, found time to write. We know that in 1529 he was appointed official historiographer of Venice (to the chagrin of his contemporary Marino Sanudo, who wanted and needed the job), covering the years 1487 to 1513. Bembo's 12-volume history of the city, written in Latin and published in Venice posthumously in 1551, describes internal politics and events as well as external affairs. Much of it is devoted to conflicts with France, Spain, the Holy Roman Empire, the Papacy and the Turks.

As a young man, Bembo wrote *Gli Asolani*, which he dedicated to Lucrezia Borgia, who was married at the time to Alfonso d'Este at the court of Ferrara. It is a dialogue on courtly love in fifteenth-century Asolo at the court of Caterina Cornaro, but it has autobiographical elements, related to his own love for **Lucrezia Borgia** (1480–1519). Their affair developed through passionate letters, one famously accompanied by a lock of Lucrezia's splendid blonde hair. That very lock of hair was admired by Lord Byron, whose imagination was fired when he saw it amongst what he described in his own letter to Augusta Leigh of 15 October 1816 as 'the prettiest love letters in the world!' Apparently Byron's attempt to steal a strand of the famous hair was witnessed by his friends Leigh Hunt and Walter Savage Landor. In spite of Lucrezia's dubious reputation, it would appear that she was ruthlessly exploited by her father, brother and three husbands. Her involvement with Pietro Bembo and their love letters make her a surprisingly more likeable character.

In 1525 Bembo wrote *Prosa della vulgar lingua*, a treatise proposing that poetry be written in Italian, which was a novelty. He wrote one of the earliest Italian grammars, helping also to codify Italian spelling. Bembo's poetry in Latin was greatly admired, but he then turned to writing in Italian – for example, his *Rime*, published in 1530. By the end of the sixteenth century, Italian had completely taken over.

Thanks to his friendship with **Aldus Manutius** (1449–1515), known also as Aldo Manuzio, who had founded the Aldine Press in Venice, Bembo was influential in bringing Petrarch into fashion: his imitation of Petrarch's sonnets started the enduring fashion of Petrarchism in poetry and his personal copy of Petrarch's Italian poems, *Il Canzoniere*, was published by Manutius in 1501. Dante's *Divine Comedy* followed in 1502. Both Manutius and Bembo collaborated on development of the printing process in Venice, and together they invented the first small book in octavo format, which could be carried around in a pocket – the first *libri portatili* were printed in 1503, forerunners of the modern paperback. In a letter to Bembo in 1514 Manutius mentioned that he 'took the small size, the pocket formula, from your library'. Bembo appeared as a fictional character in Castiglione's *Book of the Courtier*, published in 1528 by Manutius' Aldine Press.

In 1539 Bembo was unexpectedly made a cardinal and devoted the rest of his life to theology and ancient history. He spent his last years in Padua, surrounded by his superb library and works of art, including Mantegna's *St Sebastian*, now in the Ca' d'Oro collection. Bembo often visited the greatest painters, Giovanni Bellini, Giorgione and Titian, who completed at least two portraits of him. Today it is possible to see his birthplace in Venice, Palazzo Bembo, near the Rialto Bridge, as well as Palazzo Camerini where he died, near the Church of the Eremitani in via Altinate in Padua, now a museum.

Unlike Bembo, who spent little of his adult life in Venice, **Marino Sanudo** (1466–1536) never left the city of which he became a dedicated chronicler and keen historian: 'I have written and composed so many volumes of my History, beginning with the arrival of Charles the King of France in Italy, up to 1 March 1523.' Sanudo's life's work became to record life in Venice in all its aspects, and, above all, to tell the truth 'and only the truth: because this is the most important thing in history'.

Born to a Venetian patrician family in a palace on the Fondamenta del Megio, Sanudo's diaries were neglected for centuries, stolen by the Austrians and then republished in 1872 thanks only to English scholar Rawdon Brown. Reissued in 1923, they became a mine of information on life in Venice in the early Renaissance. They have the particular advantage of being written by someone who benefited from firsthand knowledge of public and everyday life. At the early age of 20 he was elected a member of the Great Council and became a senator in 1498. Having started noting everything that was said and done in the assemblies, Sanudo was a reliable witness, taking part actively in important decisions made at the time. He allowed himself on numerous occasions to give his personal opinion on various matters. The Council of Ten finally gave him permission to examine the secret archives of the state in 1515, allowing him to 'have sight of the secret books and letters in order to note down the truth'.

In the early sixteenth century the city had decided to appoint a local trusted 'public historian'. Marino Sanudo was the obvious choice, thanks to his public and political experience, his inside knowledge, his learned interests (he had a wonderful library containing priceless manuscripts and chronicles) and his friendship with Aldo Manuzio, whose death he mourned in a diary entry on 8 February 1515. He was disappointed since the Great Council appointed Andrea Navagero (who never wrote a single line, although paid very handsomely) and then in 1530 Pietro Bembo, who was away from Venice most of the time and had to rely on Sanudo's diaries to carry out his official duties, saying they were 'invaluable to throw light on so many things'. This was clearly unfair, as Bembo then reported that 'he told me that the diaries represented his life's work and that he did not want to give the result of so much effort to just anybody.' Moreover, Sanudo, who was not as well-off as Bembo, would have been grateful for the financial help the public historian's position would have given him. He died in poverty, despite the meagre pension of 150 ducats he had been granted rather too late in 1531, when the value of his work was at last recognised.

Almost everything is described and commented on in Sanudo's 58 volumes, including the function of the secretive Calza Guild (portrayed by Carpaccio and Bellini) and the banquets they organised. He wrote about the Rialto Bridge, the magnificent Piazza San Marco, the great houses, the palaces, the jewellery and glass and the general affluence: 'In the city nothing grows, yet whatever you want can be found in abundance.'

Topics dealt with in the diaries range from the wars against the Turks and the French to disasters which struck the city, including the earthquake of 1511: 'On 26 March [. . .] a mighty earthquake came upon this city of Venice. It seemed as if the houses were collapsing, the chimneys swaying, the walls bursting open, the bell-towers bending, objects in high places falling, water boiling, even in the Grand Canal, as though it had been set on fire.' He described also the disastrous fire which destroyed the Arsenal in 1509, the plagues, the *acqua alta* which flooded the city in November 1511, and again in November 1517, reporting that 'the floods have caused much damage', food shortages, poverty and famine, particularly from February to April 1528: 'So great is the misery of everyday life that on the Rialto Bridge there were 200 poor souls with their begging bowls pressed one up against the next [. . .] It is a great shame to see so many poor people, above all those from the island of Burano.' He depicted daily life, describing processions, celebrations, entertainments and successive carnivals, theatrical productions and public executions.

The diaries offer a series of local news items, almost like a tabloid newspaper, reporting priests accused of homicide, prostitutes attacked and robbed. On 2 August 1521 he graphically reported the first execution of a woman, describing how her body was quartered between the two columns of Piazza San Marco. There is even a possible reference to Shakespeare's future *Othello*, as Sanudo wrote on

26 October 1508: 'In the morning Cristoforo Moro was at the meeting, a lieutenant from Cyprus, now made Captain [. . .] because his wife had died.'

No subject was too trivial. In October–November 1506 he reported how a statue of the Madonna arrived miraculously in Venice, 'brought by an angel'. The Madonna was found by the patrician Michel Lion and taken to the Church of San Marziale, which was then rebuilt to house it. The church is worth a visit (restricted visiting times permitting), as the statue is still there, as well as the magnificent ceiling by Sebastiano Ricci. On 5 May 1515 Sanudo wrote disapprovingly of how a 14-year-old youth from Picardy was exhibited by Spaniards in Piazza San Marco as a monster: 'you paid one penny and could touch him and talk to him, even in Italian.'

Some entries read like contemporary newspaper headlines: 'Small Crowds Attend 1529 Carnival', '4 Feb 1529, Heavy Snowfall in Venice', 'Wearing of Masks Forbidden from 9–31 January 1517 Following Serious Incidents'. Sometimes indulging in personal moral judgement, he criticised the wealth and power of the bankers or noted that the courtesans were practically the only friends and confidantes of ambassadors (who were not allowed contact with Venetians). Sanudo supported the creation of the first Jewish ghetto: 'I think they should be sent to live in the New Ghetto, as it is enclosed, with a drawbridge, and surrounded by a wall' (26 March–24 April 1516). Foreign affairs were also covered; in June 1529 Sanudo even discussed the annulment of the marriage of Henry VIII to Catherine of Aragon.

Fortunately, it is possible to access Marino Sanudo's diaries by reading Labalme and White's excellent English version, *Venice, Città Excelentissima: Selections from the Renaissance Diaries of Marin Sanudo*.

Another chronicler of the city was **Francesco Sansovino** (1521–86). Francesco accompanied his father, the famous architect Jacopo Sansovino, when he came to Venice from Rome to rebuild parts of Piazza San Marco, the Church of San Geminiano, the Library and several other churches and palaces. Jacopo Sansovino was offered prestigious and convenient lodgings in the Procuratie Vecchie, in

Piazza San Marco, next to the Clock Tower, where he stayed with his family for the rest of his life. Francesco was sent to Bologna and later to Padua to study law, but chose to return to live in Venice and became a historical writer. One of his works is generally considered the first guidebook ever written: *On Venice, the Most Noble City, Described by Francesco Sansovino* (*Della Venetia, città nobilissima, descritta da M. Francesco Sansovino*, 1581).

Venice, the Most Noble City gives us not only a detailed description of the palaces, churches and works of art as they were in 1581, but also describes everyday Venetian life, commenting on the inhabitants and what was generally considered at the time as a wisely governed city, 'which foreigners marvelled at'. Thanks to his contact with his father's distinguished friends like Titian and Aretino, Sansovino played an active part in Venice's cultural and political life. At a time when in the rest of Italy and Europe religious intolerance and violence prevailed, the book presents a picture of Venice as a relative haven and model host for Muslims and Jews, Orthodox Christians and Lutherans, where anyone could express their opinions openly.

In 1573 Sansovino, in a letter to Alvise Michiel, announced that he was now prepared to write a *Vulgar History (Historia vulgare)* of the city. He felt strongly that the history of Venice should be written in Italian, 'a language which will be better accepted than Latin'. He worked as a publisher, wrote poetry and was also the author of a treatise on forms of government.

Pilgrims, visiting artists and local chroniclers all left invaluable accounts of the great city, but also fascinating are those of the foreign envoys, the *ministri degli esteri corti*, sent to Venice on diplomatic missions. 'When they weren't busy with hired killers, diplomats described the city,' wrote Fabio Isman in a 2009 review entitled 'Ambassadors, Spies and Artists – Centuries of Cloaks and Daggers'.

On the whole, ambassadors, sent to represent their countries in the city which claimed to have invented diplomacy, led a pleasant life, but tedious, since they were not allowed to mingle with members of the ruling patrician families and native Venetians, and were kept away from the centre of the city because many were – probably correctly – believed to be engaged also in spying activity. Francesco Sansovino noted, 'The ambassadors are all the eyes and ears of their states.' On the importance of foreign diplomats in Venice, Montesquieu wrote acerbically: 'There is nothing as useless as an ambassador in Venice; it is like having a shopkeeper in a quarantine camp.' Even so, ambassadors were privileged witnesses whose dispatches to their governments, letters and personal writings constitute a rich testimony of the city, until the end of the Republic in 1797.

One of the first, and undoubtedly the most famous of these, was **Dante Alighieri** (1265–1321). Little is known for certain about the great Florence-born writer, but he led most of his life in exile, caught in factional power struggles, and banished from his home city in

1   Bust of the poet Dante at the Arsenale

1302, where he had been condemned to be burned alive. The only fact we have about his connection with Venice is that he arrived in August 1321, having been sent by his patron in Ravenna, Guido Novello da Polenta, on a delicate diplomatic mission (involving smuggled salt), which he failed to complete.

Some Venetians like to think that the poet had visited Venice before, perhaps in 1312, when he is reported to have come to read a Latin oration in honour of the newly elected doge, Giovanni Soranzo. He was apparently treated to a special visit to the city's Arsenal, working at full capacity at the time. This efficient boat-building area of Venice employed up to 20,000 workers, who could build a battleship in a single day. The visit so impressed Dante that he referred to it in Canto XXI of Hell in *The Divine Comedy*, using it as a metaphor to describe the place in the eighth circle of Hell where corrupt officials are punished (he felt strongly about this, having himself been accused of fraud):

> For as at Venice, in the Arsenal
> In winter-time, they boil the gummy pitch
> To caulk such ships as need an overhaul,
> Now that they cannot sail – instead of which
> One builds him a new boat, one toils to plug
> Seams strained by many a voyage, others stitch
> Canvas to patch a tattered jib or lug.
> (cited in John Julius Norwich, *History of Venice*)

Some critics say that Dante never invented anything, and must have seen the Arsenal, in order to be able to describe it so vividly. A marble plaque and a bronze bust have been placed by the main entrance of the Arsenal to commemorate the visit which Venetians are sure he made.

The early fourteenth-century Florentine chronicler G. M. Villani reports an amusing anecdote. Invited to a banquet by the newly elected doge, Giovanni Soranzo, presumably as a part of the festivities, Dante was dismayed to notice that his plate contained only small fish, whereas other guests, perhaps more important than himself, were served larger ones. He placed one of the small fish near his ear and when the Doge asked him to explain this strange behaviour, he answered that his father had died at sea and that he was asking the fish news about him. 'What did the fish say?' asked the Doge. Dante replied that the fish and his friends were too small to know, but older ones might. The Doge got the message and ordered a plate of bigger fish to be served to the poet.

Dante's first visit to Venice may even have been as early as 1304. It is tempting to believe that he visited the island of Torcello, where the *Universal Judgment* mosaic in the Basilica of Santa Maria Assunta may have inspired his description of Hell, Purgatory and Paradise in *The Divine Comedy*. A local scholar, Cesare Augusto Levi, passionately defended this thesis in a 1906 pamphlet, *Dante on Torcello*, maintaining that 'it is quite likely that he went to Torcello during one of his periods as ambassador to Venice and Verona, and that he saw the great mosaic in the Cathedral representing the Universal Judgment.' Levi also saw in Canto VIII elements which suggest that Dante might have been inspired by the wintry bleak greyness of the Venetian lagoon, subsequently using it in some of his descriptions of Hell.

While travelling home via Comacchio in August 1321, Dante is reported to have contracted malaria in the marshes, and he died a month later in Ravenna, his journey to Venice having contributed to his death.

Foreign diplomats after Dante reported dutifully in their dis-patches on life and events in the city, as well as giving personal impressions and testimonies in letters. Their official duties consisted of negotiating treaties, arranging royal marriages and sending formal congratulations or condolences. Unofficially, they helped their employers to build up their collections of artworks, paintings, rare books and rare objects. They also had other secretive duties. The ambassador is 'an honourable spy', wrote **Philippe de Commynes** (1447–1511), himself sent for this purpose by the French King Charles VIII in 1494 and 1495. During his diplomatic mission in

Venice, Commynes observed and noted public life, published in his *Memoirs* in 1524. He was duly impressed: 'truly in religious affairs and in the beautifying and adorning of their churches it is a city of the greatest reverence that I ever saw.' He made the customary journey to the island of Santo Spirito, from where 25 men escorted him to the city on a richly decorated boat. They sailed for the monastery of San Giorgio via the 'grand rue which they call Grand Canal, which is very wide [. . .] and is the most beautiful road that I ever saw in the whole world, with the most beautiful houses [. . .] It is the most triumphant city that I ever saw, honouring greatly ambassadors and foreigners and governed very wisely.'

Although one French ambassador was reported to have lived in the sixteenth-century palace which is now the Hotel Danieli, close to Piazza San Marco, all French embassies thereafter were situated in the less central area of Cannaregio. The Palazzo Surian, one such ambassadorial residence, dominating the Rio di Cannaregio, is best known for Rousseau's entertaining descriptions of it in *The Confessions*. The Palazzo della Vecchia, built by Jacopo Sansovino by the Church of Madonna dell'Orto and used as a French embassy until 1743, was pulled down at the beginning of the nineteenth century. Its huge garden had a beautiful view over the north lagoon towards the island of Murano. In 1790 the Embassy moved to Palazzo Morosini della Trezza, which was vandalised by the occupying French soldiers at the fall of the Republic in 1797. It was situated strategically next to the Church of San Geremia, almost opposite the Spanish Embassy which was the origin of the current street name, Lista di Spagna. One can still admire the surviving Gothic gate at the entrance to its huge garden, once praised for its beauty. But perhaps the most prestigious of the French embassies was the Palazzo Michiel, occupied by a series of French diplomats in the second part of the sixteenth century. This is where the French ambassador Arnaud du Ferrier (in Venice 1563–7) famously hosted for one night **Henri III of France** (1551–89). René Guerdan in his book *The Gold of Venice: On the Splendours and Miseries of the Venetian Republic* (1967) gives us a detailed description of the lavish celebrations on the occasion of this visit, immortalised also by several paintings. The palace is in a quiet part of Cannaregio, by the Rio della Sensa, and was considered by the architect Sansovino to be 'one of the most beautiful modern residences ever'. The two façades, one on the Rio della Sensa and the other overlooking the Rio della Madonna dell'Orto, were covered in frescoes by the Venetian painter Andrea Schiavone. Its grand staircase and its main entrance were decorated with sculptures by Tullio Lombardo. It has been restored, although nothing remains of its magnificent garden.

Spying for his country was indeed an unofficial part of an ambassador's duties, and the ambassador **Henry Wotton** (1568– 1639) must have performed that part of his work with relish, since he was appointed by the court of King James to Venice three times, from 1604 to 1612, from 1616 to 1619, and lastly from 1621 to 1624. He imprudently declared on a mission in 1604 that an ambassador is 'an honest man sent to lie abroad for the good of his country'. This irreverent play on words, describing the true range of the duties of an ambassador and his view of others in the role brought him temporary disgrace, but there was some truth in it. Officially, since the end of fifteenth century, ambassadors were envoys from good families sent abroad principally to negotiate treaties, arrange marriages and defend their countries' interests and status – matters which Wotton took very seriously. Left impoverished by the death of his father in 1587, the young Wotton started travelling abroad around 1589, acquiring invaluable experience for a future career in diplomacy, probably his greatest strength, apart from writing. He started to spend most of his life abroad, also perhaps for his own political safety. Having visited France as a young man, he went on to Venice, Rome and Florence. James VI of Scotland (with whom he was on good terms) became James I of England in 1603 and offered Wotton the embassy in Venice. At first Wotton settled with his household in a relatively modest palace (Palazzo da Silva) by the Ponte degli Ormesini in Cannaregio, near the Jewish Ghetto. One of his English compatriots, the intrepid traveller Thomas Coryat,

2 *Palazzo da Silva, where Wotton lived as English ambassador*

who visited Venice in 1607, describes him in his travelogue *Crudities (Hastily Gobbled in Five Months of Travels)* as

> our most worthy Ambassador, Sir Henry Wotton, honoris causa, because his house was in the same street (when I was in Venice) where the Jewish Ghetto is, even in the street called St Hieronimo, and by a little from it. Certainly he hath greatly graced and honoured his country by that most honourable port that he hath maintained in this nobility, by his generous carriage and most elegant and gracious behaviour.

On his second visit Wotton moved from Palazzo da Silva to a grander palace, Palazzo Gussoni-Grimani della Vida on the Grand Canal, 'one of the fayrest in Venice', attributed to the architect Michele Sanmicheli and frescoed externally by Tintoretto (fragments of the frescoes can still be seen on the façade). Palazzo da Silva was abandoned because of its 'farness to the Piazze'. Like Venetian patricians and many of his colleagues, Wotton also rented a mainland villa at Noventa on the Brenta Canal, where he would retire in the hot summer months, as was then the fashion.

Wotton's regular work as ambassador would have included detailed and accurate weekly dispatches, reporting the main events in the city to the King of England. His fluent accounts were designed to amuse his gossip-loving monarch. A gifted and compulsive correspondent, he was even called the best letter-writer of his time, probably because he was not always an entirely impartial witness. To his patron Lord Salisbury he freely said what he thought of the Venetians. Referring to Doge Grimani, who had recently died, Wotton noted: 'he was generally a zealous patriot, and a great conserver of the public plenty; which is the only virtue allowed here in a prince!' To the same correspondent he wrote: 'Yesterday was the Feast of Corpus Christi, celebrated by express command of the State [. . .] with the most sumptuous procession that ever had been seen here [. . .] The reason for this extraordinary solemnity [. . .] as I conceive it [. . .] is to contain the people still in good order with superstition, the foolish bend of obedience.'

He took part in some of the most dramatic events in Venice at the time. At the end of his second mission in 1618, he was suspected of being involved in the plot to overthrow the Republic, in his own words, 'the foulest and fearfullest thing that hath come to light since the foundation of the city'. This event is usually referred to as La Congiura di Bedmar, or the Bedmar Plot. The Spanish ambassador, the Duke of Bedmar de Osuna, with collaborators from Spain and elsewhere, was suspected of attempting to overthrow the Venetian government through internal conspiracy and treachery, with the Spanish Viceroy's fleet standing by. The alleged plot was discovered, and some of the suspects summarily executed. Documents in the Venetian Archives record Wotton's friendship with the Duke of Bedmar, whom he was supposed to have met in secret nocturnal encounters. This involvement is not entirely implausible, since Wotton was poor, had to foot many expenses at the English Embassy and was saddled by debts which prevented him from returning to England at a time when he was keen to do so. Whether or not the accusations were true, this event subsequently inspired many plays and other writings, including *Venice Preserv'd* (1682) by Thomas Otway, *The Spanish Conspiracy* (*De la conjuration des Espagnols*) (1618) by Abbé St Real, *Venice Saved* (1903) by Hugo von Hofmannsthal, who wrote his own adaptation of Thomas Otway's play, and *Venise sauvée* (1940) by the French philosopher Simone Weil.

Despite this, the witty, charming Wotton was well regarded by senators and members of the Venetian Republic. He also remained on generally good terms with the doges. Doge Donato praised him as 'the kind of person whom the Republic loves and honours'. Wotton was friendly with the politically and religiously influential Servite monk and scholar, Paolo Sarpi, also resident in Cannaregio, as Thomas Coryat confirms: 'In this street also does famous Friar Paul dwell which is of the order of the Servi.' Wotton and Sarpi had secret meetings on the Fondaco Zechinelli, at the Golden Ship, a Flemish trading post in Merceria, but also a venue for liberal-minded Venetians and foreigners. A part of Wotton's mission was to encourage Venetians, if not to become Protestants, at least to reject the authority of the Pope (then Paul V). As an Anglican, he would certainly have attempted to attract possible recruits to his religion in Venice, which was firmly independent of the Pope's rule. This would have been encouraged by Paolo Sarpi, actively supporting the establishment of a Venetian Church free from Catholic rule. Having failed to obtain the unconditional submission of the Venetians, Paul V resorted to excommunication until a compromise was reached in April 1607. In October Sarpi was attacked near his convent, his attempted murder probably commissioned by the Pope. He recovered despite the fierce stabbing (15 thrusts of a stiletto) and his statue can now be seen in Campo Santa Fosca near the bridge where he was left for dead.

Venice was at a peak in the early seventeenth-century, with its 10,000 gondolas and visitors flocking from all over Europe and the East. It was a city of pomp and pleasure. Great palaces and beautiful churches had been built. Endless ceremonies, processions

3   *Statue of Paolo Sarpi by Ponte Santa Fosca, where he was stabbed*

and pageants were designed to impress the travellers. It was, after all, the most admired city in the world. Wotton frequented writers and painters, as recorded in Carlo Ridolfi's *Lives of the Artists*, which mentions works painted by Jacopo Bassano, including a painting of 'Sir Henry Wotton Englishman, standing dressed in red', and another portrait of Wotton by Domenico Tintoretto, son of the great Jacopo. A further portrait of Wotton hangs in the Bodleian Library in Oxford.

Apart from dispatches to his country and numerous letters addressed to friends, including Sir Francis Bacon, Wotton wrote frank and witty speeches. For example, in a letter of 16 January 1608 congratulating the newly elected Doge Leonardo Donato, he praised the Serenissima, with 'her orderly government, her sound institutions, her exaltation of the worthy, her punishment of evil, the reverence paid to her magistrates, the encouragement of her youth in the paths of virtue and the service of their country. I am forced to believe that, come what may, she will survive until the final dissolution of the elements themselves!'

He also gave detailed descriptions of his life in Venice, musical evenings, religious services in his Anglican chapel, his rich library, his collection of armoury, his leather wall hangings, his collection of paintings and his hired furniture (the inventory listed billiard tables, a gondola, beds, sheets, awnings and firearms, all rented at extortionate prices, according to Wotton, from the Jews living in the neighbouring Ghetto). Like his fellow diplomats, he collected precious glassware, decorative items and paintings to send to friends and patrons at home. He was a reputed connoisseur of Italian art and he helped to acquire the collections of Lord Salisbury and the Duke of Buckingham. He was a patron of Odoardo Fialetti, an Italian painter, art dealer and expert; at the end of his life Wotton left Charles I five paintings attributed to Fialetti. The 1606 painting at Hampton Court Palace of Wotton's audience with Doge Leonardo Donato is attributed to the same artist, and *The Bird's Eye View of Venice* which Fialetti painted in 1611 remained a part of Wotton's private collection. Artworks were constantly bought and sent back to England. On one occasion the enormous sum of £450 was used to buy pictures for Prince Henry. Information was exchanged for art and art for information, as art deals were often a cover for spying activities. Wotton also collected seeds of plants and flowers, and many rose cuttings were sent to the King and to friends, including the gardener and plant-lover John Tradescant.

Wotton or 'Le Chevalier Outon', as he was called, kept open house for family members, young protégés, visitors and travellers. Thomas Coryat gratefully recorded this in his *Crudities*. In his house Wotton also entertained the *bravi*, dangerous, rough young men employed to protect Italian landowners' interests, and French adventurers who were prepared to spy and betray if paid handsomely. 'I think the reason is because they know themselves to be necessary,' wrote Wotton, spying on the enemies of England, the dreaded Jesuits amongst others. One of Wotton's favourite activities was to intercept Jesuits' letters: 'I must confess myself to have a special appetite to the packets that pass to and fro from these holy fathers,' he admitted. All this was actively encouraged by his employer, King James I.

This made some of his writings on Venice exciting reading, almost forerunners to Cold War thrillers. A part of the job was to intercede in favour of fugitives, and of fellow countrymen imprisoned or in difficulty. He took this side of his work very seriously and was persistent and successful on many occasions. Embassies were often used as sanctuaries for criminals because of the diplomatic immunity they offered. There was nothing Wotton could do, however, to save Venetians from public executions: 'Tomorrow morning at the point of day [. . .] is here to be publicly beheaded one of their gentlemen of the house of Bolani for having assailed another gentleman with a pistol (himself masked).'

This widely cultured scholar was also a linguist, a poet, author of at least two famous poems (not on Venice), and his letters to Bacon reveal an interest in philosophy. Being a follower of the Protestant faith by conviction, another of his concerns was to protect Englishmen travelling in Italy from attempts to convert them to Catholicism. Thomas Coryat praised his 'piety and integrity of life and his true worship of God in the midst of Popery, superstition and idolatry (for he had service and sermons in his house after the Protestant manner, which I thinke was never permitted in Venice)'. After an eventful diplomatic life, Wotton retired to become provost of Eton College in 1624, and from there sent letters of advice to the young John Milton as he prepared to travel to Italy, stopping in Venice for three weeks. Sir Henry Wotton died in 1639.

One century later the French philosopher and musicologist **Jean-Jacques Rousseau** (1712–78) arrived in Venice to work in the Embassy, as the French ambassador's secretary, from 4 September 1743 to 2 August 1744. His experiences are described humorously, if not necessarily accurately, in his autobiographical *Confessions*, completed in 1769 and published in 1782.

Rousseau was unable to reach Venice by crossing the Alps because of the war raging between Spain and Sardinia. Forced to travel via Toulouse, he had to approach Italy by boat. On arrival in Genoa on 11 August 1743 the passengers and crew were not allowed to disembark because of an outbreak of plague. The passengers were put in quarantine for 21 days, obliged to stay either on board or in the *lazzaretto*, a special quarantine establishment set up outside important ports for ships arriving from the Mediterranean. The French philosopher recalls with pleasure this unpropitious arrival in Italy, because he was unexpectedly at liberty to dream and read as he wished for a few weeks. Rousseau was not a social animal and had a tendency to melancholia and hypochondria. Nevertheless, once in Venice, he embarked on a busy social and cultural life, in spite of the restrictions imposed on ambassadors.

His work at the Embassy, the impressive Palazzo Surian in Cannaregio, consisted of writing a report on the Venetian Republic every Saturday. The secretary was also supposed to help the ambassador in his daily business, keep a register of his negotiations and look after the ciphers (secret codes) and important papers. When the ambassador was ill or absent, the chief secretary could act for him and, in some cases, he could write or help to compose dispatches. Unfortunately, Rousseau's relationship with the ambassador, Pierre François, Comte de Montagu, was strained, and it was unlikely that such an independent spirit would have enjoyed the commitments imposed by his responsibilities.

Instead, Venice had much to offer the young 31-year-old, who could choose between several theatres, San Giovanni Crisostomo, San Samuele, San Salvatore and Sant'Angelo. The city was filled with popular music, especially gondoliers' songs or barcarolles, a real discovery for him: 'It is as if I had never seen real singing until now,' wrote the delighted young writer. A musician whose previous paid work had been to copy music scores, Rousseau also set out to compose an adaptation for flute of Antonio Vivaldi's 'Spring' from the *Four Seasons*. He rented a harpsichord and paid a group of musicians for his personal entertainment. When he went to a concert, he would not share his box with anyone for fear of being distracted or prevented from falling asleep so that he could wake again, delighted by the music: 'But who could express the delicious sensation of the sweet harmony and angelic song of the singer who woke me?' recalled Rousseau in *The Confessions*. 'What an awakening! What delight! What ecstasy when I opened my eyes and ears together! My first thought was to believe myself in Paradise.'

On this occasion Rousseau was probably attending a performance of *La finta schiava* at the San Giovanni Crisostomo Theatre (now Teatro Malibran) and the voice of the singer was that of a castrato. 'The Italian word castrato indicates the profession, whereas the French suggests only the means by which the voice is achieved,' noted Rousseau in his *Dictionary of Music*.

Visitors interested in hearing music in Venice at that time would also have visited the *scuole*, including Santa Maria della Pietà, Incurabili, Derelitti and San Lazzaro dei Mendicanti. In these institutions, which functioned as orphanages, hospitals and music schools, visitors could hear young orphan girls sing and play musical instruments from behind a grille. Rousseau did not miss the experience: 'What I resented were those infernal grilles which allowed only the Angelic sound to pass and denied me sight of its beautiful source. The Italian voice does not deceive, and the sound is as beautiful as the singer.' He was therefore cruelly disillusioned when he managed to see some of these hidden beauties, who turned out to be rather less attractive than he had imagined.

Rousseau, like so many other visitors to Venice, including Montesquieu, Goethe, George Sand, Byron and Richard Wagner, was appreciative of the quality and the variety of the music on offer. He was also impressed by the musical quality of the barcarolles sung by the gondoliers: 'Let us not forget Tasso, much of whose *Jerusalem Delivered* most gondoliers have by heart, some of whom have memorised the whole work, and which they sing through the summer nights, throwing stanzas back and forth between their boats.' Much inspired, he would later publish his *Songs from the Boats* (*Canzoni da battello*, 1753), as well as many articles on music, as his contribution to the *Encyclopedia* published in 1748–9. When his opera *Les Muses galantes* was performed in 1745, critics accused him of plagiarism: 'He was writing French music, but it was all taken from the Italian.' Rousseau himself had said that French music lacked both rhythm and melody.

Like most short- and long-term visitors to Venice, he also paid visits to the famous courtesans. One of them, La Zulietta, gave him her advice, as reported in *The Confessions*: 'Forget about the women and study instead mathematics.' He may indeed have taken heed, as it was apparently in Venice that the idea for his political work, *The Social Contract*, was conceived.

To give an idea of the open-air musical entertainments once enjoyed by the ambassadors in their residences, one can visit the garden of Palazzo Rizzo-Patarol, now a luxurious hotel in Cannaregio. The surviving garden, redesigned in Romantic style in the nineteenth century, was used by French ambassadors for entertaining their guests. **Antonio Vivaldi** (1678–1741) would have come to play his compositions on the surviving terrace overlooking the lagoon. The then ambassador, Comte de Cergy, occupied this palace from his official arrival in 1723 until 1732. Written accounts as well as paintings give an idea of the magnificent celebrations, and of the status given to French ambassadors. Welcoming ceremonies generally took two full days, and ambassadors would commission painters such as Canaletto to record these momentous events. These were significant, as they were the only public occasions the ambassadors were given. They did have unofficial contact with aristocratic nuns in their convents, and with artists and painters – as well as prostitutes, with predictable consequences. The Abbé de Pomponne, whose welcoming ceremony had been recorded by the painter Luca Carlevarijs in 1706, had to be recalled by King Louis XV for his involvement in an amorous relationship with Maria Candida Canal, a nun from the convent of Sant'Alvise, which had provoked a diplomatic crisis. Similarly the Comte de Froullay, who had been chosen to replace Cergy, had fallen in love with a 16-year-old nun from the convent of San Lorenzo. This inappropriate liaison provoked another political difficulty, as the French diplomat complained that the young nun was prevented from seeing him by the State Inquisitors. All this is well documented in the Venetian Archives and by some ambassadors' public and private correspondence. In his letters and dispatches, **François Joachim de Bernis** (1715–94), French ambassador in Venice from 1752 to 1755, complains about the boredom, but notes wisely, 'be sure that I am contented not to be involved in important matters: Europe is only happy when Ambassadors have nothing to do.'

De Bernis, the young protégé of Louis XV's mistress Madame de Pompadour, was sent to Venice to act also as a mediator between the Republic and Pope Benedict XIV, a task he performed with some success. During his three years in the city, he managed to maintain a front of respectability in spite of a somewhat shady reputation. His involvement with the fellow libertine, spy and adventurer Giacomo Casanova and two young nuns from the convent of Santa Maria degli Angeli in Murano is described in Casanova's memoirs, *Histoire de ma vie*.

On the other hand, the Spanish diplomat and former politician **José Joaquín Guzman de Montealegre** (1698–1771) kept his personal life very private and wrote little on the city, which he considered a 'golden exile', but he must have enjoyed being in Venice, as he stayed until his death in 1771. He had been sent there in 1749 to represent Spain and the Kingdom of Naples. Unlike some of his predecessors, who were not always welcome in Venice owing to the strained relationship between the Republic and the powerful Catholic Spanish Empire, Montealegre had unusually decided to settle for good. Instead of renting a suitable place for the Embassy, the Duke of Montealegre, who was very wealthy, bought from the Zeno family the palace which they had rented out to Spanish diplomats since the middle of the seventeenth century. It stood in Cannaregio, like most embassies, on Lista di Spagna. In 1739, one of his predecessors had organised a banquet there on the occasion of a Spanish royal wedding, during which Vivaldi had played the harpsichord, accompanying his pupil the singer Anna Girò. The wealthy Montealegre bought the existing fifteenth-century building with an adjoining house (then a pharmacy), courtyards and gardens. It was enlarged and converted into the impressive building known now as Palazzo Sceriman (formerly the Istituto Manin). Its unusual and impressive frescoed surviving staircase by the architect Paolo Possi was much criticised at the time by Antonio Visentini (Joseph Smith's architect and engraver) for its frivolous character. The palace, completed in 1759, still retains the magnificent original well in the courtyard.

As was the fashion, Montealegre also bought a villa on the mainland with a large garden, 'an extravagant and spectacular zoological garden, full of exotic animals'. This villa was bought from Joseph Smith, the English consul, who had it restored by Visentini, whose watercolours of it are now at Windsor Castle. In spite of being accused of spending too much time in his villa – apparently because of his failing health, but probably for a quieter life – Montealegre successfully integrated himself into Venetian life. When he died in 1771, he chose to be buried in a tomb encased in an impressive altar which he commissioned to be built in the Church of San Geremia. A requiem was even composed by Mozart's contemporary Andrea Luchesi in his honour.

Like some of his predecessors, including the Frenchman de Bernis and Henry Wotton two centuries earlier, Montealegre had excellent relationships with artists, painters and intellectuals, in particular with the most famous Venetian painter of the time, Giambattista Tiepolo, who was very much in demand by the English, French and Swedish courts, but, thanks partly to Montealegre's efforts, worked at the Spanish court for the last decade of his life.

Montealegre had met Tiepolo in 1750, when the painter had just completed the beautiful frescoes of Antony and Cleopatra decorating the palace of the very rich Spanish Labia family. After long and complicated negotiations with the Venetian government, Tiepolo, who had become 'a real friend', left Venice in 1762 with his two sons, Giandomenico and Lorenzo, to work in Madrid. They intended to stay for two years in order to decorate the Royal Palace. King Carlos III was so pleased with Tiepolo's ceiling *Glory of Spain* and other paintings that he commissioned him to work in the Aranjuez Palace, and the years in exile extended until Tiepolo's death in 1771. His son Giandomenico then returned to Venice, but Lorenzo stayed, and died in Spain.

The Spanish ambassador remained an intriguing, scheming and influential figure in eighteenth-century Venice. Tiepolo's presence in Spain had a radical influence on Spanish painters, including Francisco Goya. Bernard Berenson wrote in *The Italian Painters of the Renaissance* (1952):

> But Tiepolo's feeling for strength, for movement, and for colour was great enough to give a new impulse to art. At times he seems not so much the last of the old masters as the first of the new. The works he left in Spain do more than a little to explain the revival of painting in that country under Goya; and Goya, in his turn, had a great influence upon many of the best French artists of our own times.

Montealegre's extravagant way of life and some of his connections gave rise to much comment, to be found in spies' reports, letters and dispatches, which make fascinating reading. Unlike de Bernis or Henry Wotton, the Spanish ambassador had plenty of money to spend on splendid receptions and parties. Like Wotton he could be quite firm with the Venetian authorities, particularly when he insisted on keeping diplomatic immunity in his *lista*, his little Spanish enclave inside the city.

On the whole, however, when his health allowed, he led a discreet life surrounded by all the pleasures Venice could offer. Very little is known about his private life except for a reference to him by Casanova in his memoirs that he met 'the Spanish Ambassador, duke of Montealegre in Parma' and saw him at the theatre, where, 'on our left, the Spanish ambassador, the Marquess Montealegre was sitting with his mistress, la signorina Bola.'

On his death, Montealegre's heirs sold the Spanish Embassy to an Armenian merchant, Gianbattista Sceriman, who founded a charity, Istituto Manin, offering professional training to orphans. It now houses offices for the Region of Veneto, its extraordinary staircase and ballroom reminding us of the palace's elegant past.

Montealegre was the penultimate Spanish ambassador after a long series of more or less successful predecessors, some of whom had also established close relationships with Venetian painters, as had Diego Hurtado de Mendoza (in Venice 1539–46), a friend and patron of Titian and who introduced the famous Venetian painter to the Spanish King Philip V. Cristóbal de Salazar likewise became Tintoretto's patron in 1584.

Another art connoisseur well known to Montealegre was **Joseph Smith** (1682–1770), the English consul in Venice from 1744 to 1760, whose mainland villa he had bought. Joseph Smith's fruitful life started in Venice in the import–export trade in 1700, where he made a modest fortune, thanks to wise investments. During the 70 years he spent in the city he practised as a merchant banker, finally acting as a British consul. As his wealth increased he became an obsessive collector of books and works of art and a patron of contemporary artists and painters. The most famous was Canaletto, for whom he acted as a kind of agent from 1729 to 1735, and whose paintings he bought to decorate his own palace. He was somewhat unkindly dubbed 'the merchant of Venice' by Horace Walpole, as he arranged commissions for the numerous English visitors who were keen to take home a *veduta* (cityscape) of Venice as a memento of their Grand Tour, but he also encouraged Canaletto to leave for London in 1746 (where he spent ten very successful years). Apart from the British Royal Collections, the collections of the Duke of Bedford, Earl Fitzwilliam and the Duke of Buckingham were all connected with Smith's dealings. In 1762, after his retirement as consul, Smith encountered financial problems and sold a great part of his unique library to George III, which became the foundation of the King's Library, the core of the British Museum. The drawings, paintings, coins and prints which Smith sold to the King remain in the Royal Collections. There were 50 paintings and 140 drawings by Canaletto, and works by Anthony Van Dyck, Rembrandt and Peter Paul Rubens. When he died, Smith still owned several hundred paintings and drawings.

Smith had commissioned Canaletto to paint Palladio's buildings in Venice, and financed personally a facsimile of his *Quattro libri dell'architettura* printed at the Pasquali Press. As well as Canaletto, Smith patronised many other Venetian painters, including Sebastiano and Marco Ricci, Francesco Zuccarelli, Pietro Longhi,

Giovanni Battista Piazzetta and Rosalba Carriera. It was he who commissioned Tiepolo to paint his *Banquet of Antony and Cleopatra* before the same subject was executed as one of the frescoes at the Palazzo Labia. As a book collector, passionate about printing, he opened a bookshop in Campo San Bartolomeo, La Felicità delle Lettere, which became a meeting place for scholars. He also set out to publish classical and modern authors such as Giovanni Boccaccio, Denis Diderot, Voltaire, Niccolò Macchiavelli and Francesco Algarotti. Passionate also about music, he was a friend of Vivaldi and had a box in the San Giovanni Crisostomo Theatre near his house. He acted for a while as agent of the famous castrato Farinelli and in 1731 acted as go-between to try to persuade him to sign a contract with the Theatre Royal Haymarket in London. Although well integrated into Venetian life, having left England for good, and speaking excellent Italian, Smith tended to move in English-speaking circles. His first wife was a famous soprano, Catherine Tofts, whom he married in Venice in 1717. When she died, he courted the young Giustina Wynne, but when she rejected him, he married at the age of 76 the British resident's daughter, Elizabeth Murray.

Joseph Smith's Venetian residence was the Palazzo Balbi, a small Gothic palace on the Grand Canal which he had been renting, but eventually bought in 1740. He asked Antonio Visentini, the engraver and architect (and Rosalba Carriera's brother-in-law), to redesign it in the Palladian style, which took more than ten years to complete. In this elegant palace, now known as Palazzo Mangili-Valmarana, he entertained writers, artists and musicians, aristocrats and travellers such as James Boswell and Frederick, Prince of Wales. Like many powerful and wealthy Venetians, he also owned from 1731 an estate at Mogliano on the mainland, with a charming summer villa sold on later to the Spanish ambassador. The building was pulled down at the end of the nineteenth century.

He was buried in the Protestant section of the Lido Cemetery, where Goethe sought out his grave during his Italian trip in order to pay his respects: 'to him I owe my copy of Palladio, and I offered a

4   *Palazzo Mangili-Valmarana, home of Consul Smith at Santi Apostoli*

grateful prayer.' Smith's tombstone was later moved to the English Church in Campo San Vio in Dorsoduro in Venice. His young son's grave can still be seen in the Church of Santi Apostoli near Smith's beloved palace, which is occasionally open to the public.

In spite of his friendship with so many gifted painters, it is strange that there is no known surviving portrait of Joseph Smith, and Smith himself wrote little about Venice, apart from a very few private letters. However, much can be found about him in the works of contemporary travellers and writers. His extraordinary obsession for collecting may well have been used by Carlo Goldoni for a comedy written for the 1750 Carnival, *La famiglia dell'antiquario.* Although Smith was generally clever in his business dealings, he was occasionally the victim of swindlers, and this is the subject of Goldoni's play. It is clear, however, that Goldoni held him in high regard, as he featured him again in another play, *The English Philosopher*, dedicated to 'the illustrious Sir Joseph Smith, Consul of the British Nation. My English Philosopher is a wise man, discreet, civil, who will not sully the sacred name of Philosophy, but will exalt it, and anyone who hears it will be enamoured of it.' According to Goldoni, Consul Smith's house was a house where one found 'the most perfect union of the Sciences and the Arts'. He also appears as a cultivated, wise and witty diplomat in *L'amante del Doge* (2008), an Italian historical novel by Carla Maria Russo set in 1755, in which the young heroine Caterina Dolfin meets the powerful older Andrea Tron in Consul Smith's magnificent library, and falls in love with him.

A century later, **William Dean Howells** (1837–1920), a congenial young American writer, was appointed consul to Venice in 1861, an experience which he enjoyed to the full until 1865. He was delighted by the city and started writing daily sketches on his life there, later collected and published as *Venetian Life*, appearing in 1866. It gives a close and amusing observation of what daily life would have been for someone arriving straight from Boston and whose prior knowledge was restricted to his reading:

> I could not [. . .] dwell three years in the place without learning to know it differently from those writers who have described it in romances, poems, and hurried books of travel, nor help seeing from my point of observation the sham and cheapness with which Venice is brought out, if I may speak in literature. At the same time, it has never lost for me its claim upon constant surprise and regard, nor the fascination of its excellent beauty, its peerless picturesqueness, and its sole and wondrous grandeur.

The 22 chapters of the book cover such subjects as food and drink, cold winters and lack of comfort, but Howells described humorously the customs and foibles of local Venetians from all backgrounds. A curious visitor, he devotes great detail to the churches, museums and public buildings of the city. He played a lively part in Venice's cultural life, wondering at the variety of its inhabitants and getting to know the Jewish, Armenian, French and Anglo-American communities. His observations go far beyond the remark for which he is famous: 'Is it worthwhile to observe that there are no Venetian blinds in Venice?'

Recently married, and after a frustrating search, he found lodgings at Ca' Falier, a venerable palace on the Grand Canal, almost opposite the Accademia, from whose balcony he took great pleasure in observing the picturesque life of the city. Interested in Venetian history, Howells was pleased to occupy a palace which had belonged to the famous doge who had inspired Byron's *Marino Faliero*, beheaded for plotting against the Venetian state, and whose headless statue presided over the grand staircase in his palace.

Howells, like Byron, used to swim in the Grand Canal all the way to his office. During his last year he moved to Palazzo Giustinian-Brandolini, a magnificent palace with a beautiful garden, the home of Richard Wagner a few years earlier in 1858.

Many of Howells's observations on Venetian life are still valid today, but others would now be impossible, such as his neighbours' habit of happily spending part of their summer swimming in the then-clean waters of the Grand Canal. It is to his credit that he made sensitive remarks on Venetians' attitude to what was, for most of them, the very painful Austrian occupation, when other writers seemed almost oblivious to it.

Howells, who mixed with the Anglo-American community frequented by Henry James, probably met one of the pillars of the English community in Venice – the historian **Rawdon Brown** (1803–83). A friend and guide of the Ruskins, Brown was not a diplomat, but a dedicated historical scholar who had arrived aged 27 in Venice to find the gravestone of Thomas Mowbray (Duke of Norfolk) which is mentioned in Shakespeare's *Richard II*:

> And there at Venice gave
> His body to that pleasant country's earth
> And his pure soul unto his captain Christ.
> Under whose colours he had fought so long.

Brown seems to have failed to find the tomb, but was in Venice for the rest of his life, spending much of his time researching in the Marciana Library and the Venetian Archives, working on *A Calendar of State Papers and Manuscripts Relating to English Affairs Existing in the Archives of Venice and Northern Italy.*

It was thanks to him that Marino Sanudo's diaries were rediscovered, the Venetian chronicle giving a precious record of fifteenth-century life and events in Venice and in Europe. The originals had been removed by the Austrians, but Rawdon Brown, who recognised their importance, worked from a copy he found in the Marciana Library and then had them published. Like Sanudo, Brown was frustrated in his career, since he never became British consul in Venice, which he would have loved, and from which he would have benefited financially. Fortunately, he was commissioned by Lord Palmerston to collate the Venetian State Papers relating to British affairs, for which he received a salary.

When John and Effie Ruskin visited Venice in 1849–50, and again in 1851–2, he became a faithful and invaluable friend to both, which continued after the Ruskins' return to London and the ensuing bitter divorce. In Venice at the end of 1849, Effie wrote to her mother: 'We have found a most agreeable acquaintance in Mr Rawdon Brown who is a most agreeable, clever literary person and yet not at all grave. He knows and has seen everybody worth seeing of English [*sic*] and has lived in a beautiful Palace on the Grand Canal for the last 15 years.' In 1837 Brown had bought for £480 the fascinating but crumbling Palazzo Dario, but, defeated by the financial burden it represented, he sold it after a few years to settle in Palazzo Businello, and finally in Palazzo Gussoni-Grimani della Vida in Cannaregio, once the home of the seventeenth-century English ambassador Sir Henry Wotton, of whom he was a great admirer. Rawdon Brown was also a passionate collector, and his palace and its contents were very much admired by Effie: 'Mr Brown is exceedingly kind to us. We went to see his house the other day and were delighted with it; it was furnished in such exquisite taste [. . .] He is a curious person, extremely clever, and greatly occupied in research.'

Both Ruskins were very pleased with his acquaintance, as apart from introducing Effie to members of the old Venetian aristocracy such as Lucietta Mocenigo (who had been Byron's landlady), 'he was also of great help' to John Ruskin. Effie wrote in the same letter: 'He has much influence here and has got John already some very precious books out of the Library of St Mark's regarding the old architecture of Venice, which will be most useful to him, and is helping him in every possible way.'

Having become a great supporter of Effie (almost a surrogate father), Brown also looked after her health, as she constantly complained about all kinds of ailments: 'I have not told you that Mr Brown put me in the plan of rubbing myself with hair gloves morning and night, which I hope will promote circulation.' On their second trip, the Ruskins accepted his hospitality while they waited to move into Casa Wetzlar (now Hotel Gritti).

Brown was rather reserved in his personal life, of which very little is known. Effie found out accidentally that he had two sisters and a mother somewhere, seldom mentioned. He was undoubtedly a dedicated scholar and very helpful to English visitors, but he appeared often secretive and moody, as Effie complained on numerous occasions in her letters: 'Mr Brown never asks me to come although I call regularly [. . .] but there is something [. . .] that I can't make out at all.' Rumours circulated in Venice, and at some stage and after some strange behaviour on his part, Effie wrote, 'Mr Brown is mad and not accountable.'

When he died, he left instructions that his private letters should be burnt, and there were rumours that he might have committed suicide, perhaps linked to the tradition of violent deaths connected with occupants of the mysterious Palazzo Dario. So little is known about him. Anyone looking for his tomb in San Michele Cemetery will find only the bald inscription:

RAWDON BROWN
ANGLUS

3

Haven and Inspiration

Venice embraces those whom all others shun. She raises those whom others lower. She affords a welcome to those who are persecuted elsewhere.

(Pietro Aretino, in his address to the Doge, 1527)

As we have seen, from the start Venice was a city where foreign visitors came for relatively long periods, either to work, or in transit to the Holy Land, or to visit the innumerable religious institutions and their treasures. For early religious tourists, coming to Venice was seen as a necessary step to salvation and even as a version of heaven itself, the 'Paradise of Cities' (as Venice was called by a delighted John Ruskin).

The city continued to exert its fascination, offering visitors a spiritual experience; of course, as a worldly and mercantile city, it also benefited from this early form of tourism, later drawing crowds of artists and writers seeking refuge. The anticipation of heaven which had attracted so many of their predecessors became a haven for those who, whether by force or by choice, were seeking a safe place where they could work, write or live a freer life, denied them in their own country.

Venice the Wise, the Free, the Rich and the Just enjoyed a long reputation for democracy and tolerance. During his time in Venice, Voltaire's protagonist Candide is surprised at meeting a great number of exiled ex-sovereigns, the Turk Achmet III, Ivan 'once Emperor of all Russians', Charles Edward Stuart, Pretender to the throne of Scotland, two kings of Poland and Theodore of Corsica, all deposed, dethroned, 'all stripped of their territories by the fortune of war, had come to spend the remainder of the Carnival'. Sects and persecuted communities which, through the centuries, have used Venice as a refuge – Jews, Armenians, Freemasons, Templars, Knights of Malta, followers of Kabala and alchemists – have all left their architectural mark on the city.

The city also attracted fugitives from justice seeking sanctuary inside embassies. One such case was the Welshman **William Thomas** (*c*.1507–54), former tutor to Prince Edward, later Edward VI, who fled to Venice with money he had embezzled from his patron. He was granted his liberty by the Venetian authorities and later gained an English pardon. Apart from greatly admiring the city's famous buildings, Thomas praised the general sense of political and personal freedom experienced by everyone in the city: 'all men, especially strangers, have so much liberty.' A reformed character, he wrote his own *History of Italy* in 1549 and afterwards became political mentor to the young English King.

On the whole, Venice remained tolerant of visitors' eccentricities and misdemeanours. In 1546 the Florentine artist Benvenuto Cellini chose to take refuge there, having been accused of sodomy, a capital crime in much of Europe. But the city's tolerance had limits; the sixteenth-century writer Pietro Aretino had to leave Venice for a time, accused of the same crime. The use of masks during Carnival allowed people to move and behave in perfect anonymity, something they certainly could not do in their own countries. Venice was not at war within its own borders until 1797, so many people moved there in the wake of conflicts in their own countries, including the architect Jacopo Sansovino and writer Pietro Aretino after the Sack of Rome in 1527.

Venice was generally considered, certainly in the eighteenth century, the playground of Europe. The early twentieth century also saw many visitors choosing to stay at the Lido for health reasons, attracted by its new reputation as an elegant European bathing resort. Some stayed a few days, a few months or a few years. Some remained until the end of their lives. Others who did not die in Venice asked to be buried in the cemetery on San Michele, including Igor Stravinsky and Josef Brodsky.

Throughout the centuries, the city has also attracted painters, musicians and writers looking for inspiration (and nowadays photographers and film directors) even if, like William Shakespeare, they have never set foot in the city.

Born in Arezzo, the fourteenth-century Italian poet **Francesco Petrarca (Petrarch)** (1304–74), went to Venice to find a haven, 'mundus alter' ('another world'), 'the most marvellous city that I have ever seen'. He celebrated Venice as the 'sole shelter in our days of liberty, justice and peace, the sole refuge of the good'.

Petrarch had visited Venice as a young man, but it was only in later life that he decided to live there, attracted by the idea of a haven of freedom and peace and by his high regard for its inhabitants: 'This nation of sailors was so skilful in the handling of horses and weapons, so spirited and so hardy, that it surpassed all other warlike nations whether by sea or by land' (quoted by John Julius Norwich in *Venice, Pure City*). He arrived in Venice with his daughter, son-in-law and grandchild, fleeing the plague raging in Milan. The family settled in the beautiful Palazzo Molino of the two towers, overlooking the Bacino, which the Venetian Senate granted him in return for a promise that Petrarch would donate his impressive library to Venice after his death. The idea appealed to him, as he liked to think that 'they [his books] cannot be sold, nor separated [. . .] and kept in a safe place [. . .] far from fire and rain.' In 1364, at the festivities in the piazza to celebrate the victory over Crete, the poet was given a place of honour next to Doge Celsi. From his house he witnessed the triumphant return of the Venetian fleet after it had put down the Cretan rebellion and described the event in detail:

> It was the fourth of June – perhaps the sixth hour of the day, I was standing at my window [. . .] when one of those long ships that they call galleys entered the harbour which augured good news, for the masts were garlanded with flowers, and on the deck were young men, crowned with green wreaths and waving banners over their heads.

It was also in Venice that he put together his *Familiares*, 'a book of my letters to different people', and *Seniles*, letters written in old age.

His friend Giovanni Boccaccio visited him in Venice, but it seems that Petrarch was not entirely happy in the city, for, as he complained in a letter, many accused him of envy, and four youngsters had called him 'virum bonum, immo optimum, eundem tamen illitteratum prorsus et idiotam'. They clearly admired him, but also saw him as an ignorant old fool. It was in the early summer of 1367 that he left by boat for Pavia, taking with him some of his books, as the agreement with the Venetian government had not been respected. Unfortunately, the library was eventually dispersed, against his wishes: some books ended up in the possession of the Carrara family in Padua; others, including priceless codices, were sold. From Padua he moved to what is now Arquà Petrarca, a lovely medieval town where he died in 1374. After his death, the remainder of his library, which he had left in Palazzo Molino in Venice, was neglected for centuries. It was eventually found in poor condition in a small room above the main door of the Basilica of St Mark; some of the volumes had crumbled to dust.

The creation of the Biblioteca Marciana is sometimes mistakenly attributed to Petrarch, whose bust presides over the large reading room

5   *Bust of Petrarch*
(*courtesy of*
Marciana Library)

in the famous library (it was in fact founded in 1468 by Cardinal Bessarion, and finally completed in 1560). A plaque recording Petrarch's time in Venice can still be seen on the façade of Palazzo Molino next to San Sepulcro Bridge, on the Riva degli Schiavoni.

The poet became a model to many, including **William Shakespeare** (?1564–1616). The city is referred to in many of Shakespeare's plays, and two of his works are set partly in Venice – *The Merchant of Venice* and *Othello*. *The Taming of the Shrew* takes place in Padua on the Brenta, and *Romeo and Juliet* is set in 'fair Verona', another important city of the Veneto, but it is said that the original story which inspired Arthur Brooke's *The Tragical History of Romeus and Juliet* in 1562, on which the Shakespeare play was based, was set in Venice itself, near San Pietro di Castello. The fate of the two young Venetian protagonists of the original, Elena and Gerardo, was less tragic than that of Romeo and Juliet, as they were ultimately reunited and lived happily ever after.

Even though he probably never set foot in Italy, it may be assumed that Shakespeare, whose command of Italian was perhaps good, based his famous plays on Italian texts. He might also have had encounters with travellers who knew Italy firsthand. Like many of his contemporaries who read Italian, Shakespeare must have read Giraldi di Cinthio's story, *Gli Hecatommithi*, one of the sources for *Othello*, which was available in French and Italian, but which had not yet been translated into English in 1603, when Shakespeare's tragedy was written.

Unlike many others, Thomas Nashe in his *The Unfortunate Traveller* of 1594 wrote unfavourably of Italy, describing it as a country where 'the art of atheism, epicurizing, whoring, sodomy, poisoning' was rife. His 'Unfortunate Traveller' was taken to the house of a 'pernicious courtesan' and ended up in a Venetian prison. This darker side of Italy is portrayed more widely in the tragedies of Shakespeare's contemporaries Thomas Middleton and John Webster. On the whole, however, Shakespeare gives us a favourable view, judging from the proverb quoted by Holofernes in *Love's Labour's Lost*:

Venetia, Venetia
chi non ti vede, non ti pretia.

Venice, Venice
who does not see you, does not appreciate you.

The reputation for sexual licence in the Venetian Republic plays
an important part in the plot of *Othello*. Iago takes advantage of
this to ignite the jealousy of Othello, the foreigner and a Moor,
married to a Venetian lady in a city where women were known for
their licence and promiscuity. In the course of the play Desdemona,
Emilia and Bianca are all referred to as whores. In Act IV, Scene II
Othello taunts Desdemona:

I took you for that cunning whore of Venice
That married with Othello.

In *The Merchant of Venice* the Jew Shylock pleads for equality,
dignity and respect – basic human rights for which Venetians then
provided an example to the rest of the world:

If you deny it, let the danger light
Upon your charter and your Cities freedome.

Shakespeare seems in *The Merchant of Venice* to have excellent
knowledge of the Jewish practices of money-lending and usury, and
of the widespread anti-Semitism in the city. The play was written
in 1596, a few years before the arrival of the English ambassador
Wotton and traveller Thomas Coryat, both of whom stayed near the
Ghetto. Contemporary English visitors would probably also have
stayed in Cannaregio. The historian Brian Pullan has shown that
some of Shakespeare's scenes recount events which really did take
place in Venice in 1567. It is possible to identify two places which
may have been the homes of Desdemona: the delightful Palazzo
Contarini-Fasan, built around 1475, overlooking the Grand Canal

and almost opposite the Church of the Salute, or 'the house of Othello', near Campo dei Carmini, as described by Rawdon Brown. Although nothing is certain, the sculpture of a warrior decorating the façade of the palace might have sparked Brown's imagination.

Why did Shakespeare set his merchant in Venice? Disguises, masks and intrigues were very fashionable at that time, and the city enjoyed a reputation for decadence and immorality, but above all it was a place where money was everything and anything was possible for the love of it. Shakespeare's contemporary **Ben Jonson** (1572–1637) also set his bitter comedy *Volpone* in Venice. The play's opening is well known: 'Good morning to the day, and next, my gold!' This is as shocking as Shylock's reaction when he discovers that both daughter and money are missing from his house: 'My daughter! O my ducats! O my daughter!' We are left in no doubt about the role money played in Venice.

When Sir Politick Would-Be in *Volpone* says: 'I had read Contarine, took me a house', he was referring to Gasparo Contarini's book *De Magistratibus et Republica Venetorum libri quinque*, written in Latin, but translated into English by the politician and writer Lewis Lewkenor after 1551. Contarini's work contributed, like Sansovino's *Venezia, città nobilissima*, to the fact that many educated Englishmen – including Jonson – had sound second-hand knowledge of daily life in the Serenissima. Venice has been a source of fascination and fantasy for other writers, painters and artists who never set foot there, including Thomas Otway, whose Restoration tragedy *Venice Preserv'd* has been mentioned, and saw great success on the London stage in the 1680s.

The great eighteenth-century writer **François-Marie Arouet**, better known as **Voltaire** (1694–1778), never visited Venice either, although he had several Venetian friends, including Casanova and Algarotti. In Chapter 19 of his memoirs, Casanova related a conversation he had with Voltaire about Venice and Venetians known to him. Voltaire's short satirical novel *Candide* contains three chapters dedicated to Venice, portrayed again as the ultimate place for an easy life and easy women. The young character Paquette, now a fallen woman, says to Candide, 'I have come here to practise my profession.' But Voltaire also knew that some equality among human beings was possible there: when Candide cannot help but remark that the gondoliers 'are perpetually singing', a Venetian points out that 'indeed, generally speaking the condition of a gondolier is preferable to that of a doge, but the difference is small.'

Venice is mentioned again in Voltaire's short satirical story of 1768, 'The Princess of Babylon'. It focuses on a handsome young shepherd, Amazan, who travels the world and then proceeds to Venice:

> He embarked upon the sea of Dalmatia, and landed in a city that had no resemblance to anything he had heretofore seen. The sea formed the streets, and the houses were built in the water. The few public places with which this city was ornamented, were filled with men and women with double faces, that which nature had bestowed on them, and a pasteboard one, ill painted, with which they covered their natural face, so that the people seemed composed of spectres. Amazan despised a fashion so contrary to nature.

This version of the Serenissima appeared not only in writing but also in painting. The French eighteenth-century painter **Jean-Antoine Watteau** (1684–1721) never had the chance to travel to the Serenissima in his brief life. He is well-known for his representation of charming scenes, both fanciful and dreamlike, one of which is entitled *Fêtes vénitiennes*, painted in 1718–19. This painting, now in the Scottish National Gallery in Edinburgh, is a blend of fantasy, restrained licence, beauty and exquisite elegance. There is no doubt that it is all imagined, as Watteau left France only once and certainly never reached Venice. The background landscape with its overpowering tree is probably the garden of a villa on the mainland, rather than the garden of a Venetian palace. It is generally assumed that the young man playing the musette, sitting on the right side of the picture, is Watteau himself. It would be pleasing to think that the sick young painter fancied himself in an idyllic Venetian garden. In this painting no one wears a mask, but in the Wallace

Collection's 1715 *Voulez-vous triompher des belles*, Harlequin is wearing the typical Italian mask associated with Venetian carnivals, festivities and *commedia dell'arte*.

Staying in 1718 at the Parisian home of his friend the collector Crozat, who owned a wide collection of paintings by Italian artists, many of which were Venetian, Watteau became acquainted with the works of Bellini, Giorgione and Paolo Veronese, which were to influence his use of colour as well as his style and subjects. As the twentieth-century French art critic René Huyghe said: 'He takes his place in the line of painters who, after the Venetians, Bellini and Giorgione, know how to depict the clear music of the soul of the picture.'

Also sharing Crozat's house was a Flemish painter, Nicholas Vleughels, who had been working in Italy, visiting Venice between 1707 and 1712. It is known that Watteau copied his Venetian sketchbook, and through Vleughels he met artists, including the Venetian painter of pastels, Rosalba Carriera, whom he subsequently drew as *Rosalba Carriera à sa toilette*. He also drew a portrait of the Venetian caricaturist Anton Maria Zanetti in Paris in 1720. Carriera's own portrait of Watteau (which can be seen in the Treviso City Museum) is a moving record, as it was painted in the last year of Watteau's tragically short life. In France Watteau also met Italian actors, who were very popular at the time and performing in *commedia dell'arte* productions in Paris; some can be identified in his paintings. These works later inspired the French poet **Paul Verlaine** (1844–96) to recreate Watteau's dreamy atmosphere in his 1869 collection of poems, *Fêtes galantes*:

> Your soul is a chosen landscape
> Charmed by the masked
> Who play their lutes and dance, almost
> Sad behind their fanciful disguises!

Verlaine's Venetian poems, always praised for their musical quality, inspired in turn the composers Reynaldo Hahn, Gabriel Fauré and Claude Debussy and were set to music by Fauré as part of *Five Venetian Melodies*, written while he was staying in Venice in 1891 with Winaretta Singer, his wealthy hostess and patron.

In the poem 'Mandoline'

> The gallant serenaders
> And their lovely listeners
> Exchange bland nothings
> Beneath the singing boughs.

His patron's hope that composer and poet would meet in Venice was never realised, but she arranged for the first performance to take place in a boat on the Grand Canal.

Hahn, Fauré and Debussy were not the only musicians to be inspired in a place which had once been the musical capital of Europe. Like Rousseau, visitors were attracted not only by its concerts, but also for the more popular music heard on the Grand Canal sung by gondoliers, who – as mentioned in the previous chapter – were reputed to sing the verses of Ariosto and Tasso.

The Italian writer **Torquato Tasso** (1544–95) moved with his father Bernardo to Venice in 1559 because the city was famous worldwide for its editing and publishing activities. Tasso's father came to attend the publication of his 1560 book, *Amadigi*, now almost forgotten. Of much greater longevity and influence is Torquato Tasso's epic poem *Jerusalem Delivered* (*La Gerusalemme liberata*), which depicted events from the First Crusade. *Jerusalem Delivered* was completed around 1575, and was first published in Venice in 1580 by Celio Malespini (without the poet's authorisation, as Tasso was interned in Sant' Anna Hospital between 1579 and 1586). He had started writing his poem at the age of 15, and it is generally assumed that the inspiration for this war narrative poem goes back to the fact that Venice and other cities had been gripped in the past by the fear and almost continuous threat of Turkish invasion. The site of the famous Battle of Lepanto (1571) was not far from Venice. Another source of inspiration might be a traumatic event which happened when Tasso's beloved sister Cornelia survived a terrifying kidnapping attempt by Muslims when the family was living in Sorrento. Tasso's short tragic life was marred by bouts of depression and madness.

After publication, the long poem was repeatedly copied, some elements being used by the English Elizabethan poet **Edmund Spenser** (1552–99) in his *Faerie Queene*:

> Along the shore, as swift as glance of eye,
> A little gondelay, bedecked trim
> With boughs and arbours woven cunningly.

At the end of the seventeenth century *Jerusalem Delivered* was translated (not altogether faithfully) into the Venetian dialect by Tomaso Mondini. Subsequently (and maybe because of the translation), it became a favourite part of the gondoliers' repertoire, as illiterate gondoliers mainly spoke Venetian. Many stanzas were used, particularly the description of the deadly fight between the Christian Tancredi and the Muslim Clorinda (in love with one another in spite of belonging to opposing sides). Thus gondoliers threw defiant vocal challenges to one another in singing matches across the Grand Canal from the early eighteenth century until about 1950. 'I do not fear the battle and will kill you before sunset,' ran the threat.

The popularity of this work in Venice might also be due to the fact that the composer Claudio Monteverdi, who had put the famous final combat into music, had it performed for the first time in 1624, before Francisco Ereda in 1629 and Biagio Marini in 1637 composed their own versions. This first performance took place in the courtyard of Palazzo Mocenigo in San Stae (now the Museum of Fashion and Textiles). It was common to have concerts in the courtyards of Venetian palaces, where balconies served as opera boxes. The Paduan composer and famous violinist **Giuseppe Tartini** (1692–1770) also composed his own *Sonata del Tasso*.

This partly classical, partly popular music to be sung from a boat continued to inspire a succession of famous composers, including

Felix Mendelssohn, Frédéric Chopin, Giuseppe Verdi, Wagner and Fauré.

'If the Iliad had been written down, it would have been sung a great deal. No poet has been sung as much as Tasso in Venice, save by the gondoliers, and they are surely not the greatest of readers,' wrote an enthralled Rousseau in his *Essays on Foreign Languages in Song*. Rousseau had transcribed these tunes in his *Canzoni da battello* in 1753 and also devoted a lengthy entry to the barcarolle in his *Dictionary of Music*.

The gondoliers' song became a leitmotif in so many writings on Venice. **Joseph Addison** (1672–1719) wrote in the diary he kept while travelling in Italy in 1701–3:

> I cannot forbear mentioning a custom at Venice, which is particular to the common people of this country, of singing stanzas out of Tasso. They are set to a pretty solemn tune, and when one begins in any part of the poet, it is odd, but he will be answered by somebody else that overhears him, so that sometimes you have ten or twelve in the neighbourhood of one another, taking verse, and running on with the poem as far as their memories will carry them.

Many remarked on the sad and hypnotic quality of this strange singing. In 1782 William Beckford noted in his travelling book on Italy: 'the gondoliers, catching the air, imitated its cadences and were answered by others at a distance, whose voices, echoed by the arch of the bridge, acquired a plaintive and interesting tone.' The English musicologist Charles Burney also mentioned it in 1770 in his *Tour of Italy:* 'I had many enquiries to make, and had very sanguine expectation from this city, with regard to the music of past times as well as present [. . .] the songs of the Gondoleri, or Waterman, which are so celebrated.'

'These boatmen traditionally so easily sing and recite Latin verse, especially Tasso's poem, with a facility which stupefies the Foreigner,' marvelled Joseph de Lalande in his 1765 *Voyage en*

Italie. A few years later, in his *Voyage in Italy*, Goethe, stopping in Venice in 1786, also described these impromptu nocturnal open-air performances.

In his narrative poem *Childe Harold's Pilgrimage*, Byron sadly lamented that the gondoliers no longer sang:

> In Venice the echoes of Tasso are gone
> And the songless gondolier rows in silence.

This disappointment, shared by his friend Percy Bysshe Shelley, was reported in 1818, but a few years later Madame de Staël reported that she had nevertheless heard gondoliers sing Tasso. The French writer Stendhal's experience was different again, as he wrote in a letter (volume 3 of his *Correspondance 1812–1816*) that he had heard verses by Tasso and Ariosto, but sung by women of Malamocco (an island situated between the Lido and Pellestrina).

The tradition seems to have continued in one form or another. In 1850 Madame du Boccage wrote in her *Lettres d'Italie*: 'A gondolier starts off a couplet by Ariosto or Tasso, and his colleague takes up the second line, picked up again by the first singer.' The Spanish nineteenth-century traveller Emilio Castelar remembers similarly in his *Memories of Italy* (*Recuerdos de Italia*, 1873): 'From the gondola came forth a most harmonious song, solemn, accompanied by excellent music, the accords mysteriously amplified and softened by the resonance of the air and the lagoon.'

The exiled German composer Richard Wagner, who died in Venice, definitely heard the singing, as he recalled in his diary in 1858: 'those deeply melancholic melodies, sung in a rich and powerful voice, are carried from a distance across the water, and the echoes fade away to the horizon.' They probably inspired part of the third act of *Tristan and Isolde*, on which he was working up to 1859, when it was completed.

'Sing to me, Gondolier! Sing words from Tasso's lay!' pleaded John Addington Symonds in Venice in 1880. At the beginning of the twentieth century Maurice Barrès, the French aesthete and writer noted in *The Death of Venice* (*La mort de Venise*): 'And so the gondolier's song becomes the powerful unrefined voice of an unsophisticated people, but charged as a result with all the softness, all the richness, all the ceremony which the name Tasso summons up, the greatest in the South.'

George Sand was very keen on Italian music, and in her *Traveller's Letters* (*Lettres d'un voyageur*, 1857) also describes listening to the music, enjoying balmy evenings in a gondola in the company of her lover, Pietro Pagello, who composed a barcarolle (a popular song to be sung on the water) in her honour, subsequently adapted by Reynaldo Hahn. In 1845 Chopin, another lover of George Sand, wrote his *Barcarolle* (Op. 60), although he never visited Venice. He very probably came across this form through other contemporary composers such as Gioachino Rossini and Daniel Auber, who often introduced a barcarolle into their operas. The 'Song of the Fisherman' in Rossini's *La Donna del Lago* of 1816 is an obvious case, as is the fisherman's aria in *William Tell*. Verdi used it in *Mefistofele*, and in his Venetian historical opera, *The Two Foscari* (*I due Foscari*, 1844). The French composer Auber included it in 1830 in *La muette de Portici* and *Fra Diavolo*. One of the most famous versions is in Offenbach's *Tales of Hoffman*.

Reynaldo Hahn (1874–1947) related in his 1933 *Journal of a Musician* how delighted he was to hear the gondoliers singing heartily, keen to demonstrate their rowing ability as well as their beautiful voices. Following Rousseau's example, he wrote down and adapted into music what he heard. In a letter to his cousin Marie Nordlinger he related rather disparagingly how he wrote his six Venetian songs 'hurriedly': 'I have written some Venetian songs – vulgar, sentimental, extremely Grand Canal – neither the Venice of the Doges nor that of Byron or Guardi (except no.3). This is banal, cosmopolitan, pleasure loving Venice, floating on a tide of indolence and facile affairs.'

However, Hahn did play and sing them himself in an open-air impromptu performance, with the piano having been lowered onto a boat in a canal near Santa Maria Formosa: 'In a candlelit boat I was alone with a piano and two rowers [. . .] I sang all kinds of things [. . .] little by little the passers-by gathered,' he recalled in his *Journal*.

What would these music-lovers say if they knew that Venetian music has now almost entirely disappeared from the Grand Canal, and the main musical pieces to be heard (and specially requested by tourists) are a Neapolitan popular song, 'O sole mio', and 'Lara's Theme' from the film *Doctor Zhivago*?

It is not altogether surprising that Tasso's poem, calling repeatedly for heroism, freedom, nationalism and courage, had appealed to composers of literary and musical works at the time of the Risorgimento in Italy, as well as to Venetians impatient to shake off the long burden of Austrian occupation, which ended in 1866.

One Italian composer whose sympathies for Garibaldi and the Risorgimento were clear was **Giuseppe Verdi** (1813–1901). Apart from his adaptation of Byron's plays *The Two Foscari* and *Marino Faliero*, the most famous of Verdi's works connected with Venice is *Otello*, completed in 1887. Verdi and his librettist, **Arrigo Boito**

6   Bust of Giuseppe Verdi at Giardini

(1842–1918), did away with the first act of Shakespeare's tragedy and set the opera only on the island of Cyprus, then part of the Venetian Empire, excluding the city entirely. Venetians, however, still claim the part the city played in the tragedy, pointing out Desdemona's palace on the Grand Canal, as well as Otello's house, Casa del Moro.

The fate of Venice since 1793 interested Verdi, who regularly used stories and plots concerning freedom and independence. The 'Chorus of the Slaves' in *Nabucco* is one of the best examples, treated since its composition almost as a national anthem in Italy, now assumed by the nationalist party the Lega Nord:

> Rekindle the memories in our hearts,
> Tell us about the time gone by!
> Oh my country so lovely and lost!
> Oh remembrance so dear, yet unhappy.

Verdi's recourse to the barcarolle, once in *Rigoletto* and twice in *I due Foscari*, returns to the familiar Verdian theme, dear to Venetians, that exile is more cruel than death: 'L'esilio è più crudele della morte'.

The librettist Arrigo Boito's older brother was Camillo Boito, an eminent architect and author who is remembered mainly for having written *Senso*, a short novel of 1833 about a destructive passion, dealing also with the theme of Austrian-occupied Venice's fight for independence. The novel was immortalised in 1954 by a film adaptation shot by Visconti. It is worth noting that the film was an invaluable resource when restorers were recreating La Fenice, which had been almost completely destroyed in a fire in 1996. In the first two chapters of 2005's *The City of Falling Angels* the American journalist and writer John Berendt relived the fire and its aftermath. The opening of the film *Senso* is memorable, with its turbulent performance of *Il Trovatore* at the Fenice, where young supporters of Garibaldi and Venetian independence defy the Austrian officers attending the concert. The hopeless and fateful passion of the beautiful Venetian countess Livia for the seductive but worthless Austrian officer Remigio echoes the melodrama of an opera. At the same time it describes the tragedy of a city crushed for half a century by a foreign power.

Verdi's great contemporary, **Richard Wagner** (1813–83), could not keep away from the musical city. Like Verdi, Wagner shared a deep attachment to Venice, which was first for him a haven. Forced to leave Germany, where he had been condemned to death for his radical activities, he arrived in Venice in August 1858 as a political exile, and settled in Palazzo Giustinian-Brandolini. He was also running away from a difficult marriage and a complicated love affair with Mathilde Wesendonck, the wife of one of his supporters.

As he noted in his diary on arrival, 'I shall be able to complete Tristan here, despite the turbulent world.' He had found peace and quiet, worked hard on *Tristan and Isolde* and *Parsifal* in the morning and took short breaks in Piazza San Marco in the afternoon for an ice cream or drinks and cake at Caffè Lavena (where we are told that he 'faceva poum', or never paid his bill). He enjoyed his grand

7 Bust of Richard Wagner at Giardini

bedroom, which was decorated with frescoes by Tiepolo, and he had his piano sent from Zurich. The composer listened from his balcony to the 'ancient singing of Gondoliers' which, as he wrote in his diary, inspired the third act of *Tristan*: 'These melodies, profoundly melancholic, sung in a sonorous and powerful voice [. . .] have given me a deep emotion. Magnificent!' His haven was not to endure, as the Austrian army was on the move in Italy against Garibaldi, and Wagner had to leave Venice in March 1859. The city was still under the iron rule of the Austrian Empire, and the police followed his every move. Nevertheless, he was back in November 1861. The sight of Titian's *Assumption of the Virgin* so overwhelmed him that it is supposed partly to have inspired *Die Meistersinger*. Fifteen years later, he returned for a longer visit, taking lodgings in Palazzo Contarini dalle Figure on the Grand Canal. Because of ill health, probably heart trouble, Venice suited him, as it offered a warmer climate. He came back a further three times, finally settling in Palazzo Vendramin in Cannaregio (now the Venice Casino), where he stayed until his death.

On Christmas Eve 1882 he organised a party and a concert in the Apollonia Room at the Fenice for his wife Cosima's birthday. A few weeks later he died; according to his physician, Dr Keppler, his death 'must have been caused by a state of physical overexcitement'. There are suggestions that he might have been *in flagrante* with the maid, Betty Birkel, or that he had argued violently with his wife Cosima. His body was embalmed and transported to the railway station, and then put on the train to Bayreuth. The Venetians paid him a great tribute, escorting the funeral gondola bearing his glass-covered coffin to the station in silence. Two plaques outside Palazzo Vendramin-Calergi record his time there (one written by his great admirer, the poet Gabriele D'Annunzio). An impressive bust can also be seen in the Castello gardens, but it is incongruous to find his photograph presiding over one of the gambling rooms of the present Casino. Some rooms of the Casino are now open to the public as a small museum dedicated to Wagner, displaying personal items, letters and manuscripts, as well as a copy of the couch on which he died.

Wagner's life in Venice is well documented by his diary, and by that of his wife, who kept a detailed account of her husband's daily activities, visitors, meals, aches and pains and conversations. Much can be read elsewhere about Wagner in Venice. D'Annunzio in *The Fire* (*Il fuoco*), published in 1900, makes several references to Wagner and to the impact of his work. He wrote in his inimitable style a description of the funeral party on its way up the Grand Canal to the station to leave Venice (although he was not present in Venice at the time):

> The funeral boat moved off; the widow followed with her loved ones; [. . .] the deep silence was worthy of the departed, and transformed the forces of the Universe into an endless paean of praise for the religion of men. A column of doves, rising from the marble of the Scalzi church in a swirling flutter of wings, flew above the catafalque across the Canal, and wreathed the green cupola of San Simeone.

Wagner and Verdi apparently never met, although it is rumoured that Verdi had paid a visit to Wagner on 13 February, the day he died. The thought of such an encounter is tantalising, as it seems that Wagner never approved of Verdi. We read in Cosima's diaries that Wagner once mocked a Verdi theme which he heard sung on a canal, and we find in one of her entries, 'In the evening we heard Verdi's Requiem, about which it would be best not to say anything.'

Wagner had been a close friend of the German philosopher **Friedrich Nietzsche** (1844–1900), also a frequent visitor to Italy and Venice. Nietzsche had renounced German citizenship in 1880 but had not yet acquired a Swiss passport, and led a wandering life until 1889. He made four short visits to Venice between 1880 and 1887. On one of his stays he found a room near Piazza San Marco, which he thought was the 'most beautiful working room'. He also stayed in Palazzo Berlendis near the Fondamente Nove, then still looking across the lagoon towards the cemetery island of San Michele, from where he wrote to a friend, Overbeck, on 27 March

1880: 'Today I found lodgings ideally situated not in the Laguna, but as if it was by the sea, with the view of the island of the dead.' However, the heat, the rain, the wind and the mosquitoes made him flee, as did an outbreak of cholera on a later visit. During this period he was writing his most famous work *Thus Spake Zarathustra*, and from April to June 1884 he spent weeks working on his friend Köselitz's musical composition *The Lion of Venice*.

In his poem 'My Happiness' he expresses his pleasure to be in Venice: 'Oh my happiness, my happiness,' he declares, likening the moon hanging above the Campanile to the dot on the letter i, just as the French poet Musset had done. In *Ecce Homo*, published in 1883, a kind of autobiography, he wrote an exalted celebration of the city: 'In Venice I would live quietly, like an angel, I would not eat meat and would avoid anything which makes the soul troubled and tense. Recently I wrote to Overbeck that I love one single and unique place in the world, and that is Venice.'

For personal and ideological reasons, Nietzsche had broken off what had been for a few years an intense relationship with Richard Wagner and Cosima. He therefore did not visit them in Venice, but the news of Wagner's death upset him and made him seriously ill, especially when he learned that the death had occurred as he was finishing *Thus Spake Zarathustra*, which, as he wrote, 'was completed during the exact sacred hour in which Richard Wagner died in Venice'. This coincidence affected greatly someone who had been ill for most of his life and was already showing worrying signs of mental breakdown. It did not prevent him from writing *Nietzsche against Wagner*, however, and perhaps even prompted him to do so, as it was published in 1889. In its original edition the work had in the 'Intermezzo' section a poem dedicated to Venice and Venetian music (here in Walter Kaufmann's translation).

> At the bridge I stood
> Lately in the brown night.
> From afar came a song:
> As a golden drop it welled

Over the quivering surface.
Gondolas, lights and music
Drunken it swam out into the twilight.
My soul, a stringed instrument
Sang to itself, invisibly touched,
A secret gondola song,
Quivering with iridescent happiness
Did anyone listen to it?

Nietzsche had written in the introduction: 'Seeking to find another word for music, I inevitably come back to Venice.' Very soon after this he had a final breakdown.

The Russian composer **Pyotr Ilyich Tchaikovsky** (1840–93) visited Venice as many as four times between 1872 and 1881. On the first occasion his mood was so bleak that he found the city 'as gloomy as if it were dead', and headed straight for Rome. To recover from his disastrous marriage to Antonina Milyukova and fortified by money from his patron, Baroness von Meck, he was back again with his brother in 1877 and settled in style in the Hotel Londra Palace. During the nine days he spent there, he found inspiration, as reported in letters to his sister and to the

8   *Plaque commemorating Tchaikovsky at Hotel Londra Palace*

Baroness. He was completing the second act of *Eugene Onegin* and the first movements of his Fourth Symphony – amongst his most 'Russian' works. Nevertheless, he wrote to his brother that he found the city repellent: 'I must tell you that I find Venice unbearable. There is something awful, disgusting which I will never get used to.' The regular and healthier life he led there allowed him to work surprisingly productively, although his mood was still extremely volatile. He drank heavily during that visit. On his last trip, in 1881, he was finally reconciled to the city: 'This time I love Venice. Today, having got up, I opened the window and the day seemed to me wonderful, the air was balmy and caressing.'

The Londra Palace now bears a plaque recording the composer's stay, and has a special suite named after him, which contains a small display of copies of documents and photographs relating to the time he spent there. One of the glass panes to the left of the main entrance is an engraved copy of a hand-written letter to Nadezhda von Meck, reporting progress on his symphony. The last of his *Twelve Pieces* (Opus 40), composed in 1878, entitled 'Interrupted Dreams', was inspired by a song he heard from his hotel window on Riva degli Schiavoni. After his death, a copy of three tragedies by Euripides was found among his belongings. It was a rare edition published in 1581, and inside Tchaikovsky had written in his own hand, 'Stolen from the library of the Palace of the Doges in Venice on 15 December 1877 by Pyotr Tchaikovsky, Court Counsellor and Professor at the Conservatoire'.

Lord George Gordon Byron (1788–1824) is probably the visitor Venice remembers most. He had not come to Venice during his Grand Tour (1808–11), as he was diverted from the traditional itinerary by the Napoleonic Wars. On his return to England, his friends encouraged him to publish some of the writings he had collected during these travels, and the ensuing publication of the first two cantos of *Childe Harold's Pilgrimage* was a great success, to his surprise. He marvelled: 'I awoke one morning and found myself famous.'

In 1816 Byron fled England for Venice, trying to escape debts and avoid moral public condemnation after a disastrous marriage in 1814 and a scandal involving his sister. As one of his lovers, Lady Caroline Lamb, put it, he was generally considered 'mad, bad and dangerous to know'. During the three years he spent in the city, the English Romantic poet wrote prolifically – letters, poems and plays. The third and fourth cantos of *Childe Harold's Pilgrimage* (a fictionalised account of his travels) were also completed.

> I stood in Venice, on the bridge of Sighs,
> A palace and a prison on each hand;
> I saw from out the wave her structures rise
> As from the stroke of the enchanter's wand.

It was only a few years after the fateful year of 1797, and he recorded with nostalgia the past glories of the city:

> And such she was; her daughters had their dowers
> From spoils of nations, and the exhaustless East
> Poured into her lap all gems in sparkling showers.
> In purple was she robed, and of her feast
> Monarchs partook, and deemed their dignity increased.
> [. . .] Venice, lost and won,
> Her thirteen years hundred years of freedom done,
> Sinks, like a sea-weed, unto whence she rose!

In 'Ode on Venice' he prophesied the coming woes of a city doomed to sink, fears which are still shared two centuries later:

> O Venice! Venice! When thy marble walls
> Are level with the waters, there shall be
> A cry of nations o'er thy sunken walls,
> A loud lament along the sweeping sea!
> If I, a northern wanderer, weep for thee,
> What should thy sons do? – Anything but weep:
> And yet they only murmur in their sleep.

He had found the perfect setting for himself at this stage in his life. As he wrote in a letter to his publisher John Murray,

> Venice pleases me as much as I expected – and I expected much. It is one of those places which I know before I see them, and has always haunted me the most – after the east. I like the gloomy gaiety of their gondolas and the silence of their canals. I do not even dislike the evident decay of the city, though I regret the singularity of its vanished costume. However there is much left still.

His interest in historical events spurred him to write, after he left Venice for Ravenna, the tragic stories of the beheaded doge Marino Faliero, later adapted as an opera by Donizetti in 1835, and *The Two Foscari*, set by Verdi in 1844. Both doges are treated harshly by the Venetian state and the operas have remained to some extent unpopular in the city.

Byron, the 'northern wanderer' and romantic English incarnation of Don Juan, led a dissolute life and made the most of the decadent Venetian atmosphere, as recounted for instance in his amusing *Beppo, a Venetian Story*. Venice was also the perfect environment to work on his humorous picaresque narrative poem *Don Juan*, now generally considered his masterpiece. Shelley, who joined him there for a short period, thought Venice had a very poor influence on his friend, but conceded that he seemed to prosper in a place where he enjoyed so much freedom and tolerance. In a letter to Thomas Love Peacock dated October 1818, Shelley noted how different Byron seemed to be in Venice: 'I saw Lord Byron, and really hardly knew him again; he is changed into the liveliest and happiest looking man I ever met!' Stendhal gives us a telling (and envious) portrait of Byron in a letter:

> Venice, 27 June 1817. I was introduced to Lord Byron at the theatre. What a demi-god! No one could have more beautiful eyes. A man of wondrous form and talent. He is barely 28, and is the foremost poet of England and probably of the world. To witness him listening to music is to observe the perfect profile of the Greeks.

To be a great poet, and what's more the scion of one of the most ancient families of England is too much for our times; so it was with some pleasure that I heard that Lord Byron is also a scoundrel. When he entered Mme de Staël's salon at Coppet, all the English ladies got up and left.

This last would not have been the reaction in the more lenient Serenissima. A great success in Venetian circles, Byron received the great and famous in his house, as well as people from all walks of life: he entertained gondoliers, merchants, priests, and also conquests like Marianna ('an ordinary woman', his first landlady in Calle Frezzeria), a baker's wife known as La Fornarina and his last and perhaps most important love, Countess Guiccioli. Amorous adventures, generally with married women, were described in letters to his friends, to his half-sister Augusta Leigh and to his friend Douglas Kinnaird, to whom he wrote: 'I meant to have stopped gallivanting altogether, but the "besoin d'aimer" came back from my heart again.'

In his major biography on Byron, *The Myth of Lord Byron* (*Il mito di Lord Byron*), Vincenzo Patanè mentions that Byron, who was bisexual and had throughout his previous life formed attachments with young boys, whether at school or at university, continued such adventures in Venice. This was strongly condemned by the bewildered Shelley in his letter to Peacock: 'He associates with wretches who seem almost to have lost the gait and physiognomy of man & who do not scruple to avow practices which are not only not named but I believe seldom ever conceived in England. He says he disapproves [*sic*] but he endures.' Sodomy was harshly punished in England at the time, but Venice had been since the eighteenth century, and even earlier, a tolerant place for those who could freely indulge and remain unpunished, particularly at Carnival time when the use of masks allowed one's identity, nationality and gender to be hidden. Byron's antics seem to be remembered indulgently by Venetians nowadays.

In the monastery on the island of San Lazzaro, having befriended the Armenian monks, Byron tried hard to support their culture and language, seeing them as 'an oppressed and a noble nation'.

Every day he visited the island and took lessons in the language, helping also to translate and publish at his own cost an Armenian grammar into English. He chose the language for its difficulty, as an intellectual challenge which he considered 'an amusement', the perfect counterpart to the dissolute life he led by night.

A keen sportsman, terrified of putting on weight and spoiling his good looks, he would swim from his Palazzo Mocenigo on the Grand Canal all the way to the Lido, where he would gallop on horseback for hours on the beach and then proceed to swim the 200 yards to the island of San Lazzaro, his faithful gondolier following with his clothes. Byron also regularly visited the beautiful and clever Countess Isabella Teotochi Albrizzi, who hosted a famous salon. Hobhouse, Byron's travelling companion, called her 'the Madame de Staël of Italy'. It is probably in her salon, or perhaps at the salon of Marina Querini Benzon, that he met Countess Guiccioli.

After three years the city had lost a part of its charm and fun and had become 'an oyster with no pearl', so Byron decided to return to England, but was prevented from doing so by the illness of his daughter Allegra. He eventually left Venice on 21 December 1819 to join his ailing lover Teresa Guiccioli in Ravenna. After Allegra's death at a Capuchin convent at Bagnacavallo near Ravenna, and Shelley's tragic death by drowning at Livorno, Byron, who was probably bored and had long thought of travelling to Greece and devoting the rest of his life to fighting the Turks for Greek independence, determined to make his dream come true: 'I dreamed that Greece might still be free.' While in his lover's house in Ravenna, Byron had become involved through her brother, Conte Gamba, in the Italian Republican movement, the Carbonari. To her despair, both men left for Greece in 1824, but soon after their arrival, Byron died at Missolonghi of rheumatic fever. He was only 36 years old. He had written in *Childe Harold's Pilgrimage* (Canto IV, Stanza 137):

> But I have lived and have not lived in vain:
> My mind may lose its force, my blood its fire,
> And my frame perish even in conquering pain,

> But there is that within me which shall tire
> Torture and Time, and breathe when I expire.

He did indeed not live in vain, and left his mark on further generations of writers, fascinated by his work, his life and the myth which still survives in the city. Admirers have flocked to Venice to see Palazzo Mocenigo, where he lived from June 1818, among them the French poet François-René de Chateaubriand, Flaubert's mistress Louise Colet (who insisted on seeing Byron's writing-desk, still *in situ* in 1860), and even Ernest Hemingway, who mentions Byron's palace in his 1950 Venetian novel *Across the River and into the Trees*.

A great admirer of Byron, the American writer **Edgar Allan Poe** (1809–49) saw Venice only through dreams and readings. In a short story 'The Assignment', published in 1845 and set in an imaginary Venice, it is easy to recognise the mysterious, brave, romantic character described as 'Ill-fated and mysterious man! Bewildered in the brilliancy of thine own imagination and fallen in the flames of thine own youth.' Poe would emulate his hero by swimming across the James River in Virginia, six miles against the tide. This Byronic fascination continues to this day. An annual swimming race in the Grand Canal used to take place until quite recently in memory of Lord Byron.

'Venice is a wonderful fine city,' wrote **Percy Bysshe Shelley** (1792–1822) on arriving there. He had left England for Italy shortly after his first wife's suicide. As soon as he was in Venice in October 1818 he joined Byron and immediately realised the fame his new friend enjoyed in the city, as he described in one of his letters: 'I came from Padua hither in a gondola and the gondolier, among other things, began talking of Lord Byron. He said he was a giovanetto Inglese, with a nome stravagante, who lived very luxuriously and spent great sums of money.' Shelley was also struck by the city, which he called 'one of the finest architectural delusions in the world'.

Shelley would have been prepared to stay in Venice for ever, in the words he gives Maddalo in 'Julian and Maddalo', the narrative poem Shelley wrote inspired by the long 'conversations' he shared with Lord Byron while they rode together on the Lido beach:

> If I had been an unconnected man
> I, from this moment, should have formed some plan
> Never to leave sweet Venice, – for to me
> It was a delight to ride by the lone sea.

The two poets had first met in Geneva in 1816 and renewed and strengthened their friendship in Venice. Shelley's entourage included his wife Mary, his children and Allegra, the young child Byron had fathered but not yet seen, and her mother Claire Clairmont (Shelley's sister-in-law, and perhaps his previous lover), whom Byron wanted to avoid at all costs. Wives, mistresses, children, servants and menagerie all went to live together in Villa Foscarini dei Carmini, Byron's house in Mira on the River Brenta, and at Villa Kunkler at Este in the Veneto.

Shelley quickly became disillusioned with Venice, however, particularly when he saw the Doge's Palace and he pictured, in Gothic mood, the past horrors that had taken place in its prisons: 'I saw the dungeons, where these scoundrels used to torment their victims.' He too was disappointed at not hearing Tasso sung as he had expected by the gondoliers on the Grand Canal: 'I heard nothing of Tasso.' But he was mostly saddened and upset at the plight the recently fallen city was enduring under foreign occupation:

But Venice, which was once a tyrant, is now the next worst thing, a slave; for, in fact, it ceased to be free or worth our regret as a nation. A horde of German soldiers as vicious as and more disgusting than the Venetians themselves, insult these miserable people. I had no conception of the excess to which avarice, cowardice, superstition, ignorance, passionless lust, and all the inexpressible brutalities which degrade human nature, could be carried, until I had passed a few days at Venice.

It is therefore not surprising that Shelley left Venice for Florence and then went on to Livorno (Leghorn), where he drowned in a sailing accident near the city. His boat, built to his requirements 'as a perfect plaything for the summer,' was originally named *Don Juan*.

In spite of his disappointment with the city and the grief caused by the death of his daughter Clara, who fell ill in Este and died on arrival in Venice, Shelley found time to work on his *Prometheus Unbound* and the inspiration to write many letters and poems, including 'Julian and Maddalo' and 'Among the Euganean Hills':

> Sun-girt city! Thou hast been
> Ocean's child, and then his queen
> Now is come a darker day,
> And thou soon must be his prey,
> Lead a rapid masque of death
> O'er the waters of his path.

This extract from 'Among the Euganean Hills' laments the decadence and humiliation of a city, once so powerful and brilliant, now fallen. This was a theme dear to Romantic writers' hearts and follows Wordsworth's 1802 poem 'On the Extinction of the Venetian Republic':

> Once did she hold the gorgeous East in fee
> And was the safeguard of the West: the worth
> Of Venice did not fall below her birth,
> Venice, the eldest child of Liberty.

Wordsworth apparently never visited Venice but felt the need to lament the fall of a city which had upheld sacred values, symbolic at a time of great political turmoil in Europe. This same theme inspired a number of young writers and encouraged some to fight and to sacrifice their lives to turn the political tide.

The Italian writer and activist **Silvio Pellico** (1789–1854) was, for example, arrested in 1820 by the Austrian police for belonging to the secret resistance group Federati and condemned to death. The sentence was commuted and he was instead sent to prison for ten years. He spent one year in the infamous Venetian prison the Piombi where Casanova had been incarcerated in the previous century. These cells were directly beneath the lead roof of the Doge's Palace, heated to an intolerable temperature by the summer sun. Pellico recalled later the dreadful time he spent in prison in *Le mie prigioni*.

Born in New York, but based mainly in England from 1876, **Henry James** (1843–1916) was one of the first in the flow of new visitors after the liberation of Venice from Austrian occupation. He came to the city on numerous occasions from 1869 to 1907. During these visits he explored many areas of the city extensively, some well-known, others more obscure, on foot or by water. In a letter to his brother in 1869 he explained the merits of the gondola: 'Gondolas spoil you for a return to common life. To begin with, in themselves they afford the perfection of indolent pleasure. The seat is so soft and deep and slumberous and the motion so mild, elastic and unbroken that even if they bore you through miles of stupid darkness you'd think it the most delectable fun.'

As a guest of his American friends the Curtises, Henry James enjoyed the use of the family's gondola, which can still be seen in the courtyard of Palazzo Barbaro on the Grand Canal, by the Accademia Bridge. The rich Bostonians had settled permanently in Venice. It was a haven for them, as Daniel Curtis was considered *persona non grata* in his own country, having allegedly attacked a fellow passenger (who turned out to be a judge) in a Boston tramcar, twisted his nose and broken his spectacles. Palazzo Barbaro was probably James's preferred lodging in Venice; he had toyed with the idea of buying his own house but never made up his mind. On his numerous visits James also stayed in Pensione Wildner (on the Riva degli Schiavoni, in Ca' Alvisi, now Palazzo Michiel Alvisi), which belonged to another rich American couple, the Bronsons, or in Casa Biondetti close to the Salute. The area was, and still is, a favourite for Anglo-Americans, having as a central attraction for them St George's Protestant Church in Campo San Vio, the Accademia, and today the Guggenheim art collection in Palazzo Venier dei Leoni.

Being near or on the Grand Canal was most important for the writer, who enjoyed visiting museums, the Doge's Palace and

9 *Palazzo Barbaro, the most famous of Henry James's Venetian homes*

churches, which also made him venture further afield, looking for Madonna dell'Orto in the more humble Cannaregio, for example. He also liked sitting in places such as the famous Caffè Florian, or retracing the steps of some of his favourite writers, including George Sand at the Hotel Danieli or in Calle Minelli next to the Fenice, where she had lived with Dr Pagello. He went to the opera at the Fenice, which he found 'very bad'. He also tried to imagine the life of Lord Byron in Palazzo Mocenigo, 'where the writing-table is still shown at which he gave rein to his passions'. In his writings, letters, novels and travel notes, James always commented thoroughly and somewhat critically on what he saw and felt, finding, for example, the Church of San Giorgio Maggiore 'an ugly Palladian church [. . .] with a great deal of worn, faded-looking brickwork'.

For a writer particularly appreciated for his treatment of female characters, James seemed not surprisingly to have been attracted by a 'smallish canvas of Sebastiano del Piombo' in the Church of San Giovanni Crisostomo representing the female saints Mary Magdalene, Agnes and Catherine:

These ladies stand together on the left, holding in their hands little white caskets; two of them are in profile, but the foremost turns her face to the spectator. This face and figure are almost unique among the beautiful things in Venice, and they leave the susceptible observer with the impression of having made, or rather having missed, a strange, dangerous, but a most valuable acquaintance. The lady, who is superbly handsome, is the typical Venetian of the sixteenth century and she remains for the mind the perfect flower of that society. Never was there a greater air of breeding, a deeper expression of tranquil superiority. She walks as a goddess – as if she trod on the Adriatic. (*Italian Hours*)

He was also struck by Tintoretto's paintings in the Scuola di San Rocco: 'You get from Tintoretto's work the impression that he felt, pictorially, the great, beautiful, terrible spectacle of human life very much as Shakespeare felt it poetically – with a heart that never ceased to beat a passionate accompaniment to every stroke of his brush.'

His judgement on Titian was lukewarm, as he considered Titian's *Assumption* in the Frari a 'magnificent second-rate picture'. He was, however, a great admirer of Bellini's work. Palazzo Dario was 'delightful', and no doubt he would have liked to stay there, but the neighbouring Palazzo Corner was more disparagingly Sansovino's 'splendid pile'.

His beloved Palazzo Barbaro was the perfect setting for the Venetian section of *The Wings of the Dove*, where it became Palazzo Leporelli. Although he set this part of the novel in this palace, Henry James wrote it in 1900 at home in England and not in Venice, which he hardly visited any longer. He chose the more modest Palazzo Soranzo-Cappello for his shorter novel *The Aspern Papers*, probably for its most beautiful garden, which was important for the plot: 'It is the old faded, battered-looking, and quite homely and plain (as things go in Venice) old Palazzino on the right of the small Canal [. . .] it has a garden behind it,' he wrote in his letters. Nowadays the palace has been completely renovated and the garden, although truncated, is still magnificent, having been restored using some of the details in James's novel. In *The Aspern Papers*, published in 1888, the palace is described as 'a house of the class which in Venice carries even in extreme dilapidation the dignified name. "How charming! It's grey and pink!" my companion exclaimed, and that is the most comprehensive description of it.' James's gloomy but fascinating story has inspired four cinematographic adaptations as well as *Sciarrino's Aspern*, a modern opera, which had its premiere in Venice at the Malibran Theatre in October 2013. The American director James Ivory, who made a short documentary in Venice early in his career, is considering a further version.

In the novel Aspern is an American writer whose love letters and various papers were kept jealously by a former lover, a very old and lonely lady living in a Venetian palace. These papers are finally destroyed by the old lady's niece, who would have otherwise given them to the narrator in exchange for marriage. There is perhaps some echo of the destruction of some of Byron's very personal papers by his editor, John Murray, and it is thought that the character of Aspern is based on both Byron and Shelley. The old lady of the story might have been Claire Clairmont, who bore Byron's child and also perhaps had a short love affair with her brother-in-law Shelley. The unnamed narrator was prepared to stop at nothing to gain access to the papers and, for this purpose, rents rooms in the palace and starts lavishing time and money on the garden, but he is not prepared to go as far as marriage.

Although this book was published in 1888, it would be difficult not to have it in mind when hearing of Henry James's involvement with Constance Fenimore Woolson, a fellow American and a very successful local writer of fiction, whose frustrated desire for a closer and more romantic relationship with James might be connected with her suicide in Venice in 1894. There has been speculation about James's responsibility for this tragic event, which took place in Palazzo Semitecolo, near the Accademia Bridge on the Dorsoduro side, from where she threw herself into the neighbouring *calle*. She was depressed and felt isolated and lonely, partly because of deafness. She had become close to James, who spent much time in her company in Venice, London and Florence. Three months after her tragic death, Henry James went to Venice to help sort her belongings, 'a most devouring, almost a fatal job', as he wrote to his brother. He was especially keen to see his dead friend's papers, as he was most concerned lest some of the numerous letters he had written to her fall into the hands of others, revealing intimate details. He made sure that all his own letters were burned. The strange behaviour which followed may have betrayed a sense of guilt felt in relation to Constance's suicide. In the company of her gondolier, who was ordered to row to the furthest and deepest part of the lagoon, so the story went, James attempted to drown one by one all Constance's dresses and underclothes, but with great difficulty, as the voluminous garments refused to sink, 'like vast black balloons', even when encouraged by the gondolier's pole.

Colm Tóibín in *The Master*, his romanticised biography of Henry James, and David Lodge in his *Author, Author* (the two books

10 Window from which Constance Fenimore fell to her death

published almost at the same time in 2003–4), tread very carefully when raising the subject of Henry James's presumed homosexuality, and they both acknowledge that Constance's suicide had something to do with his reluctance to become emotionally involved with a woman. The only other two well-known women who had been close to him had been the young Minnie Temple and James's cousin Alice, both of whom died young.

Chapter 9, 'March 1899', of *The Master* deals with the part of Henry James's life in Venice connected with Constance's death. Tóibín relates the nightmarish episode of James trying to dispose of Constance's clothes: 'He did not cease pushing, prodding, sinking each dress and then moving to another. Finally, he scanned the water to make certain that no more had re-appeared, but all of them seemed to have remained under the surface of the dark water. Then one swelled suddenly some feet from them. "Leave it," Henry shouted.'

David Lodge muses about James's feelings in the 'aftermath of this ghastly tragedy': 'He groaned softly. The last thing he wanted to think about was poor Fenimore [. . .] But the creative dearth on which he had been brooding had surely been caused in part by her death. It had taken him over a year to get over it, if indeed he had yet done so.' He had not recovered from the tragedy, and Henry James's love affair with Venice had come to an end, as he returned only twice more to the city, in spring 1899 and June 1907, when it was reported that he carefully avoided walking in the area of Palazzo Semitecolo, where Constance had met her terrible death.

Very jealous of his privacy – hardly anyone among his close friends and family knew of his friendship with Constance – secretive, always fastidiously concerned about propriety and maintaining a respectable and respected front, James was very careful not to reveal anything about his deeper self and desires, nor to leave any traces. The sad example of Oscar Wilde, who had publicly acknowledged his homosexual involvements and consequently been rejected by society in 1895, must have been a warning: someone whom he had envied as a successful playwright had now lost everything.

James became very interested in another writer who had been remarkably open about his homosexuality, John Addington Symonds, whom we shall meet later. Symonds, who also had a wife and four children, inspired Henry James to write a short story based on him, 'The Author of Beltraffio' (1884). In this grisly story a writer's wife is driven to allow her son to die so that he will never grow up to read his father's work. On his deathbed Symonds wrote to his wife, 'I have written things which would not be pleasant for you to read, but which I felt justified and useful for society.'

Venice brought James both great happiness and great sadness. It also inspired his friend, compatriot and fellow writer **Edith Wharton** (1862–1937), to whom he wrote on one of his last visits that 'Venice never seemed to me more lovable.' Wharton also chose to live abroad from 1907, mainly in Paris. The story of her close friendship with James, which started properly in 1903, reads a little like their novels, as she had already met him at a dinner party in 1887, where he did not notice her, in spite of the new Doucet dress she was wearing. At another meeting in the 1890s in Venice he ignored her once again. The two American writers had much in common, and when Wharton joined the Curtises' magic circle of prestigious guests in Palazzo Barbaro their friendship developed through an exchange of correspondence and shared travel, despite the age difference between them.

One of Wharton's non-fiction works, *Italian Backgrounds* (1905), a collection of essays written during her travels in Italy between 1901 and 1904, includes at the end a nostalgic view of Venice, and her 1904 *Italian Villas and their Gardens* covers the unique botanical garden in Padua, as well as the impressive garden at the Villa Pisani at Stra on the Brenta. She also wrote a lighter short story with Gothic undertones in 1903, 'A Venetian Night's Entertainment', and later two novels, *Glimpses of the Moon* (1922) and *The Children* (1927), based partly in Venice. They express a rather censorious and moralistic view of the city, describing it as a corrupt place for already corrupted characters, the ideal setting for 'simply affording excellent opportunities for bathing and adultery' or for 'jazzing'.

It was a rather different kind of Venice that **Robert Browning** (1812–89) had come to look for at the age of 26 in 1838 to complete *Sordello* (1840), a challenging narrative poem set in Northern Italy. From the start he loved the 'Queen of Cities', where he found inspiration and a political awakening. London's Little Venice was given its name by Browning. *Sordello* also refers to 'sparkling Asolo', the small city situated at the foothills of the Dolomites in the Veneto, which the young poet then visited for the first time.

Volume 1 of *Men and Women*, published in 1855, includes 'A Toccata to Galuppi', a homage to the eighteenth-century Venetian musician Il Buranello from Burano. The poem is a reflection on life and death, with Venice's great past recorded through the composer's music:

> Here you come with your old music, and here's all the good it
> brings.
> What, they lived once thus at Venice where the merchants were
> the kings,
> Where Saint Mark's is, where the Doges used to wed the sea with
> rings?

It ends on a familiar nineteenth-century note on death and old age:

> Dust and ashes! So you creak it, and I want the heart to scold.
> Dear dead women, with such hair, too – what's become of all the gold
> Used to hang and brush their bosoms? I feel chilly and grown old.

A great admirer of Byron and Shelley, Browning had married Elizabeth Barrett in 1846, against her father's wishes. To escape his wrath the couple had eloped to Italy and lived in Florence, from where they went to Venice for a month in 1851 with their two-year-old son, Pen. Elizabeth Browning was able to enjoy the city, as she was still in relatively good health. After her death in 1861, Robert Browning started to visit Venice each year from 1878, staying at Mrs Bronson's modest palace, Ca' Alvisi.

As a widower, Browning also spent some time in Mrs Bronson's villa La Mura in Asolo, where, as did so many Venetian residents, she had a country retreat on the mainland. The small town attracted many contemporary writers and intellectuals, including the great actress Eleonora Duse and her lover Gabriele D'Annunzio. Writers, painters and artists gravitated around the American community at Mrs Bronson's palace in Venice and the Curtises at Palazzo Barbaro. Pleasant evenings in educated refined company were spent talking, reading, listening to Browning's poems, or dressing up for the fashionable tableaux vivants. The visitors also went to concerts or the theatre, Goldoni's plays being especially popular. At the time Venice was seen as one great party by Henry James, who noted in *The Aspern Papers*, 'Piazza San Marco is the most ornamented corner, and places and churches, for the rest, play the part of great divans of repose, tables of entertainment, expenses of decoration.' The period was frequently described as the Gondola Days.

Browning had become quite dependent upon the Bronsons. In 1880 Arthur Bronson became seriously ill and disappeared from the scene, and the poet became more and more attached to his wife Katharine. This seemed to have been reciprocated, but nothing came of it. Browning's poem 'Il Ponte dell'Angelo' was written while he was living in the Bronsons' palace, and in her memoirs, *Browning in Venice*, Katherine Bronson related the story of how the poet had come across a book in her house: 'a modern book was brought to his notice during his last sojourn in Venice. It is Tassini's *Curiosità veneziane*, which gives a history in brief of the old palaces, together with their diverse legends.' Browning became interested in the legend to which the bridge owed its name and looked it up in Father Boverio's *Annals of the Cappucini*. With Mrs Bronson's gondolier, he went to find the bridge near Piazza San Marco, the completed poem being a fusion of two historical sources and the more popular version provided by the gondolier.

In 1888 Browning's son Pen bought Baldassare Longhena's grand palace Ca' Rezzonico on the Grand Canal, and Browning moved in. In one letter to a friend he expressed his satisfaction: 'I don't think I have told you what an advantageous bargain Pen has made in acquiring his huge Rezzonico Palace – the finest now obtainable in Venice.' Browning was still dividing his time between London and Italy. His last work *Asolando* was completed in Mrs Bronson's house at Asolo in the autumn of 1889, and the poet died in Ca' Rezzonico, having heard that very day that the first edition of *Asolando* had sold out.

Ca' Rezzonico was also a favourite haunt for American painters like **John Singer Sargent** (1856–1925), in Venice from 1880 to 1882, and **James Abbott McNeill Whistler** (1834–1903), who used light and spacious but very cold rooms on the top floor as studios. Whistler spent a very cold winter (1879–80) in the seventeenth-century palace with his mistress, Maud Franklin. He had come to Venice with a commission from the Fine Art Society to produce 12 etchings of the city. This was intended to help him out of the financial difficulties he had incurred in his disastrous libel case against John Ruskin, who had called one of his paintings a 'wilful imposture'. In one of his 10 o'clock lectures in London Whistler thus described Venice: 'And when the evening mist clothes the riverside with poetry, as with a veil, and the poor buildings lose themselves in the dim sky, and the tall chimneys become campanili, and the warehouses become places in the night, the whole city hangs in the heavens, and fairy land lies before us.'

In Venice Whistler mixed with other painters, like the Russian Alexander Volkoff and the English painter Henry Woods, who both disliked and admired him: 'I could do with Whistler very well, but for his confounded conceit and everlasting seeking for notoriety. I cannot stand it. He has started two "moonlights" entirely from memory. They are, I must admit, remarkably true as far as they go [. . .] His etchings will be very good I think.' Although they were not delivered to the Fine Art Society on the agreed date, the etchings were indeed very good, as was a series of pastels. According to Whistler, the bitterly cold weather was responsible for the delay: 'It has been woefully cold here – the bitterest winter I fancy that I ever experienced, and the people of Venice say nothing of the kind has been known for quite a century.'

Ca' Rezzonico is now the beautiful museum of the eighteenth century in Venice. It is said that you can still find John Singer Sargent's initials engraved on a wall of the upper floor where he worked.

A little later another American, the poet **Ezra Pound** (1885–1972), moved to Europe, where he became close to many contemporary writers and poets, including W. B. Yeats, T. S. Eliot and James Joyce. His first book of verse, *A Lume Spento*, was published in Venice in 1920. Finally settling in Paris from 1921 to 1925, Pound became acquainted with the Surrealists and took an active interest in the arts and music. At that time he began to write his *Cantos*. From 1925 he settled in Rapallo in Italy, where he remained until 1945. There he found himself at the centre of a group of intellectuals and writers, some of whom were attracted by Italian Fascism, as he was. He also lived partly in Venice with Olga Rudge. She was a fine violinist, and they organised a series of concerts. During the Second World War, Pound broadcast pro-Fascist speeches for Italian radio, which at the end of the war he was to regret bitterly, as he was accused of treason and collaboration, and was incarcerated in terrible conditions in a prison camp in Pisa, held in an open cage. There the memory of Venice haunted him:

> Will I ever see the Giudecca again?
> Or the lights against it, Ca' Foscari, Ca' Giustinian,
> Or the Ca', as they say, of Desdemona [. . .]

From Italy he was sent for almost 13 years to an asylum for the insane in St Elizabeth, Pennsylvania, having been judged unfit for trial. In 1949 he received the Bollingen Prize for poetry, and after sustained efforts from fellow writers, he was finally liberated at the age of 72 and was able to recover his passport. He wandered for some time in Europe and finally settled in Venice with his daughter and

Olga Rudge, dying there in 1972. During the last ten years of his life the semi-recluse found a refuge as well as renewed inspiration, for which he was grateful:

> Old powers rise and do return to me
> Grace to thy bounty, o Venetian sun.

He was full of praise for the city which, he said,

> has given me back
> Strength for the journey, heart for the journey.

The simple-looking house where he lived in Dorsoduro, referred to in the *Cantos* as 'the hidden nest', now bears a commemorative plaque, and the poet is buried in the Protestant section of the cemetery on the island of San Michele. One of his most famous poems, 'Night Litany', for which he is best remembered in Venice, is a grateful homage to the city and its beauty:

> O God of the silence,
> Purifiez nos coeurs, purifiez nos coeurs.
>
> Yea, the lines hast thou laid unto me
> In pleasant places,
> And the beauty of this thy Venice
> Hast thou shown unto me
> Until its loveliness become unto me
> A thing of tears.

Pound knew the city in the early part of his life, and then again at the very end. He had run away from the native country he abhorred, and which showed him no mercy, reaching in Venice 'the last or at least the sixth circle of desolation'. The composition of the *Cantos* stretches over this long period of association with Venice between his first visit in 1908 and his death.

His vision of the city was coloured by the representations he found in the works of painters like Tiepolo, Turner and also the Venetian writer and film director Tinto Brass, who inspired one of Pound's poems, 'Il Ponte dei Morti' in Canto XXI, 'From boat to boat the bridge makes long its strand.' Many have still neither forgotten nor forgiven the poet for his past errors, his anti-Semitism and blind support for Fascism. His tomb is quite difficult to find in the cemetery, and it seems a pity that this great poet has been overshadowed by the more familiar names of Hemingway and Mark Twain.

The American journalist John Berendt published in 2003 a collection of essays describing the characters living in Venice at the time. One of the essays, the 'Last Canto', mentioned that Pound's widow, Olga Rudge, had recently died in Venice aged 101. Berendt suggests that she was the victim of unscrupulous misappropriation of private papers and letters, rather like Miss Bordereau, the old lady in Henry James's *The Aspern Papers*.

Many Russian writers and artists were drawn towards Venice. The poet **Alexander Pushkin** (1799–1837) was never allowed to travel outside Russia for political reasons, and knew Venice only through literature, particularly Byron's verse. He fantasised about the city's mythical assets, the freedom it advocated and its reputation as the city of love. In Canto I of *Eugene Onegin*, Pushkin dreams of the Brenta and Venice, and has the young Onegin in ecstasy at the sight of the Adriatic, as he floats with a Venetian girl 'in a mysterious gondola' and thus 'imbibes the language of Petrarch'.

His 1827 poem, reworking an original by the French poet André Chenier, 'Near the Area where Reigns Venice' compares his poet's fate to that of a gondolier:

> Near those realms where golden Venice reigns
> A lone oarsman through the night his gondola steers.
> In Hesperus' light, he sails abreast the waves
> And sings of Rinaldo, Goffredo and Erminia.

Oblivious to design or fame or hope
His chant he loves and sings alone for pleasure
And in the thrall of his tranquil Muse,
Thus knows the way his path to sweeten
O'er the fathomless watery depths.
On the sea of life where storms in the gloom
Do lash my lonely sail, like him, for solace,
And without response sing I
And secret verse to ponder do I love.

The poem conjures a poetical, dreamlike imaginary view, somewhat similar to the description Edgar Allan Poe gave of Venice in 'The Assignment', mentioned above. More fanciful evocations are to be found in Ann Radcliffe's Gothic novel of 1794, *The Mysteries of Udolpho in Venice*. She knew the city only through her reading, which probably included William Beckford's account of his experiences in Venice.

Russia's most romantic poet, **Mikhail Lermontov** (1814–41), author of the famous *A Hero of our Time*, having likewise never travelled outside the Russian Empire, would embroider on this theme in his poem 'Venetsiya'. Almost all of Russia's cultural figures at the time hailed from St Petersburg, a city founded on the edge of the sea, and often dubbed the 'Venice of the North', so they felt a certain instinctive affinity. St Petersburg was a natural substitute for Venice, similarly swathed in mists and mystery.

Many of the great nineteenth-century prose writers of Russia did manage to visit Venice, but it is interesting that their visits are not particularly well documented, and unlike the poets, they do not seem to have fallen under its spell to the same extent. Nikolai Gogol, who was enamoured of Rome, where he wrote the major part of *Dead Souls*, declared, 'Where else could one write of Russia?' and passed through Venice with almost no mention of the city.

Venice was appreciated by other writers such as **Apollon Grigoriev** (1822–64), tutor to Prince Trubetskoy's children in Italy; he started a mid-century craze with his *Venezia la bella* of

1857. **Fyodor Tyutchev** (1803–73), Russian ambassador to Turin with little to do, visited Venice frequently and also enjoyed the city. The Doge's ritual marriage to the sea, the ceremony of La Sensa, was the stimulus for one of his best poems.

Another Russian, **Fyodor Dostoyevsky** (1821–81), who in his youth had dreamed of writing a Venetian novel, journeyed through Italy in 1862 with his friend the philosopher and critic Nikolai Strakhov and visited the city. Strakhov was greatly surprised by his behaviour: 'he was perfectly indifferent to views, monuments and works of art, unless they were spectacular. Only people interested him.' A few years later, Dostoyevsky contemplated spending some time during the winter of 1868–9 in Venice, on his way to Milan and Florence. He chose Florence – where he completed his novel *The Idiot* – for economic reasons, and, according to his second wife, Anna Grigorievna, because Russian newspapers were available. In the end the couple spent only a few days in Venice on their way home through Trieste. Amazingly, as Anna recounted, her inveterate gambler husband did not go anywhere near the Casino. Instead he and Anna devoted themselves to sightseeing, spending most of their time in Piazza San Marco. Although struck by the Doge's Palace, it was the Basilica which held him in thrall; he stood in ecstasy, Anna tells us, in front of the church, and spent hours gazing at the mosaics. The Byzantine style, which recalled the Russian Orthodox tradition, held a peculiar magic for Russian visitors. Anna reported in a letter: 'I can assure you that we practically haven't left St Mark's Square, which enchants us deeply night and day.' None of this was ever reported in Dostoyevsky's own writings. The couple were constantly very short of money, waiting in vain for funds from his publisher, and were forced to borrow the cost of their fare home.

Leo Tolstoy (1828–1910) chose to set Chapter 9 of Part V of his novel *Anna Karenina* in Venice, but never visited in person. Leaving her husband and child in Moscow, the heroine elopes with her lover Vronsky, intending to live in Italy to escape gossip and public condemnation. They go to Venice and settle in an 'old neglected palazzo, with its lofty carved ceilings and frescoes on the walls, with its floor of mosaics, with its heavy yellow stuff curtains on the windows, with its vases on pedestals, and its open fireplaces, its carved doors and its gloomy reception rooms, hung with pictures'. Tolstoy does not give us anything really interesting about the city itself. To fight boredom, the frustrated Vronsky takes lessons in history of art and starts painting himself, although not too successfully, and the couple's return to Russia becomes inevitable. Many screen adaptations have been made of this novel. The most memorable one was shot by Clarence Brown in 1935, with a radiant Greta Garbo playing Anna Karenina; as she sits in a gondola, the sight of a young boy brings tears to her eyes, because she misses her son.

Anton Pavlovich Chekhov (1860–1904) is also worth mentioning for his brief visit to Venice in April 1891, documented by the letters he wrote to his sister in Russia from the Hotel Bauer on the Grand Canal. He resolutely refused to descend into tourist clichés. Instead, his friend Merezhkovsky tells us, he focused ironically and wittily on the cost of living and his fellow Russians' gripes: 'He who does not go to Venice is stupid! The cost of living here is so cheap,' he declared, as well as commenting about missing Russian food and the difficulty of finding a patch of grass to lie on. From his other travelling companion Suvorin, we learn that 'Chekhov showed little interest in art, statues, paintings, churches. He was more taken in by its originality, but above all by its daily life, and less by its Doge's Palace.'

Nevertheless the magic must have worked on him to some extent, as he wrote: 'The best time in Venice is the evening. First of all the stars, secondly the long canals in which are mirrored the lights and the stars, thirdly the gondolas, gondolas and gondolas.' He reported in a letter he wrote from a gondola that he was in the company of a double bass, a guitar, a mandolin, a violin and some singers: 'How beautifully they sing!' he enthused, 'It is just like being at the opera!'

The exception to these rather banal accounts from the geniuses of Russian literature is **Ivan Turgenev** (1818–83), who visited Venice in 1857 and stayed at the Hotel Danieli. Venice had inspired him to write one of his least-read works, *On the Eve*, published in 1860. Here, more than any other nineteenth-century Russian novelist, he waxes lyrical at the magic of the city:

> He who has not seen Venice in April cannot pretend to know all the inexpressible charm of this enchanted city [. . .] The softness and mildness of spring harmonize with Venice, just as the glaring sun of summer suits the magnificence of Genoa, and as the gold and purple of autumn suits the grand antiquity of Rome. The beauty of Venice, like the spring, touches the soul and moves it to desire; it frets and tortures the inexperienced heart like the promise of a coming bliss, mysterious but not elusive.

The story tells of two young characters, newlyweds Elena and the fatally ill Insarov, spending a few days sightseeing. They visit the Accademia 'In no time at all they had done all the rooms of this little museum', go to the opera and discover the Lido, which, interestingly, depresses them by its desolation (in the middle of the nineteenth century the island was still in the earliest stages of becoming a popular health and sea bathing resort). Did Turgenev perhaps agree with his characters, who thought that St Mark 'looked like a frog in water' in the famous Tintoretto painting *St Mark Frees the Slave*? Jerzy Skolimowski made a 1989 film adaptation of the Turgenev novel, *Torrents of Spring*, which included a brilliant final sequence of the Carnival, shot in the Doge's Palace.

Another link between Turgenev and Venice is the Spanish singer Maria Malibran, sister of Turgenev's most enduring love, Pauline Viardot. She came to sing in the city in 1831, where she was enthusiastically received. She saved the ailing theatre near the Rialto where she had performed, which is now named Teatro Malibran in tribute to her. She left an interesting legacy of correspondence, mainly about her career.

Of course it was not only the best-known Russian writers and composers who visited Venice. Many less familiar figures came, including the political exile and publicist **Alexander Herzen**

(1812–70) who arrived in 1867 and sent back a series of humorous letters to friends and family, all full of delighted impressions. He had settled in the Hotel Danieli, probably recommended by his great friend Turgenev. It was a crucial time to be in the city after its liberation from Austria, and Herzen made the most of it, even attending the Carnival, 'the first Carnival in freedom after seventy years in prison'. However, his main reason for visiting Venice was political. Earlier in London he had made friends with both Mazzini and Garibaldi, hosting a banquet for them at his house in Teddington. In 1867 he not only met Garibaldi again, but also witnessed Venice's reception of the liberator of Italy: 'The city gave Garibaldi a brilliant reception. The Grand Canal was so full of boats it looked almost like a solid bridge. I found Garibaldi neither older nor ill. But he was not cheerful, and was preoccupied and not very communicative with the Venetians who came to present themselves to him the next day.' Herzen's experience was different, as he reported jubilantly: 'Today I went to meet Garibaldi at 6 am. He was happy to see me and I was the only one he kissed.' He also wrote what he thought of the city: 'Venice is the most magnificent and absurd conceit. To build a city in the one place where it would seem impossible is already madness enough, but to erect the most elegant and grandiose city which ever existed is the madness of genius.'

Some Russians settled for good in Venice. In 1859 the Russian Prince Sergio Kotschoubef bought a substantial piece of land on the Zattere where he built a villa to remind him of his house on the bank of the Neva. The artist **Alexander Volkoff-Mouromtzov** (1844–1928), also known as Alexander Roussoff, lived from 1880 until his death in the Grand Canal Palazzo Barbaro-Volkoff, which became a meeting point for Russian exiles as well as for actors, writers and artists, including Whistler and Sargent. The Russian painted popular Venetian views and portraits, including one of his tenant and close friend, the celebrated Italian actress, Eleonora Duse. He wrote in his *Memoirs* how much he loved the city as an artist: 'Nowhere else can a painter find more favourable opportunities for his work, absolute absence of noise and of people who come in and out and annoy by their presence, and the delight of finding one's subject each day under the same conditions and under the same aspects of light and shade.'

At the end of the nineteenth and the beginning of the twentieth centuries, before the 1917 Revolution, poetry in Russia was experiencing an upsurge, and many talented poets belonging to the so-called Silver Age and World of Art movements (in both of which art was cultivated for art's sake, and political commitment was set aside) made the journey to the dream city.

The Symbolist poet **Valeri Bryusov** (1873–1924) in his 1900 poem 'Dante in Venice', written before his first visit to the city, conjured up an imaginary Dante in a dreamlike sequence. When he reached Venice in 1902, the city inspired him to write a number of further poems, such as 'The Lion of St Mark'. He was staying in Calle Valleresso, clearly before the advent of Harry's Bar in 1931 made the area so modish, since he described it as 'the street of wine shops, next to San Moisè, home for the dregs of society'.

Many Russian writers came for health reasons. They chose to stay at the Lido, which, at the beginning of the twentieth century, was just becoming a fashionable and well-organised bathing resort with 'the most beautiful beach in the world', as a Venetian poster claimed at the time. The poet **Alexander Blok** (1880–1921) and his wife came in 1909. Like most of the Russians arriving from St Petersburg, he felt at ease immediately, writing to his mother: 'I feel completely at home in Venice, and am as familiar with almost all the customs, as well as the museums, churches and canals, as if I had already been here for a long time.' Three poems on Venice were composed as a part of his *Italian Poems*, including this one, dedicated to his friend Vyacheslav Ivanov:

> A chill wind by the lagoon
> The gondolas silent coffins
> I am young and suffering tonight,
> Prostrate beside the lion on its column.

The poem is full of melancholy, but he gives a more colourful picture in an essay he wrote in 1909 on 'Lightning of Art (Thunderbolts)', published in *Italian Impressions*:

> There remain on Earth only two or three pathetic shreds of the throbbing life of the past [. . .] a Catholic girl emerging from the confessional, her eyes bright with laughter; a red sail on the lagoon; an antique yellow shawl thrown across the strong shoulders of a Venetian woman. But all of this is Venice, where there are still lively happy people.

Two other poets, **Anna Akhmatova** (1889–1966) and her husband **Nikolai Gumilev** (1886–1921) travelled to Venice in 1912. She was entirely enamoured of the city and evoked a dreamy impressionistic image in 'Venice', a poem of 1912 included in a collection entitled *The Rosary*:

> Golden dovecote by the water,
> A languishing and caressing green,
> A salty breeze erasing
> The narrow furrow of the black boats.

Her husband Gumilev, tragically fated to be executed in 1921, describes the lion on the column evoked by Blok in his own poem of 1913:

> The lion on the column,
> With splendid burning eyes,
> Bears the Gospel of St Mark,
> Winged like a Seraphim.

In the beginning of the same poem he is fascinated also by the giants on the Clock Tower:

> It's late. The giants on the tower
> Have struck their deafening three o'clock

> At night, the heart is bolder:
> Be silent, traveller, and watch.

Osip Mandelstam (1891–1938) and Andrei Belyi wrote verses celebrating the beauty and mystery of the city where they enjoyed a general feeling of freedom, albeit short-lived. Mandelstam was in Venice in 1910, where he described the city's 'frozen smile and glaucous antique gaze.' He died insane in 1938 after a year in a labour camp in Siberia.

In the summer of 1922, **Sergei Esenin** (1895–1925) stayed at the Hotel Excelsior at the Lido with his wife, the famous dancer Isadora Duncan. Others stayed at the Grand Hotel Lido (now destroyed) or at the Grand Hotel des Bains. Venice at the time was offering an elegant and extravagant lifestyle to all these foreigners. It was the golden period of the Lido, so beautifully recreated by Visconti in his adaptation of Thomas Mann's *Death in Venice*. Visitors spent carefree days there, frolicking on the beach and lounging in silk pyjamas (described disapprovingly by D. H. Lawrence in *Lady Chatterley's Lover*), hiding from the sun in their beach huts, or in the evening taking cocktails in the elegant Peplos gowns of Mariano Fortuny, as worn by the actress Eleonora Duse and her friend Isadora Duncan. However, when asked for his opinion of Venice, Sergei Esenin's verdict was 'the architecture is not bad, but it stinks!'

A youthful **Boris Pasternak** (1890–1960), at the start of his career as a writer, visited Venice briefly in the summer of 1912, recreating the 1904 journey of his father, the painter Leonid Pasternak. He recorded some of his impressions in *Safe-Conduct* (not published until 1931), dedicating the book to another lover of Venice, the German poet Rainer Maria Rilke.

Arriving at the station, Pasternak was bowled over by his first glimpse of Venice, 'brick-rose and aquamarine-green, like the translucent pebbles thrown up on to the beach'. Looking for a cheap room, which he found in Campo Morosini (now Campo Santo Stefano), he saw 'tiny squares and calm people who seem strangely familiar'. Everything is described in minute detail as he explored the city over five packed days. He wrote a stunned description of the Basilica: 'over the entrance the four horses playing in the gold of the cathedral, as if they had galloped all the way from ancient Greece and had stopped there on the edge of a precipice'. Venetian painting, familiar through his father's library, made an indelible impression on him. He felt very lucky to be able to appreciate it *in situ*: 'It was necessary to understand where [the paintings] were born, in order to see not single pictures, but painting itself [. . .] here it was like a golden marshland, a primeval pool of creativity.' On his last night, on hearing a guitar chord, he composed his mystical poem 'Venice':

> I was woken at dawn
> By the tapping of a window-pane
> The creaking of the dampening stone,
> Venice afloat on the water.

Pasternak's novel *Dr Zhivago* was smuggled out of the Soviet Union in manuscript and published in Italian by Feltrinelli in 1957. After being awarded the Nobel Prize for Literature in 1957, he chose to stay in Russia and therefore did not attend a conference in Venice dedicated to the translation of his novel in 1958. In a letter to Premier Khrushchev, he explained his choice: 'Leaving the motherland will equal death for me. I am tied to Russia by birth, by life and work.' He was never again permitted to leave. It is ironic that he had been so fascinated by the denunciation boxes used by Venetian citizens to inform on each other to the state, a sinister foretaste of what was to come in post-revolutionary Russia: 'The symbol of the lion has appeared in many forms in Venice. For example the slit in the secret denunciation box on the Censors' staircase, next to the paintings of Veronese and Tintoretto, was sculpted in the form of a lion's face. Imagine the fear inspired in the people at the time by this *bocca di leone*.'

Among these Russian visitors, three figures are especially prominent: the inspired genius of an impresario, Sergei Diaghilev, who remained enchanted by Venice; the extraordinary avant-garde

11   Box outside the
Doge's Palace used
for letters to denounce
citizens

composer, Igor Stravinsky, and the poet in exile, Josef Brodsky.
All became familiar figures in the city which they loved deeply.
All three are buried in San Michele Cemetery, where their tombs
continue to attract a stream of visitors.

Sergei Diaghilev (1872–1929) had first set foot in the city in
1890, accompanied by a cousin. This was followed by a visit during
the winter of 1893–4, where he spent most of his time in antique
shops and flea markets. But it is only from 1906 that the famous
Russian impresario became an *habitué* of the Lido. During the
'Roaring Twenties' Venice had become a world capital of diversion,
drawing celebrities and the aristocracy.

Although his Ballets Russes never performed publicly in Venice,
Diaghilev returned regularly for health reasons, to be 'rejuvenated'
and for inspiration, as well as for encounters with young men,
many of whom had turned to prostitution out of financial necessity.
The city had become an international focus for visitors seeking
such encounters, especially in autumn, lending them the name
'Settembrini'. Diaghilev's visits to Venice were almost always in
September. One of his favourite dancers, Serge Lifar, heard him say:
'Here in Venice, as ever, everything is divine. There is no place on

earth like it for me, both for restfulness and because here I conceive all my ideas, which are afterwards shown to the world.'

It is assumed that the idea for the *Prélude à l'après-midi d'un faune* took shape while Diaghilev was staying at the Hotel des Bains in 1909 with his male dancer Nijinsky and Leon Bakst, his designer. His collaboration with the Russian composer Stravinsky, whom he met frequently in Venice, was not always easy, as confirmed in Stravinsky's autobiography: 'Our friendship, which lasted twenty years, was, alas! marked from time to time by conflicts which [. . .] were due to his extreme jealousy.'

One ballet, *Le donne di buon umore*, was inspired by a Goldoni play and music by Scarlatti. Leon Bakst designed the set 'in the manner of a street scene by Francesco Guardi', according to Leonid Massine, another favourite dancer. Massine also reported in his autobiography, *My Life in Ballet*, that *The Legend of St Joseph* was inspired by the paintings of Tintoretto and Veronese, to which Diaghilev had introduced him in Venice in 1914.

In the early years Diaghilev's days were filled with work, but also with parties masterminded by Isadora Duncan and the extravagant Venetian Marchesa Casati. Bakst designed extraordinary costumes and sets for the events, which sometimes took place in Piazza San Marco, closed to the public for the occasion, or in Palazzo Venier.

It was in the ballroom of the Hotel des Bains in 1912 that Stravinsky first played for Diaghilev the music of the unforgettable *Rite of Spring*. In 1925 Cole Porter invited Diaghilev's troupe to give a private ballet performance at Palazzo Papadopoli on the Grand Canal, which he had rented for the summer. His biographer William McBrien reports the extraordinary occasion in his book on the American musician:

They constructed a stage which backed on the Grand Canal. Three vine-covered arches were installed as frames, and three statues lent by museums formed the background. Two male duets from Les Matelots were danced, along with a Tarantella and a selection from Les Biches. According to Kochno, he had to hum the music of Les

Matelots to Cole, so he could play it (on the piano), as no scores were available.

Serge Lifar was one of the performers, and in his biography on Diaghilev he described the event, which ended with a storm in the garden, accompanied by Diaghilev's violent outburst when he found that the dancers had been given presents as well as their fees. 'How dare they give presents to my artists who have no need of such paltry sops!' stormed Diaghilev, who then rushed towards Piazza San Marco to remonstrate with Cole Porter, causing a scandal which soon spread around the city. It appears that there was a certain amount of resentment and jealousy between Diaghilev and the American composer and songwriter, and it did not help that the Russian impresario disapproved strongly of jazz. To make things worse, Cole Porter had a brief affair with Diaghilev's secretary and protégé, Boris Kochno.

The American was a regular visitor to Venice between 1923 and 1927, having rented successively Palazzo Barbaro, Palazzo Papadopoli and Ca' Rezzonico on the Grand Canal, where he would throw wild parties, employing up to 50 gondoliers as footmen. He also had a *gallegiante*, a kind of floating nightclub and dance floor, installed at the Lido next to the Excelsior Hotel. No toilet facilities were provided, and the dancers could not keep their balance while they were doing the Charleston, so it was quickly abandoned. Cole Porter is now seldom mentioned in Venice, possibly because he had to leave the city in haste following a scandal involving the mayor's nephew.

In the meantime Diaghilev had serious plans to build a theatre for his dancers at the Lido, but he died before this could be realised. After his death, caused partly by diabetes, at the Hotel des Bains (or perhaps the Excelsior, no one seems to agree), his body was taken from the Lido in a funeral gondola to the Greek Orthodox Church of San Giorgio and then to the island of San Michele. His tomb still receives regular visits, with offerings including ballet shoes, sweets and Russian eggs left on the stone, as well as affectionate little notes. It bears the following inscription: 'Venice is the eternal inspiration of our peace', chosen by Serge Lifar and taken from a notebook Diaghilev had given him with the following recommendation: 'I hope that these notes will remain as unforgettable and eternal as Venice itself.'

As well as sharing much of his life with his dancers, Diaghilev was at the centre of a creative group which included the French couturier Coco Chanel, who funded the production of *Rite of Spring* (and probably also financed Diaghilev's funeral), and the society hostess and pianist Misia Sert, his designers, Alexander Benois and Leon Bakst, and a bevy of writers, poets and musicians. A traditionalist in his way (he disagreed with Stravinsky on the subject of Futurism), he was also superstitious, always avoiding passing between the two columns in the Piazzetta where executions used to take place. The superstition persists – to this day Venetians prefer not to walk between the columns.

Diaghilev had met **Igor Stravinsky** (1882–1971) in 1908 and worked with him on several projects which took shape in Venice, starting from 1912 (generally at the Hotel des Bains on the Lido). Stravinsky returned regularly to Venice for short periods, mainly for concerts. He travelled extensively in Europe and Italy but Venice 'was the city' he 'loved most'. Apart from the projects undertaken

12   Diaghilev's tomb in San Michele Cemetery

with Diaghilev, he also came to seek inspiration: he was, for example, prompted in 1960 to compose *The Flood* when the city was inundated. On this occasion he was not the guest of Princess Polignac, in whose palace he often stayed, but instead was at his favourite Hotel Bauer. The level of the water was so high that he had to be carried out of the hotel by two staff. In 1925 he was in Venice for the Biennale of Contemporary Music, this time the guest of the Princess, and performed his Sonata for Piano, an event recalled by the Venetian composer Gian Francesco Malipiero: 'The flower of international snobbery had gathered in Venice that September. At the salon of Princess Polignac in the Palazzo Contarini dal Zaffo, both men and women were paying homage to the Russian composer.' For the XXI Biennale of Contemporary Music in 1927 Stravinsky composed and performed *Oedipus Rex*, Sophocles' tragedy adapted by Jean Cocteau, whom he had met in Venice.

After spending the war in the United States, he returned to Venice in September 1951 for the first performance of *The Rake's Progress* at the Fenice. His religious compositions found a sympathetic audience in Venice, particularly his *Canticle to Honour the Name of St Mark*, a homage to Venice and to Renaissance music. On 1 August 1956, at a ceremony in the Basilica, he was welcomed by the Venetian patriarch, and for the following concert the whole of Piazza San Marco was converted into a gigantic concert hall, as the Basilica could hold an audience of only 3,000. The audience's reactions were mixed, reported by *The Times* under the banner 'Murder in the Cathedral!' In September 1956 he was seen at the piano (it is still there) of Hotel Bauer, working on *Argon*, music for a ballet, and in the same place he completed *Threni: id est Lamentationes Jeremiae Prophetae*, to be performed in the Scuola di San Rocco. He was in Venice again in 1960 for a concert in the Doge's Palace of *Monumentum pro Gesualdo di Venosa*.

In an interview with Robert Craft, Stravinsky gave his mercilessly provocative judgement on Venetian music: 'Vivaldi has been praised too much. He is tedious and wrote the same concerto six hundred times. And, in spite of my preference for Galuppi and Marcello, I consider them poor composers. Living part of the last two years in Venice, I have been forced to swallow rather a lot of this music.' Although he died in New York, Stravinsky had arranged to be buried in Venice with a memorial service in the Church of Santi Giovanni e Paolo. A funeral gondola took his coffin to San Michele, where his tomb can be visited. It lies between that of his wife Vera, and that of Diaghilev, with whom he had had a tempestuous relationship, so this proximity is unlikely to have been part of his plan. The simple stone bears his name, dates and a small golden cross.

Josef Brodsky (1940–96) followed this Russian predilection for the Serenissima, but his love of Venice started, as for so many of his compatriots, long before he visited the city, while he was living in the Soviet Union, dreaming of it over postcards, films or books. A screening of Visconti's *Death in Venice* and Henri de Régnier's writings on Venice aroused his interest. After 1972, his first year in exile from his homeland, he visited Venice annually for the next 20 years, always in winter, since, 'In winter you wake up in this city, especially on Sundays, to the chiming of its innumerable bells, as though behind your gauze curtains a gigantic china tea set were vibrating on a silver tray in the pearl-gray sky.' It was here that he was inspired to write many poems as well as *Watermark,* the book commissioned by Consorzio Venezia Nuovo, and which he presented at the Ateneo Veneto in 1989. It consists of 48 short chapters of impressions, notes and musings, expressing how much he was attracted by the uniqueness of the Serenissima: 'I think it is Hazlitt who said that the only thing which could beat this city built on water would be a city built in the air.'

In *Watermark* and his other writings, Venice is seen as hypnotic and dreamy, and uncomfortably cold. It is often swathed in fog, where loneliness has its special charm, enjoyed to a certain extent masochistically by the writer who, in 20 years, did not bother to learn Italian: 'My Italian, wildly oscillating around its firm zero, also remained a deterrent.' As a result, he mixed mainly with expatriates, often Americans – like his friend the painter Robert Morgan, to whom the book is dedicated. Otherwise social life for Brodsky was practically nonexistent: 'At night, there is not much to do here,' he commented.

He returned continually to the description of a city surrounded by water: 'There is something primordial about travelling on water.' In fact, to Brodsky Venice seemed to be a return to the womb, comforting and yet at the same time unsettling. *Watermark* was published in Italy under the title *Fondamenta degli incurabili*. This takes us back to the time when the plague and other epidemics used to kill half of the city's population, century after century. 'The name conjures the hopeless cases, not so much strolling along as scattered about on the flagstones, literally expiring, shrouded, waiting to be carted – or, rather, shipped away.' This is hardly a cheerful theme, but not altogether surprising, coming from someone who already felt condemned (*incurabile*), for quite apart from being an exile – which to Brodsky was the equivalent of an incurable disease – he was suffering from a serious heart condition which proved to be fatal. His descriptions are also full of joy and love, yet suffused with his special brand of irony. They acknowledge the special beauty of Venice, as in the final chapter: 'Let me reiterate: water equals time and provides beauty with its double [. . .] By rubbing water, this city improves time's looks, beautifies the future. That's what the role of this city in the universe is.'

On his last visit to Venice in December 1995, he stayed with a friend, Count Girolamo Marcello, to whom he dedicated what is held to be his last poem, 'From Real Life'. Brodsky died a month later in New York, where he had been living since 1972. During that last visit to Venice he had said jokingly to his host: 'When I die, I will return here as a red cat. I shall never leave this place.' Apparently Count Girolamo was visited by a red cat after Brodsky's death and with the collaboration of his Italian publisher he did in fact return to Venice to be buried in San Michele Cemetery, not far from Ezra Pound and Olga Rudge, who also featured in *Watermark*, not entirely favourably.

Venice marked the sixtieth anniversary of the birth of the Russian poet in the year 2000 with a course of lectures, poetry readings and music. He is far from forgotten. Visitors bring stones or shells to his grave in San Michele, or sometimes a bottle of vodka or whisky.

4

ILLUSION AND DISILLUSION

Venetia, chi non ti vede non ti pretia [. . .] Ma chi ti vede ben gli costa.

Venice, he who sees you not, cannot esteem you [. . .] but he who sees you pays well for it.

(Shakespeare, *Love's Labour's Lost*)

How could one resist such a glorious state, advertising itself as a necessary step for those seeking the Paradise represented in Guariento's remaining fresco fragments in the Doge's Palace? The painting, replaced after the great fire in the Palace in 1577 by the Tintoretto version (which can still be seen), portrayed a rigidly hierarchical society, an exemplary civic state in which painting, sculpture, architecture and music flourished in abundance, reflecting its heavenly equivalent. For centuries it remained a model of stability and creativity. All this self-congratulation worked until the end of the seventeenth century, when Amelot de La Houssaye, a French Embassy secretary, finally denounced the pretence in his critical *History of the Government of Venice*.

Venice does not leave anyone indifferent. Some love it, others become disillusioned, and the few who hate it consider it an inflated and deceiving myth. For many it is unreal, a dream or an illusion. In his *Invisible Cities* of 1972 the Italian writer **Italo Calvino** (1923–85) set out to write 'the ultimate love song to cities'. One of the cities he mentions, named Smeraldina, is clearly Venice in all but name:

In Smeraldina, a city on the water, a network of canals and a network of streets cross over each other and intersect. To move from one place to another you always have the choice of walking on dry land or taking a boat: it is because the most direct line in Smeralda is not straight but zig-zag and may take tortuous forms.

Venice has been referred to by Ruskin as 'Arcadia, Paradise of Cities', and by Byron as the 'Pearl of the Adriatic' and the 'City of the Heart':

> I loved her from my boyhood – she to me
> Was as a fairy city of the heart,
> Rising like water-columns from the sea,
> Of joy the sojourn, and of wealth the mart;
> And Otway, Ratcliffe, Schiller, Shakespeare's art;
> Had stamp'd her image in me, and even so
> > (*Childe Harold's Pilgrimage*, Canto IV, Stanza 18)

It is interesting that he cites writers who never knew the place, which remained for them only a dream.

For Wordsworth, who knew it only by reputation, Venice was 'The First Daughter of Freedom', and Peter Ackroyd called her 'Venice, Pure City'. For some, the romantic and lapidary beauty is, however, a contrived façade. As the Colonel says in Hemingway's 1950 Venetian novel, *Across the River and into the Trees*, 'It's a tougher town than Cheyenne when you really know it.'

The concept of the 'myth of Venice' is based on the city's widely accepted reputation for beauty, liberty, peace, tolerance, fairness and republicanism. This series of attributes has been built up by travellers through the centuries, as well as by Venetians themselves, who have flaunted and exploited this conceit in their visual arts, music and poetry. The ritual and pageantry displayed in the famous welcome offered to the French King Henri III in 1574 was public self-celebration and glorification on a grand scale. It was the greatest in a long and continuing tradition of theatrical presentations. A local contemporary poet, Lucio Zorzi, gives it the evocative name of the Peacock City.

It has been difficult to contradict this enduring image of the city. The Swiss twentieth-century architect Le Corbusier, a thorough modernist and provocative critic who loved Venice and was discussing unrealised plans for a new hospital, perhaps unexpectedly considered it a sacred place, but one which could still meet modern urban needs: 'Silence and the human voice, this is the miracle of Venice within the modern world, and remains a gift from God, always present, and which must never be destroyed.' He drew our attention to the enduring human focus of the city as it evolved: 'We have rediscovered the great law of town planning which radiates so delightfully through Venice [. . .] The pedestrian is master of the ground as he will be in the new town of our time.'

In 1611 the traveller Thomas Coryat in his *Coryat's Crudities* described a place 'of admirable and incomparable beauty', and Roger Ascham in *The Scholemaster* in 1572 saw the Venetian state as 'the seat of just laws, wise rulers and free citizens'. In 1740 the French traveller Charles de Brosses enjoyed being in 'The freest city in the world'.

But was it really that free? La Houssaye, on his return to France after three years spent as a diplomat in Venice from 1668 to 1671, set out to demonstrate how untrue it was, though we shall see that daring to criticise the Venetian myth came at a great personal cost.

As for the 'incomparable beauty', during the long and cold winter months in particular, the pervading damp and decay as well as the freezing fog can create a sense of unreality which can easily turn into a nightmare. Many have also associated the Serenissima with the darker side of human nature, cruelty, fear, secrecy, revenge, deceit and hypocrisy. H. V. Morton in *A Traveller in Italy*, published in 1964, noted:

> Centuries of guile, stealth and spying had made Venice the most cautious community on earth, a state so secretive and suspicious that one rash word might ruin a man. It was typical of the Venetian attitude to women that an ambassador might take his cook abroad, but not his wife. Venice did not trust its women: it had too many secrets.

Today the decaying fabric of the city, built by centuries of mercantile obsession, is being exploited mercilessly to feed the profits of international vested interests.

As early as the sixteenth century, visitors to Venice were seeing through the myth. The French poet **Joachim du Bellay** (1522–60), in exile in Italy, was not fooled by the Venetians. Referring to them in a sonnet from *Regrets* (1558) as 'ces couillons magnifiques', he puns on their brazen strutting attitude, mocking the tradition of the city's annual ritual marriage to the sea:

> Ces vieux coquz vont épouser la mer
> Dont ils sont le mari et le Turc l'adultère.

> These old cuckolds go to marry the sea,
> Of which they are the husband and the Turk
> the adulterer.

Two centuries before him, Petrarch's friend, the Florentine writer and ambassador **Giovanni Boccaccio** (1313–75) was far from impressed by what he saw. He had met Petrarch in Florence in 1350, and again in Padua in 1351, and came to see him in Venice in 1363. His most famous work, *The Decameron*, is composed of 100 short stories related by seven women and three men sheltering together for ten days (hence the title). The second novella of the fourth day (dedicated to unhappy love affairs) takes place in Venice, described at the very beginning as 'the city that embraces all evil'. Many of *The Decameron*'s stories describe virtues, but this one exposes nothing but vices. The main character, a scoundrel on the run called Berto della Massa, decides to start a new life, calling himself Friar Alberto. Taking advantage of the gullibility of the local population and in particular of Lisetta, a vain woman whom he meets during confession, he tells her that the Angel Gabriel has fallen for her 'celestial beauties' and that he will come to visit her at night, not in his angelic form, for fear of frightening her, but disguised as Friar Alberto himself, who explains his intentions: 'Because he is an angel and coming in the form of an angel you would not be able to touch him, and so for your enjoyment, he would like to come in the form of a man.'

Very flattered, the lady agrees, but cannot help boasting about it around town. News travels fast in Venice, and soon everyone is gossiping, leading to the unmasking of the false friar (and would-be Archangel), who ends up incarcerated in a convent. In the course of his undoing, Venetians are described as an uncharacteristically dangerous and vicious mob: 'Friar Alberto was recognised by everyone, shouted at and bombarded with all kinds of refuse.' Friar Alberto's unmasking might also be that of the whole city. A Czech cartoon made by Jiri Trnka in 1965, *Archangel Gabriel and Mrs Oca*, is a delightful and witty short film adaptation of Boccaccio's story.

The French writer and politician **Michel de Montaigne** (1533–92), famous for his *Essays* of 1588, set out on a 17-month journey in Italy (by way of Switzerland and Germany) from 1580 to 1581. After visiting Germany, he crossed the Alps in Switzerland to Italy and visited Verona, Vicenza, Padua and Fusina, before reaching Venice, where he stayed from 5 to 12 November. Having escaped political and personal problems in France, he was led by natural curiosity and was trying to find a cure for the illness which had plagued him throughout his life; he suffered repeatedly from very painful kidney stones, and one reason for this long journey was to try various spa resorts, one of which was in the Veneto outside Padua. His *Travels in Italy* is written in the third person by his secretary in a mixture of French and poor Italian. Although he was warmly welcomed and entertained in Venice by the French ambassador Ferrier in his Palazzo Michiel in Cannaregio, most of the city's charm was lost on him, as he found it 'other than he imagined and not quite so wonderful'. This disappointment was expressed again in Section 55 of Book 1 of his famous *Essays*, dealing with the subject of 'smells and odours'. He wrote: 'The principal care I take wherever I am lodged is to avoid and be far from all manner of filthy, foggy, ill favouring and unwholesome airs.' The truth is that he disliked the place and had rather unpleasant memories of it. Many more pages of his report on the Veneto are devoted to Vicenza and Padua. No comments in the few pages on Venice are made on the buildings or monuments, but rather on his disappointment that the beauty of the famous Venetian ladies did not live up to expectations. At some stage, in circumstances which are unclear, he met the famous ex-courtesan Veronica Franco, as she sent him a copy of her recently published *Letters*. Some say that she even entertained him to dinner at her house in Santa Maria Formosa.

But Montaigne's harsh judgement was tempered by the fact that he did not find the cost of living any greater than in Paris, as everyone went around on foot or by boat, not having to meet the expense of a horse and carriage. He himself indulged in the daily use of a gondola during his short and disappointing stay. According to the Venetian academic Sandro Mancini, Montaigne was fascinated by the Ghetto and the synagogues as he was, according to Mancini, 'a quarter Sephardic Jewish on his mother's side'.

He next headed towards Bologna, Florence and Rome, which he must have loved, since his stay there lasted for several months. At the end of his journey he returned home to Montaigne near Bordeaux, where he was immediately made mayor, an appointment he reluctantly accepted.

One of the most powerful attacks on the city came in the seventeenth century from **Nicolas Amelot de La Houssaye** (1634–1706). Born in Orleans in France in 1634, La Houssaye became secretary to the French ambassador in Venice from 1668 to 1671. We do not know much about him or about those three years, but he returned to Paris to write his polemical *History of the Government of Venice*, published by the King's printer in 1676 and dedicated to Louis XIV's war minister, Louvois.

We do know that in the course of his duties La Houssaye had experienced the diplomatic underworld, as well as having access to various documents and archives. His job was to write the French ambassador's regular bulletins. His book sets out to criticise in no uncertain terms the way the Venetian Republic was run. He also deals with what, according to him, were the causes of its decadence and condemns the all-pervading secrecy and the attitude towards foreigners: 'Venice is a place where the secrets of government are impenetrable to Foreigners.' He talks of 'a decadent state' destroying itself because of a general decline of moral virtue among the ruling classes. He accuses the inhabitants of being 'perfidious, treacherous, guilty of envy, venom, treachery, dissimulation and hatred of foreigners'. He is also scornful of Venetians as public citizens: 'the great reason why they [. . .] lasted so long under one Government was their Citizens knowing so well how to obey. They are People of great Order, Providence and Judgment.' He compared the Venetian state to decadent Sparta and the Roman Empire.

In spite of the book's success (it sold as well as Machiavelli's *The Prince* and was translated into Italian and English), it was considered improper and dangerous in many circles. Apart from his severe critiques, the book revealed matters which ought never to have left Venice and, following the strong protests of the Venetian ambassador Nicolas Contarini, the unfortunate author was sent to prison in the Bastille in 1677. The outrage provoked by La Houssaye's book was so great that the Venetian ambassador bragged publicly that he would bring his severed head back to the city on a plate. The work continued to enjoy some notoriety, as it was republished twice in three years. The author's troubles were not yet over, as the publication of his translation of Fra Paolo Sarpi's *History of the Council of Trent* provoked in turn the wrath of the Pope, who demanded its suppression. Eighteenth-century travellers like Montesquieu were familiar with La Houssaye's works, which they dutifully read in preparation before they set out for Venice.

Another disappointed visitor came from England. **Horace Walpole** (1717–97) was the son of the first British prime minister, Robert Walpole. Horace was a writer, poet and politician, famous for his wit and literary gifts. On leaving Cambridge in 1737, he set out on the usual Grand Tour with some friends, among whom was the poet Thomas Gray, visiting major Italian cities, including Venice. He was also on a mission to buy pictures in order to enhance his father's famous art collection. This is very well documented by the numerous letters he wrote reporting on his journey, which lasted two years and three months. His are amongst the most vivid descriptions of the difficulties which had to be overcome on the journey overland to Italy, even for the wealthier traveller:

> At the foot of the Mount Cenis we were obliged to quit our chaise, which was all taken to pieces and loaded upon mules; and we were carried in low armchairs on poles, swathed in beaver bonnets, beaver gloves, beaver stockings, muffs and bear-skins. When we came to the top, behold the snows fallen! And such quantities [. . .] that I thought we could never have waded through it.

He survived, and after the usual visits to Florence, Rome and Naples, he arrived at last in Venice in June 1741, where he spent a month with two friends – but without Thomas Gray, who had preceded him there, the two young men having fallen out. Apparently Walpole was going to too many balls and masquerades, but Thomas Gray was also jealous of Walpole's affection for a new arrival in Italy, Lord Lincoln. Walpole was very much enamoured of him, it seems, perhaps provoking the split with Gray. Lincoln joined Walpole in Venice and nursed him through a bout of quinsy. After what seemed like a miraculous recovery, the young men sat for Rosalba Carriera, as was the fashion at the time. Walpole's rather effeminate portrait can be seen at Houghton Hall, the Walpole family seat in Norfolk in England. After the usual round of balls and parties, and two weeks after attending the coronation of Pietro Grimani (the new doge), Walpole returned to England via Genoa, after splitting also from Lord Lincoln. All these traumatic events might have prevented him from appreciating Venice to the full. He referred to the city's 'pestilential air and stinking ditches', perhaps a sign that he was anxious to return home. He also mentioned a public execution:

> We have had a poor man beheaded here this morning for stealing a cup out of a church. I was told it just as going to bed, and could not sleep for thinking of the unhappy creature, who was to suffer for so trivial a fault. Had he murdered or broken open a house

he might have escaped; but to have taken from the church was death WITHOUT BENEFIT OF THE CLERGY, for they never pardon where they are concerned. And a poor man dies unpitied, with the vulgar crying out, the sacrilegious wretch!

Only a few letters document a not entirely successful stay in the city, but one which may have inspired him to write *The Castle of Otranto*, hailed as the first Gothic novel.

In 1797, the year Walpole died, **Napoleon Bonaparte** (1769–1821), on his first campaign in northern Italy, may have read La Houssaye's *History of the Government of Venice*. Not yet emperor, he certainly had very mixed feelings towards Venice and decided to stay away from the city, sending instead his first wife Joséphine to represent him. In what was considered a humiliating gesture towards the last doge, Ludovico Manin, and the dying Republic, Bonaparte chose to occupy the Doge's lovely Villa Manin at Passariano in the Veneto. This is where he signed the infamous Treaty of Campo Formio on 17 October 1797, which decided the fate of the city he professed to hate and wished to destroy: 'I will do away with the Inquisition and the Senate, I shall be an Attila to the state of Venice,' he is supposed to have shouted angrily to some Venetian envoys. On the other hand, Joséphine used all her legendary charm on his behalf to win Venetians' hearts, with some success. She spent a few days staying in the late Gothic palace, Palazzo Pisani Moretta, on the Grand Canal. (This palace is so attractive that the then Italian prime minister Silvio Berlusconi attempted to buy it in 2010.) Alas, none of Bonaparte's passionate letters to Joséphine was written in Venice, so they have no place here.

Ten years later, on 29 November 1807, Napoleon made his official entrance as emperor into a city which had been humiliated, stripped of many of its inestimable treasures and then handed over to the Austrians. He was welcomed by a triumphal arch built in his honour on the Grand Canal by the vanquished but still pragmatic Venetians. Another arch was built a few days later for a regatta which he barely acknowledged. He was doubtless very busy, and certainly did not have any time for official entertainment, nor for writing about how he spent his time in the 'drawing room of Europe'.

Others did, however. Among the huge number of historical books written on the subject, *Paradise of Cities* by John Julius Norwich (2004) includes a whole chapter on Napoleon, and *The Ten Days of Napoleon I in Venice* (*I dieci giorni di Napoleone I a Venezia*) by Ugo Fugagnollo (1982) gives a detailed description of Napoleon's intensive ten days in Venice at the end of 1807 and alludes tantalisingly to a romance with a certain Countess Nahir de Lusignan. There is some mystery about a rendezvous in the Church of San Giobbe in Cannaregio, where, it seems, they were accidentally locked in. Their encounter was marred by the fact that the lady in question was suffering from severe bronchitis at the time, and it appears that she and Napoleon spent only one night together.

There is no doubt that the Emperor had more serious concerns, and was busy depriving the city of its most precious treasures, artworks and books, ransacking and looting public and private premises before the arrival of the Austrians. One of the most interesting comments on the response of Venetians themselves to the immense damage inflicted on the city is that of the historian **Alvise Zorzi** (b. 1922) in his *Venezia scomparsa*, in which he lists the cultural losses of the city. He notes that the occupying French, who had to decide quickly what loot to take away to France, seem to have made use of the guidebooks published mainly in Italy and in France in the eighteenth century, such as Charles-Nicholas Cochin's 1769 *Journey to Italy*, and *Journey in Italy* by Joseph-Jérôme de Lalande, published in 1790.

In July 1806 a decree had ordered the immediate suppression of 34 monasteries and convents, as well as 18 churches. In 1810 another 25 monastic institutions were dissolved, and churches and religious institutions were converted into prisons, gymnasia or hostelries – or worse, pulled down. This orgy of destruction is difficult to justify, especially when it came to the Bucintoro, the magnificent boat used for official ceremonies, or the Servite Convent, to mention only two major casualties. Some spoils of war did make their way back to Venice, including the four horses of St Mark. Displayed in

Paris in 1797, they were returned in 1815, but sadly other treasures are still waiting to return, one of the most important of which is the magnificent painting by Veronese, *The Marriage at Cana*, looted from the refectory at San Giorgio, and still hanging in the Louvre in Paris.

Nevertheless, some positive and constructive decisions were taken by Napoleon, and in some cases with the reluctant collaboration of Venetians. The gates of the Ghetto were opened, for example, as were those of the prison in the Doge's Palace, and the Inquisition, trials and torture were ended. A location for a cemetery was found outside the city on the neighbouring islands of San Cristoforo and then San Michele, and new hospitals and new public gardens were established in Castello. The Via Eugenia, which subsequently became Via Garibaldi, was designed as part of general improvement and modernisation. The Riva degli Schiavoni was extended, many canals were dredged, some were filled, and the city lighting was updated and improved. Venice also benefited from the construction of several new bridges, and the creation of the first public secondary school in the former Convent of Santa Catarina. Napoleon decreed that the orphans kept in institutions like the Pietà were to be treated less harshly. They were now allowed to have family names, and the inhumane practice of marking them with a branding iron was finally abandoned. Public libraries became open to everyone, as did the city archives and museums. The Ateneo Veneto was founded as a learned society, along with the art gallery at the Accademia in what had been the Scuola Santa Maria della Carità. This latter probably contributed to the preservation of many works of art, which were retained for everyone's benefit. Works were also undertaken for the city's defences, including the sea walls at the Lido, and there were improvements to the port.

The impact Napoleon had on the city, and on its bewildered and shocked inhabitants, also provides the background to numerous novels. The romanticised life of Lucia Memmo, daughter and wife of two powerful Venetian patricians, is set by Andrea di Robilant in his novel *Lucia in the Age of Napoleon* in the once glorious city, now reduced to foreign occupation, deprived of its greatest treasures and humiliated to the last.

This fate also inspired some of the most impassioned pages of nineteenth-century European writers. The French Romantic writer Chateaubriand personified the city: 'Since then, Venice, bedraggled, with her crown of campaniles, her marble brow, her furrowed golden face, has been sold and resold [. . .] to the most recent and highest bidder, Austria. Now she languishes, chained to the foot of the Austrian Alps.' During the 2014 Carnival, the Avogaria Theatre in Venice presented a play speculating on what might have happened to the city if Napoleon had not been defeated at Waterloo.

Romantic poets like Wordsworth lamented its tragic fall in his poem 'On the Extinction of the Venetian Republic', and Byron, Shelley and many others followed suit, amongst them a former admirer of Napoleon (who subsequently became a vehement critic of the emperor), the French writer **Marie-Henri Beyle**, better known as **Stendhal** (1783–1842), who, not entirely happy in Venice, wrote in *Rome, Naples et Florence* in June 1817: 'Nothing to write: everything bores me.' In *Pages d'Italie* he too commiserated with Venice's tragic fate: 'Poor Venice! Indeed it is still a glory for her, if fall she must, to have succumbed only to the forces of Napoleon, who will be famous in History for having brought about the end of the ancient monarchies of Europe, and for changing them into constitutional governments.' Stendhal was a regular visitor but, after having worked out in great detail the possible cost of settling there, decided against it, although he did enjoy the opera and the theatre, swimming in the Giudecca Canal and meeting his Venetian friends.

The return of a statue of Napoleon, which took place quietly in the middle of a cold January night in 2003, created a stir and some controversy in the city. The huge marble statue had been commissioned in 1810 as a homage to the French emperor, sculpted by the neo-classical artist Domenico Banti. Originally placed on the Molo in Piazza San Marco, it was removed by the Austrians and left, defaced, on the island of San Giorgio, from where it eventually vanished. It reappeared after almost two centuries in an auction sale, having been found in a Californian garden, and was presented to the Correr Museum in Venice. On my first visit to the museum in 2004 it was in what appeared to be a locked broom cupboard. Nowadays it is behind glass in a case near the ballroom, perhaps to avoid possible attack. As the saying goes: 'I Francesi son tutti ladri: non tutti, ma Buonaparte', 'The French are all thieves: not all of them, but certainly Bonaparte' (or 'better part', which is a nice pun).

After Napoleon had handed over the city to the Austrians, German musicians, artists and writers arrived in droves, some also critical and disillusioned by the city, like the young composer **Felix Mendelssohn Bartholdy** (1809–47), who was in Venice in 1830 while touring Europe. He reported in a letter:

> There is no regular Opera here at this moment, and the gondoliers no longer sing Tasso's stanzas, moreover what I have hitherto seen of modern Venetian art consists of poems, framed and glazed, on the subject of Titian's pictures [. . .] besides various specimens of architecture in no style at all; as all these are totally insignificant, I cling to the ancient masters, and study how they worked. Often, after doing so, I feel a musical inspiration, and since I came here I have been busily engaged in composition.

Indeed despite his reservations about the city, he was inspired to write four *Venetian Gondola Songs* for piano between 1830 and 1841, by which time to his delight things had improved: 'the gondoliers who are now crying out to one another again, and the lights reflected deep in the water; one is playing the guitar and singing. It is a merry night.'

A few years later, another disappointed visitor came from Denmark. **Hans Christian Andersen** (1805–75) arrived for three days in 1834 and settled in Albergo Luna near Piazza San Marco. His first impressions of Venice were so negative that he compared it to 'a dead swan floating on water'. He felt that 'there was something frightening in all this, something strange, alienating.' Feeling uneasy, he left quickly and wrote as he departed: 'I left Venice with the same strange feeling of anxiety which I had as I arrived.' The experience was not completely forgotten, as he did use Venice as a background for his 1835 novel *The Improviser*. Andersen's critic Alda Manghi has even found traces of Venice in one of his most well-known works, *The Little Siren*, published in 1837: 'I am thinking of the big gothic windows of the King of the Sea's marble palace, not too different from Venetian Marble palaces, and of the canal from which the Little Siren contemplates the balcony of the palace of the prince with whom she is in love, it is a canal very different from those in Copenhagen.'

In the same year the French Romantic poet Alfred de Musset, of whom we will hear more, spent a miserable and tempestuous month in December in the company of his lover George Sand at the Hotel Danieli, a visit marred by illness, bad weather and amorous betrayals. For him, the dream very quickly turned into a nightmare and he left, never to return. 'Venise, O perfide cité!' he lamented, feeling let down by the Serenissima.

A later guest at the Danieli, the English painter and famous author of nonsense poetry, **Edward Lear** (1812–88), a keen traveller and italophile, was in Venice in 1857, and at first did not at all like what he saw: 'Now, as you may well ask me my impressions of Venice, I may as well shock you, a good thumping shock at once by saying I don't care for it a bit and never wish to see it again [. . .] Canaletto's pictures please me far better, inasmuch as I cannot smell these stinking canals. Ugh!' Apart from the smell, he also hated the unstable gondolas. While getting out of one he had unfortunately dropped a letter in the canal, and railed against those 'rickety old boats'. Moreover, his two weeks were marred by a cholera epidemic, and quarantine was imposed on visitors, who all had to be fumigated. He had first booked in at Hotel Europa on the Grand Canal, where his room looked out over a wall, and he was very disappointed by this limited view of the architecture, being more familiar with the fanciful city recreated in plays on the London stage, or in Canaletto's paintings. Fortunately the November fog finally lifted and, having moved to the Danieli, he felt more favourable: 'What a sunset, and what a dream of wonderful beauty of Air and Architecture! Earth & Heaven.' 'Strange sad lagoons of Venice,' he wrote in his diary after returning to England, 'against my will no place has so much impressed me – ever.'

He did return in 1865, as he had been commissioned by Lady Waldegrave to paint an oil landscape, but again it was winter and he was not well. Still, he sounded positive about it in spite of all the inevitable drawbacks: 'I am suffering from cold and asthma in consequence, nor must I podder any more by canal sides and in gondolas [. . .] Altogether this city of palaces, pigeons, poodles and pumpkins (I am sorry to say also of innumerable pimps – to keep up the alliteration) is a wonder and a pleasure.'

The greatest attack on the city, however, came half a century later from an Italian. The young Futurist **Filippo Tommaso Marinetti** (1876–1944) came to Venice in 1909 with radical plans to force the city into the future, recalling Napoleon's great ideas. His provocative approach was brutal. His June 1910 manifesto asked for a complete annihilation of the past, in order to make a clean start. He also called for war: 'We will glorify war, the only hygiene in the world, militarism, patriotism [. . .] and bring [. . .] scorn for women. We want to destroy museums, libraries, academies of all kinds, and fight conventional morality.' He hated what he called 'La Venezia passatista', the past-loving Venice, and subsequently proposed radical plans in futurist manifestos and lectures, and at public events.

Marinetti advocated the destruction of the old city to replace it with a new industrial metropolis:

To hell with that Venice mooned over by tourists! Damn that forgers' bazaar, that magnet for snobs and imbeciles [. . .] that jewel-encrusted girdle for cosmopolitan old sluts [. . .] that Grand Privy of traditionalism. Let us clean and cauterise the putrescent city. Let us bring back to life and re-ennoble the Venetians themselves. Let us prepare for the birth of an industrial and military might in Venice [. . .] There is no time to lose. Fill in all the stinking little canals, with the rubble of those crumbling, leprous palaces. Burn all the gondolas, those rocking chairs for cretins. The reign of the Divine Electric Light, that will liberate Venice once and for all from the venal moonshine that illuminates all those sordid lodgings.

And there was more to come. A week later 800,000 leaflets of the manifesto were thrown from the Clock Tower in Piazza San Marco by Marinetti and other Futurist artists. It was the beginning of their three-year campaign against a traditional Venice, which they accused of being stuck in the past. In August Marinetti delivered an improvised speech against the Venetians, 'Discorso contro i Veneziani', at the Fenice. This time, many Venetians could not ignore the provocation, and reacted. A violent riot ensued, with Futurists whistled at and traditionalists beaten up. Marinetti's proposals were indeed radical:

Venetians!

Let us once and for all do away with the tyranny of love in the world! Stop whispering obscenities to all the passers-by in the world! You Venice! Old procuress, bending down under the heavy weight of mosaics [. . .] Enough, enough of all these absurd masks, all this abominable bric-a brac which makes us sick.

Let us kill the moonlight. Your Grand Canal will become a great port for merchandise [. . .] Trains and trams will travel at full speed on the highways built on your canals [. . .]

These marvellous instruments of speed will always be able to sweep away some pedantic professor, sordid and grotesque under his Tyrolean hat.

It was therefore perhaps not surprising that the movement which wanted change at all costs supported the entry of Italy in the First World War. Marinetti was injured fighting on the front and returned to Venice only in 1924, this time for a more peaceful protest against the Art Biennale.

He continued to be associated with the city he had failed to destroy, and in October 1943 he was back for the last time, staying in Aretino's palace Palazzo Bollani in Cannaregio with his family. The Venetians did not bear him a lasting grudge, and he is remembered quite affectionately. An exhibition dedicated to Futurism was held in Palazzo Grassi in 1986.

The English writer **D. H. Lawrence** (1885–1930) also expressed strong negative views about Venice. In October 1920 he spent about a week there in a hotel by the Ponte delle Maravegie, a charming bridge crossing the San Trovaso Canal in Dorsoduro. From 1912 he had been living abroad, spending considerable time in Italy. (Some biographers record that he died of tuberculosis in Venice, but they confuse the city with Vence, a town in the South of France.) His letters and novels give a mixed picture, and his poem 'Pomegranate' displays his apparent revulsion at the city:

> Whereas at Venice
> Abhorrent, green, slippery city
> Whose Doges were old, and had ancient eyes.

But in letters he sounded more positive: 'Venice is lovely to look at, but very stagnant as regards life. A holiday place, the only left in Italy.' He also added, 'I'm still stuck in the middle of Aaron's Rod, my novel.' This novel has a rather ridiculous

13   *Ponte delle Maravegie – D. H. Lawrence lived in the house beside the bridge*

character, Mr French, 'an elderly litterateur [. . .] one of these English snobs of the old order, living abroad, who claims "But I can live in no town but Venice."' The snobbish Mr French goes on to explain that he is attracted by the exclusiveness of the old Venetian aristocracy. 'That is one of the charms. Venice is really altogether exclusive. It excludes the world, really, and defies time and modern movement.'

One can sense D. H. Lawrence, the class-conscious son of a miner, disapproving of and ridiculing the 'northern barbarian civilised into the old Venetian sangria', the bourgeois who thinks 'how very romantic a situation!' He clearly felt ill at ease in a place which he was probably visiting for health reasons, since he mentions going to the Lido in his letters: 'The Lido is deserted, and, in the open part, quite lovely now [. . .] Sometimes we all go in a gondola a long way over the lagoons, past Malamocco.' However, inspiration did not come easily there: 'I am sick of mouching about in Venice, and a gondola merely makes me bilious.'

In Chapter 17 of Lawrence's novel *Lady Chatterley's Lover*, Lady Chatterley goes to stay in Venice with her father and sister. Their first impressions are not favourable, as their gondolier takes them through some sordid parts of the city to their lodgings in the lagoon: 'He rowed with a certain exaggerated impetuosity, through the dark side-canals with the horrible, slimy green walls, the canals that go through the poorer quarters, where the washing hangs high up on ropes, and there is a slight, or strong, odour of sewage.' They end up spending a few blissful weeks there, seeing the sights, going out, relaxing and bathing at the Lido, and on the whole rather enjoying themselves:

This was a holiday-place of all holiday-places [. . .] It was pleasant in a way. It was almost enjoyment. The Lido with its display of bodies red from the sun and dressed in pyjamas, looked like a beach with an enormous amount of seals come together for coupling. But there was too much of it: too many people in the piazza, too many limbs and trunks of humanity on the Lido, too many gondolas

[. . .] too much sun, too much smell [. . .] too much enjoyment, altogether far too much enjoyment.

Our occasionally puritanical writer seems to have disapproved of this 1928 Venetian version of *la dolce vita*. Even so, the city exerted on most visitors its dangerous and soporific magic, like a drug, at once stimulating and lethal.

Later, also sharing Lawrence's reservations, the American writer and journalist **Mary McCarthy** (1912–89) published in 1956 a small book, *Venice Observed*, recounting in eight chapters her experiences and impressions, historical facts and daily life in Venice. Her book is not openly or consistently critical of the city, but attempts to be lucid, certainly not prepared to repeat stale clichés. The second chapter is entitled 'The Loot'. It is an interesting, original, honest account of Venice in the 1950s and, unlike so many of her contemporaries, the journalist notes and describes the deprivation and poverty she witnessed. Chapter 5, 'The Sands of Time', takes us inside a Burano lace-making school where she deplores the working conditions of the apprentice lace-makers, in danger of losing their sight and apparently working under duress, doing a poorly paid and demanding job:

a long double room with rather poor light, where silent rows of little girls in smocks sit on benches, presided over by a nun and a crucifix, pricking out lace for the Society of Jesus, a pious, charitable group of worthy ladies who pay the children 400 lire (64 cents, about the same wage they received in 1913) for an eight-hour day making Burano or Point de Venise that will sell for very high prices in Venice.

She then goes on to mention 'the ferocious looks in the eyes of the children [. . .] we came in, smiling, exclaiming to ourselves mentally, "What a charming scene!" But when we tried to shower these smiles on the children, not a muscle moved in their faces; only the raised eyes shot looks like poisoned darts.'

More recently, other American and English writers have written Venice-based mystery and detective novels exploiting what appears to some foreign visitors to be an unpleasant and menacing aspect of the city, although in reality Venice is one of the safest places in the world.

Patricia Highsmith (1921–95) located at least two of her popular thrillers in Venice, including *Those Who Walk Away* (1967). In *The Bravest Rat*, published in 1977, she focuses on the unpleasant (and real) profusion of rats in the city. Antony Minghella, the director of the latest film adaptation of her novel *The Talented Mr Ripley* in 1999, set two scenes at Caffè Florian and Hotel Westin Regina. **Ian McEwan** (b. 1948) in his 1981 novel, *The Comfort of Strangers* – adapted for the screen in 1990 – gives a disturbing view of the city (never named in the narrative):

> It had become apparent that the packed, chaotic city concealed a thriving, intricate bureaucracy, a hidden order of governmental departments with separate but overlapping functions, distinct procedures and hierarchies; unpretentious doors, in streets she had passed down many times before, led not to private homes but to empty waiting rooms with railway-station clocks, and the sound of incessant typing, and to cramped offices with brown linoleum floors.

This could almost be Kafka's Prague. Had Ian McEwan perhaps read Italo Calvino's *Invisible Cities*, in which Calvino wrote that: 'the city must never be confused with the words that describe it'? The Venetian novel by **Jeanette Winterson** (b. 1959), entitled *The Passion*, was described on its publication in 1970 by the *Guardian* as 'a fantasy, a vivid dream', also seemingly influenced by Italo Calvino's book. Set in the early nineteenth century, the novel's protagonist Villanelle is the red-haired, web-footed daughter of a Venetian boatman, who can walk on water. It describes a rather sinister but fascinating city of mazes, decadent and chaotic: 'Miss your way, which is easy to do, and you may find yourself staring at a hundred eyes guarding a filthy palace of sacks and bones [. . .] This is the city of mazes. You may set off from the same place every day and never go by the same route.'

More recently, as we have seen, the attacks have come from a Frenchman, the philosopher and journalist **Régis Debray** (b. 1940), who published *Against Venice* in 1995, translated into English by John Howe in 2002. The title says it all. For Debray, 'Venice is not a city, but a representation of a city.' This brings us back to the concept of a Canaletto painting. The famous eighteenth-century painter, who trained as a *pittore di teatro* (a theatre set designer), helped his father to design backdrops for theatrical productions. He resorted to the camera obscura for the composition of his Venetian views, in which the great buildings are carefully arranged or invented for pictorial effect. Debray saw the city of the doges as 'a permanent Living Theatre', its reality simply not taken seriously. The book unflatteringly and unfairly compares Venice to Naples, but it also goes beyond all the familiar clichés and states what many think, but do not dare to say.

For **Charles Dickens** (1812–70), the Serenissima had been an illusion, a powerful dream. He had moved his entire family to Italy for a year in 1844, taking a rest from his writing in London, and in order, as he said, to 'fade away from the public eye for a year'. The rather large travelling party consisted of his wife, Catherine, his five children, his sister-in-law, servants and two nannies. After completing *Christmas Story*, the plan was to take a 'holiday' in order to gather new ideas, and to satisfy his curiosity about a country he knew largely through his readings of Shakespeare and Byron. He did not stop writing altogether, as his 1846 *Pictures from Italy* recounting his observations and experiences abroad was serialised in the *Daily News* (of which he was an editor).

Having travelled through France, the family settled in Genoa for about a year, long enough to get to know it well. Dickens wrote very detailed, factual descriptions of that city and also visited Parma, Modena, Bologna and Ferrara, before finally reaching Venice, alone, in November 1844. He arrived at dusk after emerging from a deep sleep, which is perhaps why the city appeared to him as a mirage, 'an Italian dream', as if seen through a magic lantern: 'There lay here a black boat, with a little house or cabin in it of the same mournful colour.' Everything he described was initially dreamlike, dark and lugubrious. Indeed, the first thing he saw before entering 'this ghostly city' was 'a burial place', the San Michele Cemetery. The profusion of water and the 'extraordinary silence' amazed him. But the nightmarish and funereal quality of this arrival had dispersed by the following morning, when he was struck by the busy and vibrant city, resplendent in daylight. The nightmare had quickly turned to wonder, and he described 'a place of such surpassing beauty, and such grandeur, that all the rest was poor and faded, in comparison with its absorbing loveliness'. After having made the customary visit to the Basilica and musing about the past and lost grandeur of the Serenissima, Dickens's description returned to gloomier mood, as he visited the Doge's Palace and recalled the past horrors which had taken place in its prisons: 'Among this dungeon stronghold [. . .] licking the rough walls without, and smearing them with damp and slime within: stuffing dank weeds and refuse into chinks and crevices as if the very stones and bars had mouths to stop: furnishing a smooth road for the removal of the bodies of the secret victims of the State.' Venice's past fame returned in the description of his visit to the 'old arsenal', now abandoned, 'for the greatness of the city was no more'. The description he gave has overtones of Gothic literature: 'One press or case I saw, full of accursed instruments of torture: horribly contrived to cramp, and pinch, and grind and crush men's bones, and tear and twist them with the torment of a thousand deaths.' Shakespeare was ever-present: 'In the dream, I thought that Shakespeare's spirit was abroad upon the water somewhere: stealing through the city.'

This is an extraordinary evocation of Venice, where all sense of time has been lost. 'I took but little heed of time, and had but little understanding of its flight. But there were days and nights in it.' It is as if Dickens, interested in hypnotism at the time, were sleepwalking: 'thus it floated me away, until I awoke in the old market-place at Verona. I have, many and many a time, thought since, of this strange Dream upon the water: half wondering if it lies there yet, and if its name be VENICE.'

Later, Henry James too returned to a vision of Venice as 'the Venice of dreams', an image shared by Robert Browning and Hofmannsthal, and evoked in similar ways in Turner's paintings. It was also referred to as the 'unreal city' by T. S. Eliot in *The Wasteland*. It is a recurring theme with Dickens, and so very different from his usual factual style. 'I found that we were gliding up a street – a phantom street; the houses rising on both sides, from the water, and the black boat gliding on beneath their windows.'

The short section set in Venice of his 1855 novel *Little Dorrit* returned once again to the unreal quality of the Serenissima, where anything can happen. The young heroine's family has found there a new and unexpectedly affluent lifestyle. 'Her present existence was a dream. All that she saw was new and wonderful, but it was not real.' She perceived Venice in its 'crowning unreality, where all the streets were paved with water, and where the deathlike stillness of the days and nights was broken by no sound but the softened ringing of church bells, the ripplings of the current, and the cry of the gondoliers turning the corners of the flowing streets [. . .] The family began a gay life.' Dickens was not blind, however, to the city's real state of degradation and poverty – Little Dorrit also saw in the streets the beggars, who were 'the only realities of the day'.

In a letter to a friend, Dickens described the Danieli as having 'the sober solitude of a famous inn; with the great bell of San Marco ringing twelve at my elbow; with three arched windows in my room (two stories high) looking upon the Grand canal and away, beyond [. . .] I swear [. . .] that Venice is the wonder and the new sensation of the world!' It may well have been Dickens's interest in Shakespeare which then took the family on to Verona, the setting for *Romeo and Juliet*. Many subsequent pages are dedicated to other Italian cities to which he took his family, including Rome, and he gives a vivid account of Naples and his adventurous, if not dangerous, outing to Vesuvius, which they approached so closely that 'all three came rolling down; blackened, and singed, and scorched and hot, and giddy: and each with his dress alight in half a dozen places.'

When he returned to Venice in November 1854, Dickens chose to stay in the Danieli. 'We live in the same house that I lived in nine years ago, and have the same sitting-room, close to the Bridge of Sighs and the Palace of the Doges.' This time he was accompanied by two friends, the authors Wilkie Collins and Augustus Egg. He completed a short Christmas tale, 'Nobody's Story', and undertook the usual Grand Tour sightseeing. He also rediscovered one of his favourite painters, Tintoretto: 'There are pictures by Tintoretto in Venice more delightful and masterly than it is possible sufficiently to express. His Assembly of the Blest I do believe to be, the most wonderful and charming picture ever painted.'

For **John Ruskin** (1819–1900), whom we have already met in the context of Rawdon Brown, the city was also a source of great stimulation and inspiration mixed with a certain amount of disillusionment. On his first visit he saw a vision which was 'like Turner's, chiefly created for us by Byron'. The young 16-year-old had a rather idealised and romantic view of the city, which inspired these lines:

> I've tried St Mark's by midnight moon and in Rialto walked
>   about
> A place of terror and of gloom which is very much talked about,
> The gondolier has rowed me by the house where Byron took
>   delight.
> The palace too of Foscari is very nearly opposite.

Ecstatic on a visit six years later, he wrote in one of his daily letters to his parents:

> Thank God I am here! It is Paradise of cities and there is enough to make half the sanities of earth lunatic, striking its pure flashes of light the grey water before the window; and I am happier than I have been these days – so happy – happier than in all probability I ever shall be again in my life.

He was recovering from a bout of depression and felt exhilarated, as many visitors do, arriving in Venice. However, on his fourth visit, in 1845, his disillusion was obvious, as he wrote to his father: 'When we entered the Grand Canal I was yet more struck, if possible, by the fearful dilapidation which it had suffered in these last five years,' and the shock turned to horror, 'as we turned under the arch, behold, all up to the Foscari Palace – gas lamps! On each side, in grand new iron posts of the last Birmingham fashion [. . .] Imagine the new style of serenades – by gas light.' Now he saw this slowly modernising city in a different way and was appalled by the completion of the railway bridge which finally connected the floating city to the mainland. According to him it was 'entirely cutting off the whole open sea and half the city, which looks as nearly possible like Liverpool at the end of the dockyard wall'. He had also become increasingly concerned by the poor quality of maintenance and restoration work done at the time.

Ruskin was there for a five-week working visit, in the company of his former drawing master, James Duffield Harding. He lodged at the fashionable Hotel de l'Europe, very much liked by Turner for its wonderful position overlooking the Salute and the Punta della Dogana. Frustrated by the time-consuming and painstaking drawings he was making, and in spite of his resistance to modernity, Ruskin was happy to experiment with a new method of capturing pictures, the recently discovered daguerreotype. On 8 October 1845 Ruskin reported to his father that he had just bought from 'a poor Frenchman' some beautiful daguerreotypes of the city, and marvelled at the possibilities: 'Daguerreotypes taken by this vivid sunlight are glorious things. It is very nearly the same thing as carrying off the palace itself – every chip of stone and stain is there – and of course there is no mistake about proportions [. . .] It is a noble invention, say what they will of it.' Ruskin went on to make his own daguerrotypes and the same letter remarked on the Venetians' scepticism in relation to this innovation. We can imagine their astonishment at the sight of this eccentric foreigner, going around the city on foot or by boat, dragging huge and strange equipment (assisted by his faithful servant, John 'George' Hobbes).

He was also frenetically taking notes and drawing or painting some of the city's famous buildings. He was a great artist in his own right. Shocked by the dismal restoration which had been carried out on the beautiful Ca' d'Oro on the Grand Canal, he took it as his mission to save the city from further disasters by faithfully recording what survived in detailed drawings – a way of preserving the precious past.

After his marriage in 1845 to **Effie Gray** (1828–97), Ruskin returned to Venice with his wife in 1849–50 and again in 1851–2. Effie also wrote almost daily letters to her parents, giving us information from her own point of view, as in a letter written in November 1849: 'John is very hard at work and I think *The Stones of Venice*, if it is the work he is now preparing, will be worth something but it is not easy to find out, for he finds that he has so many things to write about that have never been written about before.' In spite of their difficult marriage, both found these two visits relatively pleasant and profitable. In Venice Effie was enjoying the kind of social life she would never have had in London (or Perth) at the time, and Ruskin, already the famous author of *Modern Painters* (1841–6) and *The Seven Lamps of Architecture* (1849), was writing perhaps his most important work, *The Stones of Venice*. On arrival in November 1849 they found a battered city only a few months after an horrendous siege and a cholera epidemic, with buildings badly damaged by the bombardments inflicted by the Austrians, who had with great difficulty secured their re-occupation, which finally ended in 1866.

As Effie was going from parties to balls and flirting with Austrian officers, John Ruskin was spending most of his time studying the city in great detail, seemingly indifferent to what his wife was up to, and to what people might have thought of her occasionally unacceptable behaviour. He was dutifully reporting to his father his healthy daily regime of hard work and rowing, while Effie described how: 'John excites the liveliest astonishment to all and sundry in Venice,' and she adds:

I do not think they have made up their minds yet whether he is very mad or very wise. Nothing interrupts him and whether the square is crowded or empty he is either seen with a black cloth over his head taking daguerreotypes or climbing about the capitals covered with dust, or else with cobwebs exactly as if he had just arrived from taking a voyage with the old woman on her broomstick.

He was also engrossed in two of his favourite Venetian painters, Titian and Tintoretto, and was studying the mosaics of the Basilica, as well as examining Venetian churches and palaces.

Effie could have had no idea of the impact her husband's work and the resulting *Stones of Venice* and other writings would have on further generations, or on visitors who would see the city through his eyes, including writers like Henry James, Oscar Wilde and Marcel Proust. She wrote: 'John is busy at his drawings and books, writing beautiful descriptions and very poetical – he goes out after Breakfast and I never see him until dinner time.' As far as she was concerned, that suited her well, as she was unusually free to do exactly what she wanted and did not seem to be too concerned by his lack of interest in social gatherings: 'He never talks to anyone and he says his great object is to talk as little and go through a dinner with the smallest possible trouble to himself.' We also discover how cold he was in his relations with 'common people': 'I never find I get the slightest harm from the people. John on the contrary finds them so filthy that he cannot bear to touch them or be amongst them.' Indeed, he himself reported with disgust to his father that

in the recesses of the porches, all day long, knots of men of the lowest classes, unemployed and listless, lie basking in the sun like lizards, and un-regarded children – every heavy glance of their young eyes full of desperation and stony depravity, and their throats hoarse with cursing – gamble, and fight, and snarl, and sleep, hour after hour, clashing their centesimi upon the marble ledges of the church porch.

They both nevertheless shared a *modus vivendi* which included many happy times, with Effie revealing to us an unexpected Ruskin, prepared to play ball and fool around to keep warm in the freezing Hotel Danieli where they were staying:

John and I have been playing at ball for an hour and a half, which is the most famous exercise, thanks to Mama's hint, and the way we do it is this: we sit in a very large room, and although we are at a dreadful expense for wood, we cannot keep ourselves warm all these rainy days but by exercise; John stands at one end of the room and I at the other, we catch each other's balls and it is so exciting and warming that we do not tire until we are very hot. We also have a kind of cricket, and a kind of shell practice.

We learn that Torcello, to which Ruskin dedicated a chapter in *The Stones of Venice*, also became a playground. Effie recalls that they had a picnic there and 'after dinner, to show us that the champagne which they certainly did not take much of, had not gone in their heads, they ran races round the old building and so fast that one could hardly see them.' The picnic and the racing around the church presumably took place after Ruskin had gone in to admire the mosaics and described

the Last Judgment, the other the Madonna, her tears falling as her hands are raised to bless, and the noble range of pillars which enclose the space between, terminated by the high throne for the pastor and the semicircular raised seats for the superior clergy, are at once of the deep sorrow and the sacred courage of men who had no home left upon earth, but who looked for one to come, of men 'persecuted but not forsaken, cast down but not destroyed'.

Similarly, an outing to the Lido was the happy and relaxed occasion for a crab race:

We all went to Lido on Saturday. It was a most exquisite day. The gentlemen joined us and we had great fun catching little crabs which were feeding on the mussels in scores. We each caught one and setting them in a row made them run a race. The two men were exactly like children and John [Effie's brother] would have been greatly amused with the boat races they had by drying the large empty shells and setting them to sail on the water.

In spite of her apparent indifference to what Venetians had endured during the siege and ensuing occupation by the Austrians, Effie showed some kind of emotion when her Austrian admirer Paulizza confronted her with the obvious destruction which had just taken place: 'Yesterday we were taken by Paulizza to the island of St. Giuliano from which he threw all the bombs into Venice. I never in reading realised what war could do.'

On the Ruskins' second visit, they moved into Casa Welzlar, (now Gritti Palace Hotel) and after the expiry of their lease moved to Hotel San Marco, a stay marred by the robbery of Effie's jewellery. In the unpleasant and complicated situation which followed, involving one of her suitors, Ruskin was even challenged to a duel. The Ruskins' presence was now unwelcome, with friends like Rawdon Brown strongly advising them to leave Venice as soon as possible. It was a humiliating and unpleasant way of departing, as John wrote to his father: 'I don't think I shall want to come back here again in a hurry.'

But after more unpleasantness, their divorce in 1854 and Effie's subsequent marriage to Ruskin's former friend and protégé, the painter John Everett Millais, Ruskin did return on various occasions, staying again at the Danieli with some friends in 1870 and 1872, and at the Grand Hotel (next to the Gritti) in 1876. At this stage he was already suffering from fits of madness. He had become obsessed with Carpaccio's 1490–6 series of paintings, *The Legend of Saint Ursula*, which were kept at the Accademia. Although married, the young Saint Ursula remains a virgin; it has been suggested that she reminded Ruskin painfully of the young Rose de la Touche, whom he had planned to marry, and who had died the previous year. At his request, the Carpaccio painting was taken down specially to allow him to copy it.

In 1877 he stayed at the Pensione Calcina on the Zattere, which now bears a plaque commemorating the visit. He had also befriended a young Venetian, Count Alvise Piero Zorzi, also involved in efforts to save the city from disastrous restoration and damage inflicted on historical buildings. In a letter to Zorzi written in May 1877, Ruskin acknowledged that he was now suffering from dementia, referred to again in a letter sent from his last visit to Venice in 1888, when he wrote: 'I forgot all I knew about it – and don't care to – and can't learn it over again – and my old favourite pictures are nothing to me.'

He finally collapsed a year later. Count Zorzi wrote a warm tribute to him as someone who deserved to be accepted as a true Venetian: 'English by birth, Venetian by heart, Ruskin has a true right to Venetian citizenship, for but few of my compatriots have loved our fatherland as he had loved it, and after having visited and loved it as a youth, studied, wrote of it and illustrated it over a course of thirty years.'

14   *Pensione Calcina, one of Ruskin's Venetian homes*

After the divorce, Effie returned to Venice in October 1865 for a delayed honeymoon with Millais, which turned out to be a disappointing trip. Their stay was plagued by mosquitoes, and Millais did not share her enthusiasm for Rawdon Brown, or for his palace.

Ruskin's writings on Venice, with his preference for the Gothic style, his ridiculing of the 'corrupted' and 'ridiculous' Renaissance, his dismissal of Palladio's buildings as 'completely lacking in architectural imagination' and his profound hatred of the baroque, influenced architectural style in England and had a profound effect on the way some travellers, like Henry James and Oscar Wilde, were to see Venice. In his essay, 'The Critic as Artist', Wilde said of Ruskin's writings:

> Who cares whether Mr Ruskin's views of Turner are sound or not? What does it matter? That mighty and majestic prose of his, so fervid and fiery coloured in its noble eloquence, so rich in its symphonic music, so sure and certain, is, at least, as great a work of art as any of those wonderful sunsets that bleach or rot on their corrupted canvasses in England's Gallery.

Ruskin was probably one of the first to denounce the disastrous situation of Venice at the time. His sombre outlook on the future of the city sounds rather prophetic when one witnesses nowadays the uncontrolled arrival in the city each year of millions of visitors:

> I have said that the crowds of travellers of different nations, who have lately inundated Italy, have not yet deprived the city of Venice of much of its original character, although its change of government and withering state of prosperity had brought the shade of melancholy upon its beauty which is rapidly increasing, and will increase, until the waves which have been the ministers of majesty become her sepulchre.

His drawings, paintings and daguerreotypes have also contributed greatly to the careful restoration which has taken place since his collaboration with Alvise Piero Zorzi, and they are still used for reference.

The Model Wife is a 2010 novel by Suzanne Fagence Cooper using Effie's correspondence to write her fictional biography. In 2012 Richard Laxton shot *Effie Gray*, a romanticised approach, and *Untouched* is another cinematic project of the same story, with Keira Knightley as Effie.

One of John Ruskin's favourite painters was **Joseph Mallord William Turner** (1775–1851), whom he met in 1840. Turner was a great admirer of Titian and Canaletto, and greatly influenced by Goethe's colour theory. He was 44 when he first visited Venice in September 1819, after three months spent in Rome and two weeks in Naples. He checked into the historical hotel on the Grand Canal, Al Leone Bianco, but stayed only a week, during which he produced an impressive 100 drawings and watercolours, done mainly from a gondola on the Grand Canal. Advised by his friend James Hakewill, author of *Picturesque Views of Venice*, he explored the city on foot, looking for churches in which he spent some time copying various Venetian masters, as well as in private houses such as Palazzo Pisani, where he found and copied the famous Veronese painting *Family of Darius before Alexander* (now in the National Gallery in London).

He returned briefly to the city in 1833, and was there again for two weeks at the end of August 1840, staying at Hotel de l'Europe (also called Hotel Europa, now the Biennale headquarters) which he knew from his 1833 visit, from where he had probably sketched *Venice, La Piazetta with the Ceremony of the Doge Marrying the Sea*. Forty studies of nocturnes were done from the roof of his hotel. It is extraordinary to think that Turner managed to produce in the space of no more than four weeks so many paintings, as well as to recreate on canvas the famous Venetian ceremony of La Sensa. From his gondola Turner painted, among other scenes, Piazza San Marco, the Giudecca Canal, a sunset on San Giorgio, La Dogana and La Salute. He would sketch and make schematic drawings, which he would then develop into full-scale paintings back at

15   Palazzo Giustinian, formerly Hotel de l'Europe

home in London. His views from his hotel or the gondola were never intended to be realistic or accurate, as he was more interested in suggesting the change of colour and light. His watercolour technique was particularly suited to creating in a magical way the subtle impression of the city's precariousness and intangible quality, as well as its beauty. This was especially true of the work he did during his last visit, when he spent little time looking at Venetian paintings and thus freed himself from their influence. He developed his extraordinary use of light and suffused colours to an extreme, his paintings starting to become more abstract. As a result, Venice is portrayed as a mirage, a 'floating city'.

Much of his inspiration in Venice came from Byron's *Childe Harold's Pilgrimage*, in vogue in England at the time. The painting *Approach to Venice* shows gondolas and boats crossing the lagoon in mist, the city dissolving in the light provided by the setting sun. It was greatly admired by Ruskin, who praised the 'most beautiful piece of colour of all that I have seen produced by human hands'. In the 1844 Exhibition catalogue, Turner presented this painting alongside a quotation from *Childe Harold's Pilgrimage*:

> The moon is up, and yet it is not night,
> The sun as yet disputes the day with her.

A painting of *Jessica Closing the Window* was another literary reference for Turner, this time from Shakespeare's *The Merchant of Venice*. He also used Piazza San Marco as a background for his 1836 painting *Juliet and her Nurse*, depicting the two small figures on a balcony, to the contemporary critics' horror not in Verona, but overlooking a light-suffused Piazza. His approach was never realistic, and he took liberties, for example with *The Dogana from the Steps of the Europa*, where the statue of the winged Fortune is far bigger than in reality.

Ruskin was aware of the importance that Venice had on Turner's style and knew how it had liberated his use of light and colour, and how it had opened him to 'the freedom of space, the brilliance of light, the diversity of colour, an impressive simplicity of general form'. Turner had adopted this revolutionary painting style as he was, according to William Makepeace Thackeray: 'suffering an excess of representations of gondoliers in red bonnets, posts, distant blue horizons, too many white palaces before purple skies', and wanted to give an entirely fresh view of the city. An important retrospective 'Turner and Venice' was held in the Correr Museum in Venice in September 2004, displaying thousands of drawings, pastels, watercolours and oil paintings.

William Etty (1787–1849), another English painter, was also attracted by Venice, where he spent several months painting and copying Venetian masters. 'Dear Venice,' he wrote rapturously, 'Venezia, cara Venezia, thy pictured glories haunt my fancy now! Venice, the birthplace and cradle of colour, the hope and idol of my professional life. I felt most at home in Venice though I knew not a soul.' This ecstatic homage sounds surprising, particularly when one remembers his most famous Venetian picture, *The Bridge of Sighs*, painted between 1833 and 1835, representing the bridge at night with macabre images of bodies being taken out of the infamous Doge's Palace prison, to be dumped unceremoniously in the canal. This striking work now hangs in York City Art Gallery.

The fictional painter Elstir who appears in *In Search of Lost Time* (*A la recherche du temps perdu*) by **Marcel Proust** (1871–1922) is based partly on Impressionist French painter Claude Monet (also a visitor to the city), but also shares many features with Turner, who, Proust said, was careful 'not to reveal things as he knew they were, but to suit the optical illusion which shapes the way we respond to things we see'.

Proust's two visits to Venice had a huge impact on his writing, which he acknowledged in a letter: 'When I went to Venice I found that my dream had become – incredibly, but quite simply – my address.' On his first visit in 1900 he arrived on a beautiful May morning, a few months after John Ruskin's death, to spend three weeks with his mother, having possibly chosen to stay at the Danieli, one of Ruskin's favourite hotels. 'My mother had brought me for a few weeks to Venice and – as there may be beauty in the most precious as well as in the humblest things – I was receiving there impressions analogous to those which I had felt so often in the past at Combray, but transposed into a wholly different and far richer key,' he wrote in *The Fugitive* (*Albertine disparue*).

Aged 29, he was finally in that 'temple to beauty' which he had sought all his life. During the train journey Proust's mother read him pages from Ruskin's *Stones of Venice*. Ruskin's writings, which Proust had first encountered a few years before, greatly affected how he would perceive the city. This is how Ruskin gave his own first view of the city:

> When first upon the traveller's sight opened the long ranges of columned palaces – each with its black boat moored at the portal – each with its image cast down, beneath its feet, upon that green pavement which every breeze broke into new fantasies of rich tessellation [. . .] Time and Decay, as well as the waves and tempests – had been won to adorn her instead of to destroy, and might still spare, for ages to come, that beauty which seemed to have fixed for its throne the sands of the hour-glass as well as of the sea. (*Stones of Venice*)

Proust's prior knowledge of the city was otherwise based on Venetian painting: 'through prints of Titian's work and photographs of Giotto which Swann had given me at Combray some time ago'. The French writer decided, perhaps ambitiously, to embark on a translation of Ruskin's *The Bible of Amiens* into French. He did not know a word of English, but his mother was willing to help him.

Proust was disappointed with the façade of the Basilica, as the reality did not quite match Ruskin's description. He had also imagined 'a gothic city surrounded by a sea [. . .] and [. . .] an oriental church'. He became gradually disillusioned with Ruskin's views as a result. Fortunately, 'an ideal friend' was waiting for him, in the form of the composer Reynaldo Hahn, a regular visitor to the city, who was there with his cousin Marie Nordlinger. In the morning, the sunlit angel on the top of the Campanile beckoned warmly to him: 'glittering in the sun so much that one could not look at him, with arms wide open he was making me a promise of delight more certain than that which he had once been charged with offering men of good will.'

In 1902 the Campanile crashed to the ground almost without warning, but miraculously there was no loss of life and, according to legend, the golden angel, almost undamaged, landed by the main entrance to the Basilica. Ten years later it was replaced on the rebuilt Campanile, 'dove era e come era', just as it was originally.

Proust settled into a regular routine with his mother, getting up at ten in the morning to walk in and around San Marco and the rest of the city. He spent studious afternoons sitting in the piazza translating Ruskin's *Bible of Amiens* assisted by Marie Nordlinger, who was an English speaker and had met Ruskin personally. Afterwards they would relax on gondola rides in the company of Reynaldo Hahn, who rowed and sang at the same time.

In *Against Sainte Beuve*, Proust, a great music lover, also remembered the gondoliers' singing on the Grand Canal: 'It seemed that the serenade could never end, nor the sun set, as if my fears, the crepuscular light and the edge of the singer's voice were melded for eternity in a poignant fusion, equivocal and immutable.' They sought out Venetian churches, dutifully following in Ruskin's

16 *The angel made Proust 'a promise of delight'*

footsteps: 'Blessed days, when, with the other disciples of the Master, we went by gondola through Venice, hearing his homilies beside the water, and alighting at each of the temples which seemed to rise up from the sea to offer us the subject of his descriptions and the very image of his thoughts.' Proust also visited the islands of Murano and Torcello, and explored the city at night, 'like a character from the Thousand and One Nights' in the 'enchanted city'.

Proust had the opportunity of meeting Hahn's Spanish relative, Cecilia de Madrazo y Garetta in her Palazzo Martinengo, a Gothic palace on the Grand Canal, where she would proudly show her visitors her wonderful collection of fabrics, kept in a large chest. There he also met her son **Mariano Fortuny de Madrazo** (1871– 1949); Proust was already very familiar with Mariano Fortuny's wonderful blue-and-gold fabrics, inspired especially by a painting by Vittore Carpaccio, *The Miracle of the True Cross* from 1494, which he very much admired:

But they say that there is an artist in Venice called Fortuny, who has rediscovered the secret of making certain materials, and that in a few years women will be able to go about in brocades as sumptuous as the oriental designs which clothed the Patrician ladies of the past [. . .] Carpaccio is a painter whom I know well, and I have spent whole days in San Giorgio degli Schiavoni and before St Ursula, and have translated everything Ruskin has written on this cycle of pictures [. . .] there is not a day when I do not look at my reproductions of them.

Proust had a great admiration for Fortuny, 'this Venetian genius', a designer, artist, inventor and collector. Fortuny had become besotted with Wagner's music as a young man living with his family in Paris, but had never met him, as he moved to Venice in 1889 after Wagner's death. Much inspired by the German composer, he started working on a cycle of 46 paintings and etchings, the *Wagnerian Cycles*, as well as new ideas for stage sets, fabric designs and costumes. One year, returning from Wagner's opera house in Bayreuth, where he had been disappointed at the quality of the productions he had seen, and with the new possibility of using electricity on stage, he started to work on a new lighting technology, resulting in the innovation of an indirect stage-lighting system: first the reflector lamp and then the celestial vault, the latter used for the first time in a 1901 production of *Tristan and Isolde* at La Scala in Milan for which Fortuny also designed the sets. Fortuny's innovative lighting techniques were used more extensively in subsequent productions of *Tristan and Isolde* in Vienna in 1903, and thereafter at Bayreuth. The bicentenary of Wagner's birth was marked by an exhibition at Palazzo Fortuny in Venice in 2013, highlighting the connections between Wagner and Fortuny. The fascinating Museum Fortuny, once Fortuny's home and workshop, which had been languishing for some time, has now come back to life with regular Biennale exhibitions and several cultural events.

Fortuny was also the designer of the Peplos and pleated dresses, as well as of elaborate brocade coats which became so fashionable and desirable in the early twentieth century: 'He lifted them from the shoulders of the young members of the Calza and threw them round those of so many,' wrote Proust. The sumptuous garments worn by these 'Parisian ladies', Madame de Guermantes and Marcel's lover Albertine in *The Fugitive*, were for the writer a representation of the elusive and desired city: 'The Fortuny gown worn that evening by Albertine was to me the enticing spirit of that invisible city, Venice.'

Just like his character and alter ego Marcel in *The Fugitive* and in *In Search of Lost Time*, Proust had longed to see Venice since his childhood. The trip had had to be postponed several times, owing partly to the narrator's poor health and to his father's fears for him. 'It must still be cold on the Grand Canal (at Easter), you would be wise to pack your winter coat and a thick jacket.' The dream was made possible by the loss and subsequent death of Albertine.

One of the figures in the Carpaccio paintings in the Accademia, *The Legend of Saint Ursula*, the same paintings which had entranced Ruskin earlier, reminds Proust of another dominant woman in his life, his own mother, his companion and guardian angel on this first trip. When in the novel she decides, after an altercation, to return to Paris without him, Marcel finds himself abandoned in Venice, his isolation and disillusionment echoed by the gondolier's Neapolitan song 'O sole mio', which he can hear outside the hotel. 'In this solitary place, unreal, glacial, alien, where I was to be alone, the sound of O Sole Mio rose like a lament for the Venice I had known, and shared my misery.' Venice had ceased to be the city he had dreamed about and entranced him. It was now the 'Second-rate city full of deceptive conceits'.

But the Venice which had made him happy would be revived later in *Time Regained* (*Le temps retrouvé*), when, in as powerful a moment of memories recalled as that of the madeleine which took him to his earliest childhood, he stepped on an uneven stone in Paris, which brought back to him in an instant the paving stones of the Baptistry of the Basilica.

On his rather enigmatic second (and last) visit to the city, a few months later in October 1900, Proust stayed at the Hotel de l'Europe. Apart from the photograph of Proust sitting on the terrace of what is now the headquarters of the Biennale, very little concrete is known of this second visit, recorded only by his signature in the visitors' book of the Armenian monastery on San Lazzaro. Elio Zorzi, in his *Osterie veneziane*, relates that the writer was spotted having dinner at the Taverna della Fenice: 'As it happened, together with the society painter Kees van Dongen was a pale sickly man who I understood was called Proust, Marcel Proust.' Trying to avoid draughts, the hypochondriac Proust kept changing tables. He probably travelled alone, possibly incognito most of the time and spent more time in working-class areas of the city, seeking encounters: 'the desire not to lose certain young things for ever overwhelmed me with almost febrile intensity in Venice.' He mentions meeting a young woman whom he described as being 'straight out of Titian'.

During this second visit, according to a friend, the writer Paul Morand, Proust/Marcel could have been trying to find ways of asserting his independence from his mother as well as from Albertine: 'For Proust, Venice is the city of his subconscious. It will remain a symbol of freedom, first from his mother, and then from Albertine.' Enriched by these two short but memorable trips, Proust started his masterpiece *In Search of Lost Time* in 1907–8, which includes an important (but unfinished) section on Venice.

Although he planned to return in 1908 and again in 1917 (when, according to his biographer George Painter, he toyed with the idea of going to live in a palace in Venice with his favourite string quartet to get away from the war), he never did, except in his dreams and fantasies, which he describes in *Time Regained*: 'when we arrive [in Paris], in the opaque haze of a moonlit night just like those in classical paintings of Venice, with the dome of the Institut silhouetted against it, it reminds me of the Salute in the paintings of Guardi, and it gives me an illusion of being beside the Grand Canal.'

5

THE GRAND TOUR

*According to the law of custom, and perhaps of reason, foreign travel
completes the education of an English gentleman.*
(Edward Gibbon, *The History of the Decline
and Fall of the Roman Empire*)

From the sixteenth to the twentieth century, Venice attracted a
constant stream of curious, intrepid, often enlightened travellers. A
visit to the city was considered an essential part of a young person's
education. It was often one stop on a journey which took as long as
two years and also included time spent in France.

English travellers would leave England from Dover, heading for
Paris, and then stopping in other cities in France before tackling
the difficult crossing of the Alps to reach northern Italy. During
the Napoleonic Wars, however, France was not safe for the English,
which was why Byron, one of the most famous Grand Tour
travellers, approached Italy via Geneva. He was among the first
writers to report on Venice after the fall of the Republic.

Young men were sent abroad on the Tour, generally after
university, to study the antiquities, arts, languages, tradition and
politics. Apart from its rich cultural history, Italy offered a great
choice of exciting cities with plentiful museums, monuments,
churches and archaeological sites. Until the end of the eighteenth
century, Venice and Naples, with their opera houses and theatres,
also offered the best music in Europe.

Many of these travellers sowed their wild oats abroad, preferring
to go to balls, entertainments, parties and carnivals, indulging
in all types of pleasurable activity, including visits to courtesans

or prostitutes. It was possible to indulge freely in what would be discouraged, forbidden or even criminal activity at home, particularly if they came from England, where laws were very strict in relation to licentious or transgressive sexual behaviour. Indeed, some were sent abroad specifically to avoid embarrassment to their families, hoping that, after two years abroad, their misdeeds might be forgotten. That was the case for Byron, for example, who, suspected of adultery, incest and homosexuality, left for good. Some were more forcibly sent away or temporarily banished, like the young William Beckford.

Other undesirables or outcasts from society, bankrupts, libertines or homosexuals resorted to the Grand Tour as an escape, as in the case of Scottish financier and speculator John Law, who moved to Venice having provoked a financial crash in France in 1720. Six years after arriving in the city, he died there a pauper. His tomb is now in the Church of San Moisè. Some, like Thomas Coryat, travelled on behalf of a patron (the young Prince Henry, in Coryat's case, who for his own safety as heir to the throne was not himself allowed to travel abroad). Many were sent in order to buy books, paintings, coins and casts of statues for their family collections. Displaying these spoils at home was an obvious way of demonstrating wealth. Some would then have huge mansions and houses built, enlarged or decorated, their gardens designed by Italians, or local artists trained in Italy. Houghton Hall, the Walpole family seat, still contains many of the works gathered by the three sons who were dispatched to Italy and Venice. The Grand Tour had a great impact on the evolution of taste: the young aesthete Dorian Gray, Oscar Wilde's eponymous hero, lives in a London mansion where visitors are met at the entrance by a 'huge gilt Venetian lantern, spoil of some Doge's barge, that hung from the ceiling of the great oak-panelled hall of entrance'.

Up until 1797, Venice was considered the best place in Europe for both study and enjoyment. It offered an example of good government, influencing promising young men who would later pursue a career in politics. As Henry Wotton said in his formal reception as English ambassador in 1616:

She [Venice] is governed now from some thousand two hundred years in the same fashion, with an unfailing display of the highest qualities [. . .] each time I think of her orderly government, her sound institutions, her exaltation of the worthy, her punishment of the evil, the reverence paid to her magistrates, the encouragement of her youth in the paths of virtue and the service of their country, I am forced to believe that, come what may, she will survive until the final dissolution of the elements themselves.

More than any other city, Venice was also a special place for travellers who came to experience its pleasures before visiting the more austere Rome. It stood as a corner of liberty in Italy, undisturbed by war. In the early seventeenth century England had resumed diplomatic relations with the Most Serene Republic, which had been interrupted during the Protestant reigns of Edward VI and Elizabeth I.

For nineteenth-century Romantic travellers, Venice provided the ideal place to reflect on past or passing glories, and a warning of the dangers of excess and subsequent inevitable decay. The voyage itself was not without its dangers; the risk of disease was high. Many members of William Beckford's party, including his personal harpsichordist, died of cholera or malaria. His friend, the painter John Robert Cozens, took a month to recover from illness. Apart from catching other diseases, such as venereal infections, travellers ran the further risk of being plagued by mosquitoes, attacked by *bravi* or criminals, or even pelted with eggs by courtesans. Travellers seldom went about alone, but were accompanied by a tutor, a chaperone or a *cicerone* ('bear-leader'). The particularly wealthy were attended by a whole retinue of doctors, servants and friends.

After 1797 travellers became increasingly fascinated by the fall and humiliation of a once-powerful state, now subjected to foreign occupation. It then offered a different kind of political and ethical lesson. The fame spread of inspired writers like Byron, the Romantic poets and Ruskin, who wrote on Venice's decadence, and it made the journey a kind of literary and political pilgrimage, attracting visitors to reflect on the fate of empires and on life and death. Many English visitors, but also French travellers, started to see the city through Ruskin's eyes. They admired the Gothic buildings but ignored or criticised Palladio and baroque churches. Taste and interests altered. Initially travellers had not been very interested in pre-Gothic or 'Byzantine' style, and until the end of the nineteenth century provincial cities like Ravenna were therefore often overlooked.

The visitors themselves changed in other ways too. Up to the mid-nineteenth century, only wealthy men could afford the high cost of years spent abroad with a whole retinue. The completion of the railway line to Venice in 1846 changed this, and brought in less affluent travellers, with different interests and agendas. For cultural and economic reasons, very few women had hitherto ventured abroad. A major exception was **Anne Louise Germaine de Staël** (1766–1817), who spent a year travelling in Italy as early as 1802. Her most famous novel, *Corinne*, is set partly in Venice. Generally women travelled abroad in order to conceal an unwanted pregnancy or illegitimate child, as was the case for both the Duchess of Devonshire and Lady Elizabeth Foster in the eighteenth century. By the late nineteenth century this had largely changed, as reflected in the novels of Henry James, Edith Wharton and later E. M. Forster, which featured adventurous and emancipated women travellers, but they were still vulnerable and almost invariably accompanied by a relative or a chaperone.

Thomas Coryat (1577–1617), a gifted linguist, travelled through France and Italy long before the notion of a Grand Tour was established. He was the son of a clergyman who had him educated at Winchester College and Oxford. In 1603 he joined the court of the young Prince Henry and in 1608 he set out on foot on an incredible five-month round trip to the Continent, travelling through France and northern Italy, returning through Switzerland, Germany and the Netherlands. He recounted his adventurous journey in *Coryat's Crudities*, which he subtitled *Hastily Gobbled in Five Months of Travels*, a travelogue published at his own expense in 1611, but with Prince Henry's support. The book was met with ridicule from courtiers, however.

'The total betwixt Venice and Odcombe 1023 [miles] [. . .] The total of my whole journey forth and back 1975 [miles].' Thus Thomas Coryat summarises the distance he covered during this extraordinary journey using a single pair of shoes, 'the thousand miles shoes', which were on display as a memento (but since lost) in the church in Odcombe, the Somerset village of his birth.

Having crossed France, he arrived in Italy and visited Turin and Padua on his way to Venice. His first view of Italy was gratifying and cheering: 'Italy, being a country replenished with all manner of commodities, necessary for man's life [. . .] is wholly plaine, and beautified with such abundance of goodly rivers, pleasant meadowes, fruitful vineyards, fat pastures, delectable gardens, orchards, woods, and what not, that the first view there did even refocillate my spirits, and tickle my sense with inner joy.' With the endearing curiosity of an ignorant tourist, he even describes his wonderment at a crocodile skin which he saw in a monastery.

He was equally struck by his arrival in Venice: 'When I came to the foresaid Lucie Fesina [Fusina] I saw Venice, and not before, which yieldeth the most glorious and heavenly shew upon the water that ever any mortal eye beheld, such a shew as did even ravish me both with delight and admiration.' He was so enthralled with the 'Queen of Christendome' that he stayed for 'the space of sixe weeks, which was the sweetest time [. . .] for so much that ever I spent in my life'. These six weeks he spent in a house in Fondamenta San Girolamo in Cannaregio, very near the Ghetto and the house of the English ambassador, Sir Henry Wotton.

Thomas Coryat described in great detail the Rialto Bridge, Piazza San Marco and the Doge's Palace, where the paintings left him completely cold. The adjacent prison was more impressive: 'I thinke there is not a fairer prison in all Christendome.' Always interested in curiosities and etymology, he noted 'the statue of Barthelmew Coleon (who had his name from having three stones, for the Italian word *coglione* doth signifie a testicle)'. He visited

San Giorgio, 'which is situated [. . .] in a very delectable Island about halfe a mile Southward from Saint Marks place [. . .] the fairest and richest Monastery without comparison in all Venice'. His outing to the island of Murano was described as one of the most memorable, as there he ate the best oysters of his life and saw the famous glassworks. The unfamiliar profusion of food and vegetables and fruit amazed him, and he was tempted to sample watermelons and figs.

He also gave a detailed description of the Venetian School of Music and he was, like many visitors to Venice, intrigued by the castrati voices. A concert at San Rocco particularly impressed him: 'the third feast was upon Saint Roches day being Saturday and the sixteenth day of August, where I heard the best musicke that I ever did in all my life, so good that I would willingly goe an hundred miles a foote at any time to heare the like.' At the theatre, which he judged inferior to what he was used to in London, he was surprised to find women on the stage: 'For I saw women act, a thing I never saw before.'

He took great notice of people's clothes, those of women in particular, and criticised the wearing of *chopines* or 'chapineys', the tall shoes worn by many Venetian women, as a 'a foolish custom': 'For I saw a woman fall a very dangerous fall, as she was going downe the staires of one of the little stony bridges with her high Chapineys [. . .] but I did nothing to pitty her, because shee wore such frivolous and [. . .] ridiculous instruments, which were the occasion of her fall.'

Apologising for so 'lascivious a matter', he dutifully visited one well-known and much-reported attraction of the city, the Venetian courtesans' houses, where he met these famous ladies (one called Margarita Emiliana), whose 'fame [. . .] hath drawen many to Venice from some of the remotest parts of Christendome [. . .] I went to one of their noble houses (I will confesse) to see the manner of their life, and observe their behaviour.' Indeed, he seemed to have made a thorough observation, as his descriptions are full of detail about the courtesans' number, their living conditions, clothes, economic power and social standing. A printed illustration of his experience there shows him being pelted with eggs by the same famous ladies. Although he saw few drawbacks to life in sixteenth-century Venice, he did criticise strongly the public execution which he witnessed in Piazza San Marco, where two men were 'tormented with the *strapado*', which repelled him. He referred also to the dangers caused by the presence of the *bravi*, the city's 'dreadful and desperate villains' in the streets, the street fights which he 'utterly condemned', and he complained that 'the heate was intolerable'.

Coryat also witnessed celebrations, like La Sensa on Ascension Day, and a grand festival in San Lorenzo in Castello. He was interested in the variety of liturgy in use in Venice and gave a description of the Orthodox Mass in the Greek Church of San Giorgio, and of the Jewish customs he observed when living close to the Ghetto, where he became involved in a theological debate with a rabbi, ending with his speedy escape:

> [...] fearing lest they would have offered me some violence, I withdrew myself by little and little towards the bridge at the entrance into the ghetto with an intent to flee from them, but by good fortune our noble ambassador Sir Henry Wotton passing under the bridge in his Gondola at that very time, espied me somewhat earnestly bickering with them, and so incontinently sent into me out of his boat one of his principal Gentlemen Master Belford, his secretary, who conveighed me safely from these unchristian miscreants which perhaps would have given me just occasion to forswear any more coming to the ghetto.

Coryat writes about an important friend of Wotton, Brother Paolo Sarpi: 'I mention him because in the time of the difference betwixt the Signiory of Venice and the Pope, he did in some sort oppose himself against the Pope.' Coryat is a lively source of contemporary detail and is even responsible for introducing to England the word umbrella (from the Italian *ombrellone*) and the use of the fork. His descriptions of the Church of San Geminiano in Piazza San Marco (pulled down on Napoleon's orders to make room for the Royal Palace, now the Correr Museum) and the state barge of the doges, the Bucintoro, 'the most sumptuous galley in the world!' make evocative reading.

Thirty years later, the budding politician **John Milton** (1608–74) set out in May 1638 on a 15-month trip to France and Italy. He was well prepared, having studied Italian and read the works of Bembo, Tasso and Petrarch. A contemporary described him as a 'young stranger, good-looking, and with the promise of genius in his face'. He moved quickly through France, since, as his assistant Cyriack Skinner explained, Milton did not approve of the French regime. He did stop in Paris, bearing various letters of introduction, including one from the former ambassador to Venice, Henry Wotton, who had by then become provost at Eton College. Wotton offered him prudent advice: 'Don't let anyone see what you are thinking.' Milton's first stop in Italy was Genoa, and he proceeded to Florence, where, despite his Protestant ambivalence towards Roman Catholicism, he flourished in the intellectual and artistic environment and was feted for his Latin verse. It is assumed that it was in Florence that he found his vocation as a poet, although he remained strangely unresponsive to painting and architecture. The high point of his Italian journey was meeting Galileo Galilei, old and blind, and under house arrest: 'There it was that I found and visited the famous Galileo, grown old, a prisoner to the Inquisition for thinking in astronomy otherwise than the Franciscan and Dominican licensers thought.' This sentence was contained in a pamphlet which he addressed later to the English Parliament on the subject of censorship, 'an undeserved thraldom upon learning'. He referred on several occasions to the famous astronomer and his theories in *Paradise Lost*. He would have known that, 30 years earlier, Galileo had been in Venice to demonstrate his telescope from the top of the Campanile.

Milton hastened to Venice, which he considered the most tolerant state in Europe, later praising its republican form of government. The visit to Venice between April and May 1639 was important in the development of his political ideas. It is known that in Venice he purchased many books which he shipped to England, among them a history of Venice in Latin and various musical books. After this formative journey, the young writer was ready to start on his successful literary and political career.

A few years later, another English traveller, the diarist **John Evelyn** (1620–1706), arrived in Venice for almost a year (May 1645 to March 1646). Better off than Milton, he stayed at the Black Eagle Inn near the Rialto. His diary, kept diligently, claimed to give us 'the fairest fairly complete picture of Italy'. It sounds ambitious, but he did provide some useful information on the Serenissima. On his arrival he enjoyed a Turkish bath, 'where you are treated after the Eastern manner, washing with hot and cold water, with oyles and being rubbed with a kind of strigil of seal's skin, put on the operator's hand like a glove'. He was impressed by the Rialto Bridge, 'a piece of architecture much to be admired', and was entertained by music on the Grand Canal – 'the Canal where the Noblesse goes to take the air, as in our Hide-park'. He was then taken to the Fondaco dei Tedeschi, 'where many of the merchants, especially Germans, have their lodging and diet as in a college. The outside of this stately fabric is painted by Giorgione da Castelfranco and Titian himselfe.' He much admired 'the famous Piazza of St Marc' and the Clock Tower. The French ambassador Monsieur de Grémonville took him to see the Treasury of San Marco, 'which very few even of travellers are admitted to see'. Like Thomas Coryat, he was interested in ladies' fashions and commented on the absurdity of the extravagant *chopines* worn by Venetian ladies: ''tis ridiculous to see how these ladys crawle in and out of their gondolas by reason of their choppines.' He also did the customary round of visiting the Arsenal, attended a public execution in Piazza San Marco and was entertained by the Carnival: ''tis impossible to recount the universal madnesse of this place during this time of licence.' Among the dangers he encountered in Venice, he mentions pelting with eggs – 'filled with sweet water, but sometimes not over sweet' – and 'the barbarous custom of hunting bulls about the streets and piazzas'.

At some stage it appears that he was even shot at. He attended a Jewish wedding in the Ghetto, noting: 'at this ceremony we saw divers very beautiful portuguese Jewesses with whom we had some conversation.' On departure he was laden not only with books as Milton had been, but also with 'pictures, castes, treacle'.

As already mentioned, **Thomas Gray** (1716–71) accompanied Horace Walpole, with whom he had had a close relationship since their schooldays. Walpole's father financed the voyage and, unusually, without a tutor to accompany them, they set out on the standard adventure. The trip lasted two years and three months. Before they reached Venice, however, the two friends quarrelled, so Thomas Gray continued alone, first to Venice and then to return home. The reasons for the split, which turned out to be permanent, are unclear, as Walpole destroyed almost all letters referring to that period. The two young travellers were very different, one rich, frivolous and spoilt, and the other a 'studious and diligent traveller', from a much more humble background. In *Walpoliana* Walpole takes the blame: 'The quarrel between Gray and me arose from his being too serious a companion. I had just broken loose from the restraint of the university, with as much money as I could spend; and I was willing to indulge myself. Gray was for antiquities, &c, whilst I was for perpetual balls and plays, the fault was mine.'

Another wealthy and spoilt traveller to Venice was **William Beckford** (1760–1844), also a Gothic novelist inspired by his Venetian experiences. This unconventional young aristocrat had left England for his first Grand Tour in 1780. He was 20, and *persona non grata* at home, as he had been involved in two scandalous entanglements. Strongly encouraged to go abroad, he left for Venice, whose history he knew well. Beckford travelled in style, accompanied by his physician, Dr Projectus Errhardt, his tutor and factotum John Lettice, his harpsichordist John Burton, his friend the painter J. R. Cozens (son of the famous English painter Alexander Cozens), and a number of servants.

Arriving in the city in August 1780, he was completely enchanted, describing himself 'stalking proudly about, like an

17   *Ca' da Mosto, formerly Al Leone Bianco*

actor in an ancient Greek tragedy'. He also loved his hotel, the famous Leone Bianco on the Grand Canal near the Rialto: 'The rooms of our hotel are spacious and cheerful; a lofty hall, or rather a gallery, painted with grotesque in a very good style, perfectly clean, with a marble stucco.' The Leone Bianco, also known as Ca' da Mosto, remained a prestigious inn until the beginning of the nineteenth century. It is one of very few surviving Byzantine palaces, built probably at the end of the twelfth century, still with its original reliefs on the canal façade.

Venice seemed exotic to Beckford, with 'St Mark's a mosque; and the neighbouring palace, some vast seraglio.' At night from his balcony he was entertained by an impromptu *sons et lumières*:

As night approached, innumerable tapers glimmered through the awnings before the windows. Every boat had its lantern, and the gondolas, moving rapidly along, were followed by tracks of light, which gleamed and played on the waters. I was gazing at these dancing fires, when the sounds of music wafted along the canals, and, as they grew louder and louder, an illuminated barge, filled with musicians, issued from the Rialto, and, stopping under one of the palaces, began a serenade, which was clamorous, and suspended all conversation in the galleries and porticos; till rowing slowly away, it was heard no more. The gondoliers, catching the air, imitated its cadences, and were answered by others at a distance, whose voices, echoed by the arch of the bridge, acquired a plaintive and interesting tone.

A keen musician, Beckford was taken by a Venetian friend, M. de Benincasa, to the Mendicanti, 'one of the four conservatorios, which gave the best musical education conceivable to near one hundred young women'. The concert remained with him, 'I still seem to hear its sacred melody.'

He also marvelled at the convenient way Venetians were able to retire to their 'casinos':

Many of the noble Venetians have a little suite of apartments in some out of the way corner, others near the grand piazza, of which their families are totally ignorant. To these they skulk in the dusk, and revel undisturbed with the companions of their pleasures [. . .] Surely, Venice is the city in the universe best calculated for giving scope to the observations of a Devil upon two sticks. What a variety of lurking-places.

The pleasure he took in the exotic atmosphere of the mysterious city, with all its hidden treasures, was dampened by his visit to the prisons in the Doge's Palace. He was appalled at the sight of the prisons and the Bridge of Sighs: 'Horrors and dismal prospects haunted my fancy upon my return. I could not dine in peace, so strongly was my imagination affected; but snatching my pencil, I drew chasms and subterraneous hollows, the domain of fear and torture, with chains, racks, wheels, and dreadful engines in the style of Piranesi.' These nightmarish sights did not, however, completely spoil his enjoyment of the city: 'I like this sad town of Venice and find every day some new amusement in rambling about its innumerable canals and alleys.'

Never far from trouble, he became involved with the widow of the Austrian ambassador, Giustina Wynne, or Madame de Rosenberg, who had a dubious reputation in the city. She introduced him to Venetian salons, where the young English aristocrat, although not a stranger to scandal, was himself scandalised at the sight of women 'negligently dressed, their hair falling freely about them, and innumerable adventures written in their eyes', and at men 'lolling upon the sophas, or lounging about the apartment [. . .] Their nerves, unstrung by disease and the consequence of early debaucheries, impede all lively flow of spirits in its course, and permit, at best, but a few moments of a small and feverish activity.' Beckford, despite his own proclivities, is surprisingly shocked at Venice as 'the resort of pleasure and dissipation'. This did not prevent an intense love affair with a young boy from a doge's family, probably the Cornaro. This he alluded to in his writings, where he described himself as 'a frail, infatuated mortal', haunted by 'strange fancies and imaginations'.

On this first visit he kept a diary from 26 October to 3 November 1780. To the notes he had made he added seven letters from his second visit (May to November 1782). The 'criminal passion' for the young Venetian noble which urged him to return to the city in 1782 was, he admitted, enduring and irrepressible. As he wrote in a letter to his friend, Bartolomeo Benincasa: 'One image alone possesses me and pursues me in a terrible way. In vain do I throw myself in Society – this image forever starts up before me. In vain do I try to come up to the great expectations formed of me. I am dead to everything else.'

The diary and letters became *Dreams, Waking Thoughts and Incidents*, an account of his experiences, of which he printed 500 copies at his own expense. Most were destroyed, probably because of family pressure, and an expurgated version was published only much later, in 1834. Of only six surviving copies of the original, one is now in the Bodleian Library in Oxford.

In the eighteenth century Venice was a popular destination for serious advocates of the progressive ideas of the Enlightenment.

One such figure was the politician and writer **Charles Louis Montesquieu de Secondat** (1689–1755), who visited Italy between August 1728 and July 1729. Already 39 years old, the former member of the French Parlement was planning his greatest work, *The Spirit of the Laws* of 1748. His other famous work, *Persian Letters*, had been published in 1721, where he had already mentioned Venice:

'Here I am in Venice, my dear Usbeck,' wrote the character Rhedi (the fictionalised Montesquieu):

> One may have seen all the cities of the world and still be surprised on arriving at Venice: one will always be surprised to see a city, towers and mosques rising from beneath the sea, and to find a numberless population in a place where there should be only fish. I am learning the secrets of commerce; the interests of princes and their way of government; I do not neglect European superstitions; I apply myself to medicine, science and astronomy; I study the arts; at last the veil which covered my eyes in the country of my birth is lifting.

It is likely that this knowledge of Venice before setting foot there was thanks to Abbé Conti, a Venetian whom Montesquieu knew in Paris, and who was also to become his guide in 1728. When he arrived, he found rather more than fish, and did exactly what Rhedi had planned to do in the city, making thorough enquiries and noting down statistics, to a point where the Inquisition became alarmed and had him followed. Reassurance came from a French minister who confirmed that Montesquieu was: 'A man of letters who has much intelligence and knowledge and who is travelling as he claims out of curiosity'. From the testimony of one of his travelling companions, Lord Waldegrave, we know he was in earnest:

> When he arrived in Venice, Montesquieu, serious and active, was accustomed to rise early, and to rally forth to examine everything worthy of notice, whether relating to public edifices, or the

government of the country, or the customs of its inhabitants. On his return home he would write down the minutest details of all he had seen or heard and daily read his observation to Lord Chesterfield.

This forensic approach did not, however, spoil his thorough enjoyment of the city: 'The first sight of Venice is charming and I know no other city in which one likes most the first day for the novelty of the sight and its pleasures.' His curiosity and interest were boundless: 'Everything interests me, everything astonishes me.'

The four weeks were spent noting down facts and figures, almost manically: 'I arrived in Venice on 16 August. On the Giudecca Canal were eight ships. There are a further six galeasses, of which four are still at sea.' After touring the Arsenal he visited the glass factories of Murano, where he counted: 'two furnaces for the manufacture of mirrors, eighteen where glass is made. Each furnace employs between 18 and 20 people.' He counted 150 islands and 56 streets in just one area, 500 bridges, and 48 shops on the Rialto Bridge alone. The aspiring engineer proceeded to study the maintenance of the canals and the lagoon, and the functioning of the Arsenal. He did not seem insensitive to such sights as Veronese's magnificent painting *The Wedding at Cana*, then on the island of San Giorgio, but the philosopher remained unmoved by the relics of the Basilica.

He praised the relaxed atmosphere of a peaceful civilised city, noting that 'There are no police at the spectacles and there is no disorder at all; no brawling can be seen.' One senses some disapproval of the lax attitude in relation to courtesans: 'More freedom may be enjoyed here than most honest men would wish to have: going about with prostitutes in broad daylight, marrying them, not having to observe the days of obligation, to be entirely anonymous and independent in one's deeds.' He felt this was going too far, and was to him debauchery; to his friend the Duke of Berwick he wrote that Venice 'is a city with nothing more left than its name: no more forces, trade, riches, laws: only debauchery is there known as liberty.'

This did not prevent him from approaching courtesans himself, however unimpressed he might have professed to be: 'The whores of Venice, execrable whores, bent on instilling disgust in the most resolute; much indulged and with but little beauty; possessing the faults of the profession to a greater degree than any other in the world.' But he fell nevertheless under their spell: 'I am here at the mercy of a beauty who always says "Ah! My love!" Since she has used all my condoms, I will renounce her and leave her to M. Jacob.'

Montesquieu was disappointed at the idea of Venice as a republic, which he qualified more accurately as 'aristocratic republicanism', although 'Venice is one of those republics that have made the best use of law to correct the inconveniences of a hereditary aristocracy.' He met John Law, gambling away whatever remained of his former fortune. Montesquieu enjoyed the encounter: 'his mind always focused on projects, his head always full of calculations and numeric or representative values'.

As Montesquieu was preparing to leave with his invaluable treasure of detailed notes, facts and figures, a foreigner called on him and said: 'I am here, Sir, to reveal an important secret. Your position as a foreigner, and your researches, your questioning of every aspect of Venice have made the Government suspicious of you. By order of the Council of Ten, your papers are to be seized, and you will be arrested by night.' It was only after he had destroyed his compromising notes on the Inquisition that Montesquieu discovered that it had all been a joke in poor taste, planned by his friend the Count of Chesterfield.

Much less politically involved and more pleasure-seeking was **Charles de Brosses** (1709–77), a young French parliamentary adviser, who arrived with two friends in Venice in 1739, staying for three weeks. He kept a detailed diary of his travels and wrote many letters, published posthumously in 1885 as *Letters from Italy* (*Lettres familières d'Italie*). A future president of the Burgundian Parlement, de Brosses was seeking an intensive and varied adventure, but was disappointed on arrival: 'If truth be told, my first encounter with this city did not surprise me as much I had expected. The effect it had on me was not dissimilar to that of any coastal city.' Whether his accommodation was at the famous Leone Bianco or Lo Scudo di Francia, both strategically placed near the Rialto Bridge, is uncertain, but he was pleased with it: 'We are lodged in what I may call the Fort of the Street of St Honoré.' Generally passionate about boats and travelling on water, he waxed lyrical about the merits of the gondola: 'No carriage in the world can equal a gondola in comfort [. . .] one sits within as in one's own room, in which one can read, write, talk, make love, eat, drink.'

He had arrived from Padua on the Burchiello, the boat service on the Brenta, which he greatly enjoyed. The culmination of his visit to the Arsenal was an ecstatic description of the Bucintoro, the superb barge used by Venetians for special occasions, destroyed in 1797.

As he toured the city, he gives us a dismissive description of the Basilica, concluding rather brusquely: 'Above the portal of the church are the four bronze horses of wonderful beauty. They are the only things throughout the whole building worthy of admiration.' He was not much impressed by the palaces, commenting: 'The interiors of the palaces are very gorgeous without showing much taste.' He was, however, invited to the magnificent Palazzo Labia in Cannaregio, which

is the only one that appeared to me well arranged and comfortable. The lady of the house, once a beauty, and very fond of the French, showed us all her jewels, probably the finest owned by any private individual in Europe. She has five complete sets of emeralds, sapphires, pearls and diamonds [. . .] but she is not allowed to wear them, for the ladies of the Venetian nobility are only allowed to wear jewels and coloured dresses during the first year of their married life. I offered to take her with me to France as well as her jewels.

He also remarked maliciously upon the mean sense of hospitality, noted by many other foreign visitors:

The Venetians, with all their show and their palaces, do not understand the first rudiments of hospitality. I have looked in sometimes at the conversazione of the Marchesa Foscarini, who lives in a superb palace; she is a most gracious lady, but for refreshments we were offered at eleven at night by twenty valets, a large kind of pumpkin, cut into quarters, served on a huge silver dish, which they call here a water-melon, a most loathsome dish. This with piles of silver plates; everyone throws themselves at the table, takes therewith a little cup of coffee, and returns home with an empty stomach to have supper at midnight.

His letters, full of irony, are highly entertaining, at once critical and admiring: 'In a word, the city is so singular in its construction, its customs, its most ridiculous way of life, the freedom they enjoy, that I do not hesitate to rank it the second city of Europe' (Paris naturally came first).

The future politician and friend of the philosophers of the Enlightenment could not but be impressed by the general mood of tolerance: 'In no other place in the world does so much liberty and licence exist so entirely as here. Do not meddle with the government, and you can do as you please. Whatever is considered a bad action in the high moral sense is allowed with impunity.' He continued, 'despite the opportunity offered by the wearing of masks, going about at night, the narrow alleys, and above all the bridges with no railings, from which one may surprise and overcome a man and push him into the water, there are not four such incidents [. . .] you may judge by this how ill-founded our ideas of Venetian stilettos are.'

Still, he could not help regretting the general attitude of distrust shown towards foreigners: 'The visitors are somewhat at a disadvantage, for the patricians are not accustomed to ask them to their houses or their parties.' He was nevertheless granted the privilege of attending a session in the Great Council Chamber, an opportunity not extended to everyone, when the patrician Donato was chosen as the new doge. At the end of a long detailed description he concludes: 'The whole ceremony was got through with the greatest rapidity, and in less time than it takes to describe. It was very comical, as we left the place, to see Donato's profound bows, and the way he was kissed right and left; the kisses could be heard as far as the middle of the square.'

De Brosses did not miss the opportunity to visit the renowned courtesans – 'compared with Paris, all are so sweet-natured and charmingly polite,' he wrote. A great music lover, he also befriended Vivaldi: 'Vivaldi has made himself one of my intimate friends, probably in order that he may sell his concertos expensively.' He might have seen through Vivaldi's charms, but he falls under those of the singers in the Ospedaletti, which are

charitable establishments. Of these there are four, all containing natural daughters, female orphans, or those girls whom their parents are unable to educate [. . .] They can sing like angels, and play the violin, the flute, the organ, the hautboy, the violoncello and the bassoon. I can assure you that there can be nothing more charming than to see a young and pretty nun, dressed in white, with a bunch of pomegranate flowers in her hair, conducting the orchestra and beating time with the greatest skill and precision.

De Brosses was also very struck by the natural quality of the acting he witnessed in the theatres:

The gesture and the voice inflection are always wedded to the subject; the actors come and go, they speak and move as if in their own houses. This action is natural in a very different sense and wears an air of truth [. . .] very different from that which is seen when four or five French actors, arranged in a line like a bas-relief on the foreground of the stage, recite their dialogue, each speaking in turn.

The Italians love theatre more than any other nation; as they have no less love for music, they hardly distinguish the two with the effect that very often tragedy, comedy and farce are all opera for them.

Like many of his wealthy contemporaries, he was keen to buy works of art and also to have his portrait done by Rosalba Carriera, but was put off by her high prices, Her meeting with him was so unpleasant that she recorded it in a letter. Parting reluctantly from his 'sweet inn of delights' (the gondola) and a whole seraglio, de Brosses left Venice with regret:

> Tomorrow I must leave my sweet gondolas. I am there now in dressing gown and slippers, writing to you from the glorious middle of the Grand Canal, rocked occasionally by angelic music [. . .] What is worse, I must leave my beloved Ancilla, Camilla, Faustoli, Zulietta, Angeletta, Caltina, Spina, Agatina, and a thousand other dear things, each prettier than the next.

A more serious Grand Tour traveller, the English musicologist **Charles Burney** (1726–1814), embarked in 1770 on a trip through France to Naples, having set himself the ambitious task of making a thorough study of music in Europe. The result of seven months on the road was a work in four volumes, published between 1776 and 1779, the first printed history of music. From his letters and his *Tour of Italy*, based on his diary and notes, we know what he did, what he thought and what he saw and heard in Venice during his seven-day stay in August 1770.

Having travelled by boat down the Brenta, where he visited the famous Villa Pisani, he experienced a little tinge of disappointment, as he wrote that what he saw 'did not at all answer my expectations'. We also know where he stayed – 'I took my abode at the Scudo di Francia, on the Grand Canal within twenty yards of the ponte di Rialto'– and that he wasted no time before going shopping: 'At the Inn I found by agreement my Italian Merchant, Signor Moiana, my fellow traveller. And after dinner not having time pour m'adoniser [to put on evening dress] I went in my travelling dress with him [. . .] to see the famous glass manufactory of Briati, which produces very beautiful and cheap furniture and ornaments of all sorts.'

He enjoyed the novelty of gondolas: 'The gondolas are most admirably contrived for ease, convenience and pleasure.' He revelled also in picture galleries and museums, but showed little interest in or understanding of the architecture of the city.

Although a dedicated and resilient traveller who walked around 'at a season when it is said that only Dogs and English Gentlemen are seen out of doors at noon, all else lie down in the middle of the days', he was almost defeated by the insects: 'such myriads of gnats, or rather mosquitoes came in as both stung and devoured me. The sufferings of those thus situated, seem greatly to exceed those described in Dante's Purgatorio.' He added later, 'This morning I was too much disfigured to go out.'

But he did go out, to see the Basilica:

> I went to see the Church of St Mark, and the Piazza, or square, and though neither of them was quite what I expected, yet I found them very rich and splendid [. . .] The cathedral of St Mark is too full of fine things; it seems loaded with ornaments; which though inestimable in their intrinsic worth, yet being jumbled together they have less effect than half the number would have, if well placed.

Music was his first priority and Venice fulfilled his expectations from the start:

> Venice has likewise been one of the first cities in Europe that has cultivated the musical drama or opera: and, in the graver stile, it has been honoured with a Lotti and a Marcello. Add to these advantages the conservatorios established here, and the songs of the Gondoleri, or Watermen, which are so celebrated, that every musical collector of taste in Europe is well furnished with them, and it will appear that my expectations were not ill grounded.
>
> The first music which I heard here was in the street, immediately on my arrival, performed by an itinerant band of two fiddles, a violoncello, and a voice, who, though unnoticed here as small-coalmen or oyster-women in England, performed so well, that

in any other country of Europe they would not only have excited attention, but have acquired applause, which they justly merited.

He attended numerous concerts in the *scuole*:

> The city is famous for its conservatorios, or musical schools, of which it has four, the Ospedale della Pietà, the Mendicanti, the Incurabili, and the Ospedaletto at St Giovanni e Paolo, at each of which there is a performance every Saturday and Sunday evening, as well as on great festivals [. . .] the performers, both vocal and instrumental, are all girls; the organ, violins, flutes, violoncellos, and even French-horns, are supplied by these females. It is a kind of Foundling Hospital for natural children, under the protection of several nobles, citizens, and merchants, who, though the revenue is very great, yet contribute annually to its support.

On Saturday 4 August at a concert at the Pietà, he did not share the unreserved enthusiasm expressed by previous visitors such as Beckford, Rousseau and de Brosses in their writing: 'The composition and performance which I heard to-night did not exceed mediocrity; among the singers I could discover no remarkable fine voice, nor performer possessed of great taste', but he was delighted to hear a violin concerto at San Lorenzo: 'The first violin of Venice, [Nazari] is certainly a very neat and pleasing player; his tone is even, sweet, and full; he plays with great facility and expression, and is, on the whole, one of the best players that I had heard on this side of the Alps.' He befriended Galuppi (Il Buranello), the celebrated composer from Burano who was at the time the second *maestro di cappella* at the Basilica, better known in his day than Vivaldi, and with whom Burney stayed in touch.

Apart from the sightseeing and the music, he found that on the whole the city offered but 'few amusements', as riding or walking in fields were out of the question, but he made the most of the night life, always associated in some way with music:

The people here, at this season, seem to begin to live only at midnight. Then the canals are crowded with gondolas, and St Mark's square with company [. . .] If two of the common people walk together arm in arm, they are always singing, and seem to converse in song; if there is company on the water, in a gondola, it is the same; a mere melody, unaccompanied with a second part, is not to be heard in this city: most of the ballads in the streets are sung in duo.

He was relieved to note that the infamous lions' mouths used for denouncing citizens during the Republic were now archaic: 'I could not look at them without horror; till I observed that his mouth was full of cobwebs.' He enjoyed himself greatly, marvelling at the open markets: 'There is a great air of industry and business in every place and countenance. Fruits of all kinds abound here; enormous Melons, Peaches, Nectarines, Grapes etc from the Venetian states on the Continent.' Unfortunately, though, his time in Venice was marred by the serious and ultimately fatal illness of a companion.

A few years after his return to England in 1774, Charles Burney proposed a scheme for a music school at the Foundling Hospital in London along the lines of the Venetian *scuole*. The failure of his scheme was a terrible blow, and Britain remained without a school of music until the Royal Academy of Music was founded in 1823.

Johann Wolfgang von Goethe (1749–1832) was in Venice just before the French Revolution. He was the greatest of the German thinkers and writers to travel there, and it was one of the first cities he described in his *Journey to Italy*, published in 1816–17. The book was based on the detailed diary he had kept while travelling in 1786–8. The young German author and administrator, his reputation already established, reported impressions, notes, observations and sensations in his *Diary*, as well as in letters written to family and friends, above all to Charlotte von Stein. He had 'slipped away' from his duties at the Weimar court and the close emotional and intellectual friendship they had shared since

1776. Just after leaving Weimar, Goethe informed Charlotte in a letter dated 14 October 1786 that he was keeping a diary which he would send her gradually, and also asked her to keep it secret and return it to him later, with a view to publication. Trying to restore, as he put it, 'my elasticity of spirit', he felt liberated from emotional ties and professional duties, which he had left behind at the Weimar court, where he had been working since 1775. Initially Goethe felt an exuberant enthusiasm for everything he saw during this journey, planned on the Grand Tour model, letting himself be guided by his precious Volkman guidebook, which was very popular with German travellers at the time. Unlike other Grand Tour travellers, he was often alone, journeying incognito, going by the name of Filippo Miller, trying to mingle unrecognised with the local crowds.

His arrival by boat at sunset for a four-week stay was a major event in his life: 'It was written then, on my page in the Book of Fate, that at 5 in the afternoon on the 28th day of September in the year 1786, I should see Venice for the first time as I entered this beautiful island-city, this republic built on water as by beavers.' He had dreamed of this fateful moment from his boyhood, when he had admired a miniature gondola:

18   *Plaque on the site of the former Hotel Regina d'Inghilterra, where Goethe stayed*

My father had a beautiful model of a gondola, which he had brought back with him [from his own travels in Italy]. He set great value upon it, and it was considered a great treat when I was allowed to play with it. The first prows of polished metal, the black gondola cabins, everything greeted me like an old friend; and I experienced again a warm impression missing since my youth.

This strange Venetian means of transport inspired him to write his Venetian Epigram 8, a metaphor for life and death:

> I compare this gondola to a gently rocking cradle,
> And its cabin is like a capacious coffin.
> So it is! For we sway and hover between cradle and grave
> Borne carefree along the Grand Canal of life.

But the city was also the place where he experienced many other strong emotions. It was here that he saw the sea for the first time. Goethe, who apparently liked to survey any place he visited from its highest point, lost no time in climbing the Campanile:

> I saw the sea gleam, and the sweet waters glitter.
> Lively sails crossing it, with a following wind.

At some stage, the painter Johann Heinrich Tischbein accompanied him to look at pictures in churches and palaces, among others the Palazzo Pisani-Moretta, where he admired Veronese's *Family of Darius before Alexander*.

He was a fanatical devotee of Palladio, whose buildings he had already seen in Verona and Vicenza. While in Padua, to his great delight, Goethe had acquired Palladio's complete works and now visited Palladio's Venetian churches, Redentore, San Giorgio and San Francesco della Vigna, as well as La Carità, where Palladio had originally planned to build a convent.

There was also time for relaxation and entertainment, and his rhapsodic description of the gondoliers singing Tasso's verses on the

Grand Canal is memorable. He was deeply moved by the experience and described

> a lament without sadness: it has an incredible effect and is moving even to tears [. . .] and yet it is quite likely that a listener standing nearby would find little pleasure in listening to these voices compete with the waves of the sea [. . .] It is the song sent out into the distance by a lonely individual, in the hope that someone else in the same mood will hear and answer.

The future director of the Weimar theatre also went to plays and concerts, as well as a Mass, attended by the doge himself, celebrating the famous victory against the Turks at Lepanto, in the Church of Santa Giustina (now partly destroyed, and currently a secondary school). Very keen to hear a concert at the Mendicanti, he was enchanted by the lovely singing, but not by 'the accursed Maestro di Capella'.

He also retained his critical sense of the theatre, enjoying plays at the San Luca Theatre. He particularly appreciated Goldoni's *Le Baruffe*, a play about warring families set in Chioggia, which he had visited the previous day, and especially liked *commedia dell'arte* productions, with the characters wearing masks. He commented, 'I have not often seen more natural acting than that of these masks.'

On a visit to the Lido, he 'found the grave of the noble Consul Smith and his first wife,' explaining its importance: 'I owe my copy of Palladio to him, and I thanked him for it, standing at his unconsecrated grave.' As he strolled on the beach, Goethe, who later wrote *The Metamorphosis of Plants*, studied the flora and fauna with great curiosity, referring to the crabs and stones he encountered: 'At the Lido I have also found various plants whose similar character has led me to a better understanding of their nature.'

He enjoyed giving a full picture of the city, including practical details of his hotel. He had stayed at Alla Regina d'Inghilterra (now gone, but the building bears a plaque commemorating Goethe's visit) on Ramo dei Fuseri. He did not always comment too kindly on the people he met, and could not find strong enough terms to express his disgust at the lack of hygiene in the city with its 'disgusting sludge' and 'vile-smelling muck [. . .] I could only wish that they keep their streets a little cleaner. The filth is intolerable.'

Very different was his second journey to Venice in March– May 1790, as were its circumstances, for he came, almost under duress, on a semi-official mission. He had been sent by the Duke of Weimar to meet and accompany home the Duke's mother, the Duchess Anna Amalia, who was returning from a trip to Rome. In a letter reporting her pleasurable stay, he implies his own disillusion with the place: 'The Duchess is well and contented, as one is when one returns from Paradise. I am now used to it, and this time I was quite happy to leave Italy.' He was no longer in 'Arcadia' and probably missing home, Christiane Vulpius and their newborn son. His disillusion and 'distempered time', according to his biographer Nicholas Boyle, are apparent in his *Venetian Epigrams*. Longing to return home, he wrote in Epigram 96:

> How many treasures lie Southward! Yet one in the North
> Like a great magnet draws me irresistibly back.

But perhaps he was suffering from lack of inspiration, as he seemed to imply in Epigram 17:

> All Nine often used to come to me, I mean the Muses.
> But I ignored them: my girl was in my arms.
> Now I've left my sweetheart: and they've left me.

Visits to *spelunca* (or brothels) are mentioned in Epigram 68:

> So now you want to know what a spelunca is?
> Well, this book of epigrams is getting rather like a dictionary.
> They are dark houses in narrow little streets;
> The pretty creature takes you in for 'coffee',
> And it is she, and not you, who does the work.

There are more than 100 of these short poems, which remain as almost the only record of this second visit. Most of the letters he wrote on this trip were destroyed, apparently considered too revealing and personal. As for the *Venetian Epigrams*, it is a wonder they have survived at all, considering the daring content of some of them. Many were censored and had to wait a century to be published – not surprisingly as, apart from expressing the longing for home, their very explicit sexual and often cynical content was unusual and even shocking for the time.

Goethe was never to return to Venice, but it is generally assumed that, apart from the *Italian Journey* of 1816–29 and the *Venetian Epigrams*, these two periods in Venice and the time he spent in Italy contributed to the writing and completion of some of his most important works, *Iphigenia in Tauris* (1787), *Egmont* (1788), *Torquato Tasso* (1790), *Metamorphosis of Plants* (1790), *Roman Elegies* (1790), and parts of his masterpiece, *Faust* (1808).

As well as attracting English, French and German visitors, all quite well recorded in the city, Venice was very popular with Spanish travellers, who also left written testimonies which tend to be rather less well known. From the beginning, possibly because of their Arab past, Spaniards tended to consider the Serenissima as a crossroads between Europe and the East.

The earliest Spanish visitors to the city included pilgrims like **Pero Tafur** (1410–84) and Ignatius Loyola. Other travellers were also seen in the city, some openly hostile to it because of Spain's dominance and support for the Pope, which complicated the situation. They were suspected of espionage, as was the famous seventeenth-century poet **Francisco de Quevedo** (1580–1645), whose relationship with the Spanish ambassador in Venice, the Marqués de Bedmar, and his patron the Duke of Osuna, Viceroy of Naples, made him a suspect for involvement in the famous conspiracy against the Serenissima in 1618, the Bedmar Plot. Although he maintained his innocence in the matter and no real proof was produced against him, the fact remains that Quevedo was never sympathetic towards the city. His aversion to it and its inhabitants is clear: 'Venetians wherever their interests lie, whether it be with Christians or with Turks [. . .]; if a Turk might be in their interest, they would welcome him with open arms,' but he was also capable of praise in his writing (*Satire against the Venetians*): 'La Serenissima, which, for good sense and wisdom, is the brain within the body of Europe, that member country where resides the court of justice.'

In spite of the prevailing hostility between Spanish and Venetian governments, not all seventeenth-century Spaniards were hostile to Venice. Indeed, the author of *Don Quixote*, Miguel de Cervantes (1547–1616), who probably never saw Venice, remained throughout his life proud of the injury he suffered in his youth while taking part in the famous Battle of Lepanto in 1571, fighting with the armies backing Venice against the Turks. In his *Exemplary Novels* (*Novelas ejemplares*) he admiringly referred to the Serenissima: 'It appears that its wealth was infinite, its government wise, its situation impregnable, its resources great, finally, everything in it and in its parts [are] worthy of the fame and strength which are its reputation in the whole world.' His contemporary, the playwright **Lope de Vega** (1562–1635), never visited Venice either, but like Shakespeare, had a thorough knowledge of Venice, probably acquired through accounts of contemporary travellers and his own reading. Some of his plays, most notably *The Pious Venetian* and *The Slave of Venice,* take place in Venice.

A small number of Spaniards ventured on the Grand Tour in the seventeenth and eighteenth centuries, many sharing the belief that 'a self-respecting person must not leave Italy without having a look at Venice.' The Jesuit in exile **Juan Andrés** (1740–1817) arrived there from Mantua in 1788 and spent two weeks visiting the libraries. Back in Mantua he wrote eight letters, *Cartas familiares*, in 1790, packed with facts and figures on life in the city: he counted 140,000 inhabitants, described the numerous bookshops, praised the government and marvelled at the wealth of the city.

At the end of the eighteenth century, keen to experience a more liberated environment, the young wealthy Spanish nobleman

Leandro Fernández de Moratín (1760–1828) spent two months in Venice in 1796 with a friend, Antonio Robles (who had been living in Italy since 1793). A polyglot, poet and playwright, Moratín's aim was to explore the theatres while wandering in Europe, with a view to revitalising the Spanish theatre, which was stagnating at the time. Like other travellers he kept a diary and wrote many letters home, which give us a detailed description of his experiences, impressions and many theatre visits. Moratín was lucky, as he arrived in Venice in 1796, and the theatre scene was still very vibrant; the city could boast at least 16 public and private theatres, some dedicated only to music. After 1797 the drastic new regulations allowed only four theatres to continue.

He was immediately taken by the lively bustle of popular life around Piazza San Marco and its cafés: 'At Venice they have the habit of taking coffee around seven or eight times a day.' The playwright saw the square as a vast stage, with its extraordinary variety of activities and popular entertainments, including merchants making a sales pitch for up to three hours at a time:

> One, standing on a table before a screen on which, badly painted in red ochre and gesso his own portrait appeared, and by his side a trunk full of bottles of perfumes, papers of powders and pastes for eyes, shoes, worms, teeth, stains, callouses, smelling salts [. . .] Indeed, for any kind of affliction which might occur in this mortal life.

Investigating the Venetian stage, he was surprised at the more liberal attitude towards women, who did not necessarily have to be accompanied, and at the free admittance granted to gondoliers and servants on Sundays, as well as for premieres in some theatres. Although convinced of the superiority of the French theatre, Moratín nevertheless considered the Italian a close second. We see in his writings critical and detailed descriptions of the plays he saw in various theatres – San Giovanni Crisostomo (now the Malibran), San Moisè, Sant'Angelo, San Luca and the recently built Fenice, which he described as still unfinished in parts. Before arriving in Venice he had made a point of meeting Goldoni, then in exile in Paris, whom he considered 'in spite of all his faults, the best dramatic poet in Italy'.

His stay in the city was profitable and pleasant, and his last overall impression was very positive, describing the Venetians as unusually content, which he attributed to their government's ability to secure the affection of the masses: 'the Venetian people live, enjoy themselves and work, and do not grumble about their leaders.' This comment sounds rather poignant, considering that it was made a few months before the French army moved in. Moratín wrote successful plays on his return to Spain. However, this was his undoing as his 1805 comedy *Maiden's Consent* led to his denunciation by the Inquisition, and like Goldoni he died in exile in Paris.

Drawn by his reading of Romantic French writers, the novelist **Pedro Antonio de Alarcón y Ariza** (1833–91) visited the city for two weeks in 1860, staying in San Marco. His observation of the city is coloured by his reading of Chateaubriand, but he also became aware of the politically tense situation which prevailed. Venetians were increasingly impatient to shake off Austrian rule and its occupying troops: 'The way they look at themselves, the way they look at foreigners, reflects the terrible drama affecting their emotions so strongly.'

In his poem 'Venecia', the fallen city yearning for freedom 'cries' under the 'sad moon'. It was not to regain its freedom for another seven years.

6

LUST AND LOVE

Venise, notre amour en forme de ville – Venice, our love in the form of a city.

(Diego Valeri, *Mes carnets vénitiens*)

Anyone who has visited Venice, or read about it, cannot fail to know of the dubious reputation it has acquired, with its legendary prostitution and loose sexual behaviour, notorious since the Renaissance. At the end of the sixteenth century, of a total population of 130,000 there were 3,000 female patricians, 2,000 middle-class women and 2,500 nuns, but no fewer than 12,000 courtesans.

The gondoliers (who are obliged to take a test on aspects of Venetian history) are always eager to tell tourists that the city kept an official catalogue of its courtesans, the *Tariffa delle puttane di Venezia*, which included their addresses, merits and charges, an example of how the Republic tolerated widespread prostitution whilst keeping a tight control over everything. The courtesans' worldwide reputation for beauty and skill became a powerful draw for male visitors, as their time in the city generally included paying them a visit even – as Thomas Coryat claimed – just out of pure curiosity. The mythical fame of the 'honest courtesan' for being cultured and gifted in music and literature faded somewhat over time, when travellers in the seventeenth century started describing them as ordinary prostitutes. Many visitors, like Montaigne, as well as his compatriot François Maximilien Misson, wrote of their disappointment. In his 1688 *Journey to Italy* Misson lamented:

There are whole streets filled with filles de joie, who give themselves to the first-comer, and while all people's clothes are black and dark, these are dressed in red and yellow, like tulips, with a generous décolleté and they wear make up on the nose; they always have a bunch of flowers around the ear. You see dozens of them standing at doors and windows.

In the same chapter, however, Misson denounced the degrading way in which women were treated and exploited in the city. These were young women, not much more than children, who were married off or sent to convents at an early age without their consent. He also condemned the way some parents encouraged their children into prostitution, to the extent of selling them.

Sometimes the boundary between the respectable patrician woman and the courtesan was difficult to define in fifteenth-century Venice. Carpaccio's painting in the Correr Museum was known for centuries as *Two Courtesans*, until the missing half of the painting (now at the Getty Foundation) was discovered, demonstrating that these so-called courtesans were, in fact, respectable Venetian ladies waiting for their husbands to come back from a hunting trip on the lagoon. Signs and symbols, completely misinterpreted for centuries, should have given clues to their social and moral status. Their clothes and décolleté, their jewellery, their shoes and the white handkerchief, as well as the presence of certain animals (a pigeon, a peacock, a loyal dog), and the fruit on the table were all symbols of respectability.

In Letter XIV of his lively *Letters from Italy*, Charles de Brosses related how he was recommended by a gondolier to visit the house of La Bagatina, a courtesan, only to be told by the chambermaid on arriving at a beautiful palace, 'a vast magnificent apartment, richly decorated and seeming even better than that of a princess', that the lady had gone to a *conversazione*, a gathering usually reserved for respectable women in Venice. The lady in question was presented as Marchesa Abbati, respectably married to a Venetian noble. Nevertheless, he was invited to return on the following day, which he did, and found that she was indeed a courtesan, as he had initially presumed: 'I saw a tall lady, well-made, around 35 years old, noble, handsome, splendidly dressed and laden with jewels.' So impressed was he by this apparition that he 'doubled the number of coins, not wanting to have placed anything mediocre into a hand beringed with diamonds'.

So Venice was universally recognised as the city of Venus, Venezia – *città galante*. Lucien d'Azay, author of a short book on Venice, *The Ashes of the Fenice* (2000), goes as far as to see in its architectural features indisputably female shapes: 'The five fleshy domes of St Mark, but also those of St Zaccaria, Saints Giovanni and Paolo, St Pietro in Castello, St Giorgio, the Zitelle or Redentore remind us constantly that the celebration of a beautiful breast [. . .] is one of the most attractive and pleasing aspects of Venetian folklore.' Surprisingly, he omits to mention the lovely Church of Santa Maria Formosa, the name of which is widely understood to mean beautiful or shapely. According to the legend, the church was built when the Virgin appeared to Saint Magno, who was struck by her stunning beauty. The miraculous scene was painted by the eighteenth-century woman painter Giulia Lama and can be seen in the church.

The so-called Ponte delle Tette, near the Rialto Bridge, had been, according to the local historian Giuseppe Tassini, a very busy area of prostitution, recognised by a decree of the Major Council. The story goes that the girls would lean out of their windows with their breasts (*tette*) uncovered in order to attract prospective customers. Tassini also suggested that this practice was warmly encouraged by the city rulers, who were seriously concerned about the widespread unofficial practice of sodomy – 'abhominabile vitium sodomiae', according to accounts of chroniclers such as Sanudo. The Venetian Archives contain reports of men caught *in flagrante* who were arrested, tried and hanged between the two columns on the Piazzetta and their corpses then burned.

The attitude to this particular crime relaxed in the seventeenth and eighteenth centuries, when the authorities' tolerance of the practice started to attract visitors from Germany, England and other countries where sodomy remained a serious crime. Many on the Grand Tour were attracted to Venice for this reason, at least as much as by the city's art and architecture.

Visitors were also surprised, if not shocked, by what seemed to be an eighteenth-century Venetian institution, the *cicisbeo* or *sigisbée*, a gentleman escort to ladies, with the husband's open consent. They wondered at this relaxed and sexually charged behaviour, described by Venetian historian Pompeo Molmenti in 1882 in *Private Life in Venice*:

> The patricians were often accompanied by their housemaids, and they exchanged with the gentlemen, who followed them on another gondola, winks and smiles, tying intrigues of love on this unique 'street' of the world, between palaces of brown marble, water and the sky in smiling colours. At night, serenades went through the Grand Canal, and they saw smart feminine faces taking shape on the luminous balconies.

The traveller Charles Baldwyn did not mince his words in 1712:

> They enjoy a sort of liberty but it is only to be libertines and they are grown so scandalous that I think their whole city may well be term'd the Brothell house of Europe, and I dare say virtue was never so out of countenance or vice so encouraged in any part of the World and I believe not in any age as at this time in Venice.

From the date of its foundation on 25 March 421 (also the Day of the Annunciation), Venice formed a cult dedicated to the Virgin Mary, the foremost patroness of the city. It remains strong, judging from the crowds of Venetians who every year on 21 November visit the Church of Santa Maria della Salute. It was there on 21 November 1670 that the sacred icon representing the Virgin was placed in the main altar of the church, built for the Virgin, who had been asked to rid the city of the plague in 1630. The unusual circular shape of this church was specially conceived by the architect Baldassare

Longhena to resemble the Virgin's spectacular crown supported by two putti, their heads and wings emerging from the waters of the Grand Canal. 'O great Virgin, look down upon this city which you have elected here on Earth as the principal object of your Maternal Love,' invoked a Venetian friar in 1746.

Her ubiquitous presence is also felt in many other ways: Annunciation scenes, such as the one decorating the Rialto Bridge, and a great number of *capitelli* (little shrines) and signs of popular devotion. Among the 541 shrines around the city, 217 are dedicated to the Virgin. Many are still lit at night and in thirteenth-century Venice they provided useful public lighting. A local popular saying has it that 'each reflection of the light on water is like the birth of a love story.'

The city has also been and has remained the perfect setting for passionate love affairs, too often tragic, a fact which does not seem to have discouraged the steady flow of amorous couples of all ages and origins who descend on Venice, still the ultimate romantic destination. Many sad stories have taken place through the centuries, the most famous perhaps that of Othello and Desdemona in Shakespeare's tragedy, and subsequently in Verdi's opera *Otello*, produced again in Venice in 2013 after an absence from the stage of 47 years.

Among the relatively few happy love stories which have occurred in Venice and are still remembered is that of **Bianca Cappello** (1548–87), a beautiful young girl born into the powerful Venetian Cappello/Morosini families. She fell in love with a young Florentine clerk in 1563 and eloped with him to Florence, bringing shame on her family, although she was duly married. The Venetian government tried hard to have her arrested, but to no avail, as she was protected by Florence's Grand Duke Cosimo. As problems started to arise in her marriage, she happened to meet Cosimo's son, Grand Prince Francesco, who fell passionately in love with her. Already married and father of several children, he kept her as his mistress. When Francesco succeeded his father he installed Bianca in a palace, where their son and heir Don Antonio de' Medici was born. In 1578

Francesco's wife died, and on 12 June 1579 he married Bianca at the Palazzo Vecchio in Florence, with the Venetian authorities publicly attending the wedding festivities. So she seemed to have been forgiven, no doubt for political reasons. The happy ending was not long-lasting, however, as the couple both died on the same day in October 1587 from malaria, or more probably poisoning. This story was the source for many works, starting with a sonnet written by Venetian poet **Maffio Venier** (1550–86) celebrating this beautiful spirited lady who braved the wrath of her family and the Venetian state for love:

> Pale dawn of love from whose beautiful serene face
> Glow rays of light which turn a humble dwelling into
>   Paradise.

Also inspired by the story, the English playwright **Thomas Middleton** (1580–1627) wrote *Women Beware Women*, a tragedy (published posthumously in 1657).

The nineteenth-century French writer **François-René de Chateaubriand** (1768–1848) was influenced by this story. Walking through the city he came upon the Bianca Cappello Bridge (now called Ponte Storto). It stands near the palace where Bianca was born, behind the Bridge of Sighs. In 1806 he wrote: 'by the bridge of Bianca Capello I imagined a perfect romantic novel. Oh, how young I was!'

Yet more famously, Venice was a place where erotic writers flourished, like Pietro Aretino, Giorgio Baffo and Giacomo Casanova, to name only the most notorious. Now largely forgotten, the poet **Pietro Aretino** (1492–1556) had to leave the papal city since his biting tongue as an outspoken satirist and erotic writer had made him many enemies in Rome. He arrived in Venice on 25 March 1527. What was intended to be a short visit lasted for most of his life. For him Venice was a haven which tolerated his libertine behaviour and writing which would have led to prosecution anywhere else. He immediately developed strong friendships with many of the best painters, including Sebastiano dal Piombo and Titian, whose generous hospitality was renowned. This friendship between the great Venetian painter and the poet was immortalised in numerous poems which Aretino dedicated to Titian, and in the famous portrait which Titian painted of his friend in 1548 (now in the Frick Collection in New York).

Aretino's origins are somewhat unusual, as his father was a cobbler, and his mother Margherita dei Bonci della Tita a courtesan and model for painters and sculptors. These humble origins meant that Aretino was always short of money and dependent on patronage, even resorting on occasion to scrounging and extortion. In 1530 he settled in Palazzo Bollani, a small palace on the Grand Canal in the parish of Santi Apostoli, not far from Titian's house, which he greatly envied and admired, the remnant of which still stands in Biri Grande, near Fondamente Nove. Although he managed never to pay any rent for his lodgings, he remained there for 22 years. His bedroom ceiling was specially decorated for him by Tintoretto in 1545 (probably also free of charge). When he was finally forced to leave in 1551, he moved to a much grander house, Ca' Dandolo, on Riva del Carbon by the Rialto Bridge, which belonged to the powerful Dandolo family. This time the rent was paid by his patron and

19 Plaque commemorating Aretino at the Rialto Market

friend, Cosimo de' Medici. Aretino died there five years later and was buried in the nearby Church of San Luca. A portrait of Aretino can be seen on the façade of the Pescheria Nuova in the Rialto Market. It is a modern terracotta relief copied from a medallion by the famous sculptor Alessandro Vittoria. It is meant to commemorate the fact that he lived in Palazzo Bollani, which faces the market. It also represents an inkwell and a quill, alluding to Aretino's skills as a polemical writer and quoting one of his famous sayings: 'Veritas filia temporis' ('Truth, the daughter of time').

Many of Aretino's writings had a Venetian background, although his play *La cortigiana*, published in Venice in 1534, had been written nine years earlier in Rome. Two characters in the play, Valerio and Flaminio, are comparing Rome (and life in the corrupt Roman court) and Venice, which they believe preferable, being praised for its justice system and pleasant lifestyle, as: 'only in Venice does justice keep balanced scales [. . .] And the ease of her gondolas, it is a hymn to comfort. Why ride horses? Horseback riding is the mockery of shoes, the despair of the family, and an injury to one's body.' There is praise also for the variety of entertainment the city offers: 'I was astounded by the triumphal pageants of the Compagnie de la calza [. . .] by so many illustrious senators, so much nobility, so much youth, so much wealth.' Ambassadors are also mentioned, as well as the artistic scene: 'I have bypassed the crowd of painters and sculptors [. . .] Here is the glorious, miraculous and great Titian, whose colours breathe no differently than flesh which pulsates with life [. . .] and the worthy Sansovino, who has exchanged Rome for Venice.'

Sansovino, Titian and Aretino, the architect, the painter and the poet, belonged to a circle of writers and artists who frequented the Casa degli Spiriti, whose name is sometimes attributed to the clever intellectuals and artists who gathered there, and sometimes to the ghosts alleged to haunt it. The friends also met in Titian's house at Fondamente Nove. It was reported that Titian had invited his friends to a summer party in his garden, which in his time had a wonderful view of the northern lagoon. J. A. Crowe's *Life and Times of Titian* (1881) contains a description: 'the house was on the extreme northern edge of Venice, by the sea, from which you looked out towards the distant little island of Murano and other beautiful sights.' Titian died in this house in 1576. Behind the Fondamente Nove, now a busy embankment offering transport to the islands and the airport, little remains of the house in Campo Tiziano, and the wonderful view has been lost.

In Venice Aretino was in his element, always surrounded by a retinue of friends, protégés, lovers and servants. His daring writing resulted from the extraordinary artistic freedom allowed him by undemanding patrons: 'Better a gondolier in Venice than a servant in the courts', wrote Aretino in one of the thousands of letters he sent to friends, acquaintances and benefactors, published in 1538. The final publication of his letters was so successful that over the following five years there were ten further editions. They give a firsthand insight into literary and artistic Venice in the first half of the sixteenth century, covering political, religious and cultural life in the city, as well as pouring praise on Venice as the true republic. For this, Aretino is sometimes considered the first journalist and publicist of the modern world, 'the first great adventurer of the Press'.

Aretino is probably remembered nowadays mainly for his salacious writings, particularly the 16 erotic sonnets, *I Sonetti lussuriosi*, written to accompany the obscene prints *I modi* designed by Giulio Romano and engraved by Marcantonio, all published in Venice in 1527. But Aretino also wrote plays, serious poetry and religious writings. He never ceased to praise the city which had welcomed him: 'One could call Venice the substance of cities and peoples as the sun is substance of things, so that her eclipse would be a universal loss.' In a letter to his friend, the architect Sansovino, he also praised its tolerance: 'here, a good foreigner is accepted not only as a citizen but even as a gentleman.'

Amusing, intelligent and well-connected, Aretino enjoyed the support of some of the most powerful Venetians, including Doge Andrea Gritti. Also a gifted art dealer, he liked to style himself 'international' as, unlike Venetian patricians, he was allowed to mix with foreign diplomats, whom he befriended, and for whom

he would find paintings, art objects, rare books and introductions
for their royal patrons. He received many gifts from the French
ambassador for helping him to find manuscripts and books for the
French king, François I. However, his position was not always easy,
and one of the series of beatings he received throughout his life was
administered in 1547 at the instigation of the English ambassador
to Venice, William Harvel, who was offended by the accusation that
he had diverted a payment sent by Henry VIII to Aretino. But it was
Charles V of Austria who granted him a pension, and they even met
in 1543. Grateful for this generosity, a few years later Aretino named
his illegitimate daughter Austria (his first daughter was called Adria
in honour of the Venetian sea). Aretino had a hand in encouraging
Titian to work for Charles V, and he certainly contributed to
Titian's fame abroad. However, he provoked jealousy and made
many enemies in Venice as 'he willingly speaks ill of nobles and
others' (according to Marino Sanudo) and twice had to leave Venice
to escape charges of blasphemy and sodomy. Nevertheless, he seems
to have managed a fine balancing act in Venice between permissible
and illicit behaviour. Two years after his death, his entire works were
placed on the Catholic Church's Index of banned literature.

Surrounded by the most beautiful and desirable women, including the courtesan Veronica Franco and women from high society,
the libertine poet was not immune to falling in love. He cohabited
with Adria's mother, Caterina Sandella, for most of his life, but had
a succession of serious affairs. Some poems Aretino published in
1537 were addressed to a mistress, Angela dei Tornibeni, the wife
of one of his friends. After the end of the affair in 1536, he wrote a
broken-hearted letter:

> I wanted her to be entirely mine and I have lost her entirely. But
> I shall live for ever, since I have not died of losing her, or rather I
> shall bear Death since I tolerate the suffering which is tormenting
> me. I did not love her by force, nor did I deceive her with
> sweetness. Possessing her I adored her humbly and supported her
> with generosity.

He did recover quickly, however, and at the age of 45 he became seriously enamoured of a 14-year-old girl, Perina Riccia. He was completely enchanted by her qualities: 'her grace, manners and virtues are such that you would think Heaven had raised her.' When she was ill, to entice her to come to live with him, he wrote: 'Have you forgotten that here you will recover better than anywhere else? My house is the Fount of Eternal Youth, the very centre of Venice. Women long for an invitation to my parties. Titian is amongst my guests. Princes send their messengers to my door.' But she was already married to Paolo Bartoloni, one of Aretino's protégés, and the tension in Palazzo Bollani caused her to run away, provoking his fury and despair. As she was seriously ill with tuberculosis, she did return, and he nursed her, without being repulsed by her illness: 'The dreadful sight of her gaze, the horror of her cheeks and the repulsive lips were (yet) as if her eyes, her features and her mouth had lost nothing of their habitual splendour, their familiar colour and their inner grace.'

Once recovered, the fickle Perina ran away again, plunging Aretino once more into a deep state of despair, his thoughts 'constantly fixed upon Her'. He consulted the best doctors in town to try to save her when she returned in a desperate state. As he confided to her mother when Perina finally died, 'I loved her, I love her and I shall love her until Judgement Day. You were her mother through ties of blood, I her father by those of affection.' To a friend he said, 'I am telling you the truth when I say that I died when she died, that I shall live for ever with this great pain of love.'

Giorgio Baffo (1694–1768) was another writer of erotic literature in eighteenth-century Venice. He remains relatively unknown, although greatly praised by the French poet Guillaume Apollinaire: 'The famous Baffo, his face marked by syphilis, dubbed "the obscene", who can be considered the greatest priapic poet who ever lived and at the same time one of the best 18th century lyric poets, wrote in this Venetian dialect as seen in a number of remarkable works of all kinds.' Apollinaire considered Baffo the 'poet of love who sang with great freedom and with grandeur of language'. From the little that we know about him, he was a patrician and even a member of the powerful Quarantia (the Council of Forty which acted as a Supreme Court). He openly criticised Pope Clement VIII, and denounced lascivious priests and inept officials. He also engaged in a polemic against Carlo Goldoni's reform of the theatre.

In spite of Apollinaire's attempts at reviving the poet's reputation in *Infernal Lovers* (*Les diables amoureux*) (1910), Baffo has remained almost completely forgotten, partly because of the disapproval of moralising critics and powerful enemies, partly because his sonnets were best appreciated in their original language, the Venetian dialect. Moreover, his writing can be very crude, but Apollinaire thought that he 'deserves to be known and appreciated [. . .] even though he is certainly obscene, but with a kind of obscenity which one might say is full of nobility'. The French poet also attempted to shed some light on Baffo's life and informs us that 'he possessed a palace, the work of Sansovino, where he lived in a corner of the kitchen.' This palace, where he spent his last years, was Palazzo Bellavite-Soranzo in Campo San Maurizio, probably built by Sansovino and originally decorated with frescoes by Veronese.

Apollinaire praised the fact that Baffo wrote in Venetian: 'The Venetian dialect has a unique sweetness of sound. Grace and softness coexist in such harmonious proportions that above all they encourage erotic lyricism, although literature in dialect is almost always satirical.' He also referred to Baffo's relationship with his contemporary and fellow libertine, Giacomo Casanova: 'Casanova knew him at Venice in his youth, and it is thought that the beauty of Casanova's mother, an actress, attracted Baffo, whom Casanova called above all "my father's great friend".' Casanova, in his *History of my Life* (*Histoire de ma vie*), mentions Baffo's close friendship with both his parents, but ignores the possibility that the poet might have been his natural father. Baffo certainly showed him much kindness when he was a child.

Among the proliferation of libertines in eighteenth-century Venice, the most well-known are Mozart's librettist Lorenzo Da Ponte and Giacomo Casanova, both inveterate gamblers. Mozart, who met Lorenzo Da Ponte in Vienna and Casanova in Prague, does not really qualify as a libertine, but he did frequent many of the same haunts, with a special passion for billiards. They were restless travellers, and chose, but were more often forced, to spend part of their lives in exile. They were probably all Freemasons, as were many of their patrons.

Often penniless and in dire need of work and money, their livelihoods depended constantly on the capricious patronage of aristocrats and royalty. From relatively impoverished backgrounds, they were not active advocates, but rather supporters in general of social change. After giving concerts to entertain the nobility, for example, Mozart was usually sent to eat with the servants. The gifted composer did not readily accept this unfair situation: 'It is man's heart which gives him nobility, and even if I am not a Count, I enjoy greater honour than many a Count; and valet or Count, if he insult me, he is a villain.' The Venetians Casanova and Da Ponte, although they were guests in the houses of Venetian patricians, and mixed with aristocracy in the rest of Europe, were in their turn often ill-treated by the nobility and by the states which banished them from their cities, including Venice.

The French playwright Beaumarchais had denounced this situation in two plays, *The Barber of Seville* and *The Marriage of Figaro*, and it is not surprising that Mozart and his librettist Da Ponte chose to adapt the latter as an *opera buffa*. It was a brave choice, as the play emphasised personal, professional and political freedom.

Some claim that one inspiration for Mozart's opera *Don Giovanni* could be the legendary **Giacomo Casanova, Chevalier de Seingalt** (1725–98), born in Venice, near the Church of San Samuele. His parents were actors, and after his father's death his mother left to pursue her career as an actress in various places in Europe, ending up in Dresden. She practically abandoned him, leaving him to his grandmother's care. Casanova lived in her house in San Samuele and also in Campo San Maurizio at the house of Baffo.

Sent to study classics, music and finally law (which he hated – he would have preferred medicine) in Padua, Casanova then took

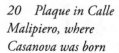

20   *Plaque in Calle*
Malipiero, where
Casanova was born

minor orders, and back in Venice considered an ecclesiastical career. In 1745 he gave sermons in the Church of San Samuele which were well-attended, and he was rewarded with love letters and generous collections from the ladies of his congregation. After some mishaps he decided that he was not really suited to this career, having realised that 'women are my ruling passion'. He then briefly tried the army, but eventually became a violinist at San Samuele Theatre (now gone). Following the festivities celebrating a wedding between two powerful Venetian families at which he had been playing, Casanova had the good fortune to save the life of a rich and powerful patrician, Senator Matteo Bragadin. The grateful Senator adopted him and continued to finance him, letting him live with him in his beautiful palace, Palazzo Bragadin in Castello, from 1746 to 1755. Now installed there, with his own gondola and a lavish monthly allowance, 'La bella vita a Venezia' started properly for him. Casanova accumulated conquests and debts and spent much time at the gambling table and behaving badly, as he admitted: 'I became a bit of a ruffian.' He claimed in his memoirs, for example, to have gone out under cover of darkness to cut the mooring ropes of gondolas. Now that he could afford to travel, he visited Rome, Corfu, Constantinople and France, where he became a Freemason and where he went by the name of Chevalier de Seingalt, and learned French properly. Back in Venice, he was making enemies, and in 1755 he was arrested and accused of depravity and blasphemy, whereupon he was condemned to be incarcerated for five years in the Piombi, the dreaded prison situated directly under the lead roofs of the Doge's Palace. He managed, in somewhat extraordinary circumstances, to escape in October 1756 after little more than a year, and returned to Paris as a hero, feted and now famous for his adventures. 'He has gained admittance, I don't know how, to the best Parisian society,' wrote an astonished Giustina Wynne in 1758. 'He is quite full of himself and stupidly pompous. In a word, he is unbearable [. . .] except when he speaks of his escape, which he recounts admirably.' It was a good time for him. He became rich for a time, having contributed to the introduction of the lottery in 1757, and also managed, less successfully, a small silk business. He travelled next to England, Germany, Spain and Russia – his friend de Bernis, the former French ambassador to Venice, was sending him abroad on small paid missions as a spy or informer. He was finally allowed to return to Venice in 1774 after many years in exile: 'My arrival in Venice after nineteen years caused me to delight in the best moment of my life.' As he was in urgent need of money, he worked again as an informer between 1774 and 1782, this time for the Venetian Inquisition, but was not particularly talented and was not really trusted. By the end of 1782 he finally left Venice, disillusioned, having apparently offended too many people. A friend, Prince Charles de Ligne, gave a description of him in 1784:

He would be a good-looking man if he were not ugly, he is tall and built like Hercules, but of an African tint, eyes full of life and fire, but touchy, wary – and this gives him a ferocious air. It is easier to put him in a rage than to make him gay. He laughs little but makes others laugh. He has a manner of saying things which reminds me of Harlequin or Figaro and which makes them sound witty.

In Vienna he worked briefly as secretary to the Venetian ambassador Foscarini, and when the ambassador died Count Waldstein, another Freemason, offered Casanova a position looking after his library in the neighbouring Dux Castle, to which he moved.

But he visited Vienna frequently, where he saw Da Ponte again, and he finally met Mozart in Prague in 1787, a few days before the official opening of Mozart's latest opera, *Don Giovanni*. The story goes that the libretto was unfinished and that Mozart was under great pressure to complete it. Da Ponte had been called back to Vienna, but Casanova was in Prague to save the situation, and helped Mozart to complete the libretto. According to the testimony of some musicians who were there at the time, Casanova visited the theatre during rehearsals, where Mozart was struggling to produce the last parts of the music. The cast members became so frustrated that they locked Mozart in a room and told him he would not be freed until he finished the opera. Casanova apparently persuaded them to release him, and was supposed to have fine-tuned the libretto in several key scenes. This story was published in 1876 in a book, *Rococo Pictures* (*Rococo-Bilder*) by Alfred Meissner. It would be difficult to assess how true the story is, or the extent of Casanova's contribution, but the fact remains that some sheets of paper written in Casanova's hand were found in the Dux Archives in 1924, with notes on Scene X of Act II of the opera.

After the first performance, which Casanova attended, a friend asked whether he had seen the opera, at which he was supposed to have laughed and replied 'Seen it? I practically lived it!' It is tempting to believe that the opera *Don Giovanni* has something to do with him, the greatest seducer of all time, the ultimate womaniser. Originally it was based on a play written in 1613 by the Spanish playwright Tirso de Molina, who had chosen to set it in Seville, and it then inspired many different versions including Molière's *Don Juan*. But Mozart and Da Ponte's version had certainly adopted many Venetian features, acknowledged in various productions.

The designer Simon Higlett recently chose to set his Edinburgh production of *Don Giovanni* in seventeenth-century Venice, saying, 'It's an opera about intrigues, disguise and the masquerade. I can't conceive of *Don Giovanni* being set anywhere else.' In 1979 Joseph Losey similarly shot his film of *Don Giovanni, Il dissoluto punito* in Venice and at La Rotonda near Vicenza in the Veneto.

In the last scene Don Giovanni is swept into hell in a Murano glass-blowing furnace.

Likely alternative models for Mozart's Don Giovanni include Count Francesco Falletti Castelman. Mozart stayed in 1771 in Palazzo Molin, the upper floors of which had been the Count's apartments. In a letter, he calls it Casa Cavalletti, a clear phonetic reference to its local name of Ca' Falletti. The Count had been condemned to death in 1752 for sexual licence and blasphemy.

Casanova published *The Story of My Escape from Prison* (*Histoire de ma fuite des prisons*) in 1788, and was encouraged by its success. Ill and depressed in Dux, where he felt he was 'buried alive', his doctor had advised him to write the story of his life as an antidote to depression: 'the only remedy to keep me from going mad or dying of grief'. Old age was catching up on him, he had lost his looks, his charm, his teeth, in short his seductive powers. He was apparently very keen to return to see Venice after the fall of the Republic but did not manage it, as he died in Dux in 1798. The manuscript of his memoirs written in French, covering his life up to 1774, when he was allowed to return to Venice, was not released by the family until 1822, and many shortened versions were published in German and then retranslated unsatisfactorily into French, in up to as many as 500 editions. The complete *Histoire de ma vie* appeared only in 1960–2, followed in 1966–71, two centuries after it was written, by the first English edition, *The History of My Life*. This could explain why for a long time Casanova was not treated as a serious writer, but rather as a pornographic author, probably because the truncated editions of his memoirs appearing in Germany and elsewhere included quantities of erotic illustrations, perpetuating also the myth of Venice as a city of vice.

In fact the full memoirs are lively, funny and generally entertaining, revealing many aspects of the times and of countries explored by Casanova during his adventurous life. He has become one of the most notorious myths of the city and continues to be the subject of a vast quantity of literature and at least 30 films, including the famous 1927 version of his life by Alexander Volkoff, Fellini's controversial

Casanova (1976), and most recently Lasse Halmstron's *Casanova*, shot in 2005 with Heath Ledger in the title role.

Many books have been published retracing Casanova's whereabouts in the Serenissima, starting from the church where he was baptised, the Church of San Samuele, between Palazzo Grassi (now owned by French art collector Bernard Pinault) and the impressive Palazzo Malipiero with its outstanding garden packed with roses, lending a touch of colour to the Grand Canal.

Casanova was not in Venice when **Wolfgang Amadeus Mozart** (1756–91) arrived in the city for four weeks with his father Leopold on 11 February 1771, at the close of the Carnival. The visit was part of a long trip to Italy which had started at the end of 1769. Il Signor Cavaliere Filarmonico, as the Italians called Mozart, was then aged just 15, and had already composed about 100 musical works. His father rented an apartment in Ca' Falletti by the Ponte dei Barcaroli and close to several working theatres which they attended, San Moisè, San Benedetto, San Samuele and the Ridotto Nuovo. It may be because the San Benedetto (now Cinema Rossini) burned to the ground a few years later, in 1774, that the new theatre built nearby was given the name 'Fenice' – the phoenix rising from the ashes – when it was completed in 1792, too late for Mozart to see it. They were guests of Johannes Wilder, a German silk trader, and his Venetian wife Venturina. The Mozarts had been introduced by Johann Lorenz Hagenauer, owner of their house in Salzburg and a great financial supporter of them. In a postscript to a letter he wrote to Hagenauer, Leopold Mozart added: 'I am writing this from the house of M. Wilder, a gentleman [. . .] and where last evening we celebrated the end of the Carnival by dining before dancing and going with the pearls [Wilder's daughters] to the New Ridotto, which pleased me greatly. I very much like Venice.' They visited the Arsenal, churches and convents (always in search of music), stopped at Caffè Pasquali for ice cream and went to the opera. Apparently the young Mozart also played in the beautiful but somewhat over-restored Palazzo Cavalli-Franchetti next to the Accademia Bridge which contained its little theatre, and in Palazzo Balbi, also on the Grand Canal, on the Dorsoduro side. Thanks to some useful contacts, they were received by the prestigious Venetian Grimani, Mocenigo and Dolfin families. The Valier family and Giovanni Bragadin, the city's patriarch, showered them with presents.

There has been some debate on the actual location of Mozart's stay in Venice. A book recently published by an Italian musical scholar Paolo Cattelan, *Mozart: One Month in Venice* (*Mozart, un mese a Venezia*), attempts to clarify the facts. It is now accepted that the plaque which anyone coming from the Fenice can see on Casa Ceselletti, by Ponte dei Barcaroli, should have been placed on the nearby Ca' Falletti, in which the Mozarts had stayed.

They left Venice on the Burchiello, which took them up the Brenta to Padua, and went on to Verona and Milan. When Mozart returned to Italy three years later in 1772, however, he did not stop in Venice, where Lorenzo Da Ponte, his librettist-to-be, was to arrive a year later in 1773. The two did not meet until much later, in Vienna, where Da Ponte had been appointed poet to the Imperial Theatres by Emperor Josef II, after being exiled from

IN QVESTA CASA OSPITE DI AMICI
IL QVINDICENNE
WOLFGANG AMADEVS MOZART
SOGGIORNO' FESTEVOLMENTE
DVRANTE IL CARNEVALE 1771
LA CITTA' DI VIVALDI E DI GOLDONI
VVOLE QVI RICORDATO
IL FANCIVLLO SALISBVRGHESE
NEL QVALE LA GRAZIA DEL GENIO MVSICALE
E IL GARBO SETTECENTESCO
SI FVSERO IN VNA PVRISSIMA POESIA

NEL SECONDO CENTENARIO
IL COMVNE DI VENEZIA
E L'AZIENDA AVTONOMA SOGGIORNO
1971

21   Mozart's plaque was mounted on the wrong house at Ponte dei Barcaroli

the Serenissima in 1779. Da Ponte promised Mozart he would write something for him, which Mozart related, not altogether convinced, in a letter to his father: 'But who knows whether he will keep his word – or will even want to? For you know what these Italian gentlemen are like: very civil to your face [. . .] But how dearly I should love to show what I can do in an Italian opera!' Fortunately the promise led to their collaboration on the three great operas *Marriage of Figaro* (1786), *Don Giovanni* (1787) and *Così fan Tutte* (1790).

It may well be that during his only stay in Venice, Mozart heard of **Giordano Bruno** (1548–1600), the free-thinking Renaissance philosopher, mathematician and astrologer. While working as a tutor for the powerful Venetian Mocenigo family in 1592, Bruno was denounced to the Inquisition by his host Giovanni Mocenigo and arrested on charges of blasphemy, immoral conduct and heresy, and, most importantly, for his free thinking. His trial in Rome lasted seven years and, since he refused to recant, he met a fate similar to that of Mozart's Don Giovanni and was engulfed by flames, in his case those of the stake. Certainly the notion of resistance based on individual freedom ('Viva la libertà!' cries Don Giovanni) was attractive to Mozart.

Lorenzo Da Ponte (1749–1838) was born Emanuele, the son of a Jewish cobbler, Conegliano. He was born in the small town of Ceneda, known now as Vittorio Veneto, on the mainland just to the north of Venice. The young Emanuele took, as was then customary, the name of the local bishop Monsignor Lorenzo da Ponte, who baptised him and his siblings in 1763. Lorenzo left the family home and was sent to study at the Portogruaro seminary, although he later said becoming a priest was 'wholly contrary to my temperament, my character, my principles and my studies'. Nevertheless, it was as a priest that he arrived in Venice in 1773, a position that did not prevent him leading a thoroughly dissolute life in what was then widely considered the city of pleasure: 'A little mass in the morning, a little gamble in the afternoon, and a little lady in the evening.' This is amusingly (but not always accurately) described in his memoirs which he wrote in French towards the end of his life. The handsome and intelligent young man also enjoyed writing. In 1777 he first came across Casanova in Palazzo Memmo Martinengo at San Marcuola, which belonged to a powerful Venetian, Bernardo Memmo. Here Da Ponte was employed as a tutor. He also worked in Pietro Zaguri's house in Campo San Maurizio, where he was secretary. Both Memmo and Zaguri were apparently also Freemasons and great supporters of the playwright Goldoni, and entertained in their houses free-thinkers like Giorgio Pisani, who openly advocated the ideas of the Enlightenment.

Referring to his meeting with Casanova, whom he emulated, Da Ponte wrote: 'I had the opportunity of making his acquaintance and having intimate talk with him sometimes at Zaguri's and sometimes at Memmo's, both of whom loved what was good in him and forgave what was ill, and taught me to do the same [. . .] This singular man never liked to be in the wrong.'

Da Ponte was making the most of Venice. 'At this juncture I was loved of women, esteemed of men, cosseted by patrons, and full of brightest hope.' While serving in the Church of San Luca near the Rialto, he was living in sin nearby in Campo San Luca with Angioletta, a married woman, with whom he had two children. Both offspring were promptly sent to the Pietà orphanage at birth. It was also rumoured that he was having an affair with Memmo's young mistress. His *mala vita*, his immoral life and seditious writings, led to banishment from Venice in 1779 following his denunciation by an anonymous letter through the *bocca di leone* in San Moisè. So, at the age of 30, he was exiled from Venice, never to return. He was also banished from Treviso for having written a Rousseau-inspired tract, *L'Uomo per natura libero* (*Man is Free by Nature*). After some years of wandering, he found a kind of haven in Vienna in 1782, where he was employed by the enlightened Emperor Josef II, who allowed him to start a fresh career, writing libretti for composers, including Salieri. Here he met Mozart and their famous collaboration began. Da Ponte was keen to enhance in his memoirs the part he played:

Wolfgang Mozart, however blessed by Nature with a musical genius possibly greater than any composer in the world in the past, present and future, had never been able to burst forth with his divine genius in Vienna because of enemies and cabals; he remained obscure and unknown, like a precious stone buried in the entrails of the Earth, the secret of its splendour hidden [. . .] I can never think without rejoicing or pride that only my perseverance and my energy were in great part the cause to which Europe and the world owed the complete revelation of the marvellous compositions of this incomparable genius.

He also related that, after the success in Prague of the first performance of *Don Giovanni*, the opera was not so successful in Vienna. The Emperor said to Da Ponte: 'that opera is divine, it is perhaps more beautiful than *Figaro*, but it is not a morsel for the teeth of my Viennese. I told Mozart this and he was not upset, and he said "Give them time to chew on it."'

Josef's successor Leopold II, who was not a lover of the arts, did not like Da Ponte and dismissed him. Da Ponte then spent a long period in London, after which he travelled to New York, where he introduced *Don Giovanni* (and other works of Mozart) to the American stage for the first time in 1826: 'The opera was well received from start to finish: words, music, performance, actors, all was admirable, and especially La Malibran in the role of Zerlina.'

He wrote his memoirs in his seventies and eighties, *Memorie di Lorenzo Da Ponte da Ceneda scritte da esso*. Although not necessarily accurate, they give an entertaining account of life in eighteenth-century Venice, Austria, London and America, where Da Ponte died in 1838.

A literary guide to Venice cannot omit **Carlo Goldoni** (1707–93), one of the best-known Venetian writers, whose plays remain popular. Like his contemporaries, Vivaldi, Casanova and Tiepolo, also successful and prolific in their home city, he chose eventually to leave Venice in 1762, moving to the French royal court in Paris,

22 Statue of Goldoni in Campo San Bartolomeo

where he died in poverty, almost forgotten, during the French Revolution, having lost his pension after the execution of his patron Louis XVI.

Having given up an early career as a lawyer in Venice, Goldoni joined successful theatre companies and started to produce numerous comedies to be performed at the San Angelo Theatre. In 1750 he managed to write and direct 16 new comedies in a single year. Some of them, adapted to suit modern taste, are still played, such as *A Servant of Two Masters* (*Arlechino servitore di due padroni*) (1745), performed in London and New York under the title *One Man, Two Governors*. The playwright will also be remembered for his attempts to reform the theatre with proposals he published in a pamphlet in 1751, *Teatro comico*. A great admirer of Molière, he proposed a theatre with fewer masks and without the burlesque elements traditionally used in commedia dell'arte, replacing them with an attempt to portray deeper and more realistic situations, characters and emotions. His plays are now best remembered for their satirical view of eighteenth-century popular Venetian society: *The Coffee House* (*La bottega del caffè*) (1750), *The Landlady* (*La locandiera*) (1753). His characters speak in Venetian dialect, and sometimes even a local dialect such as the one from Chioggia, an island Goldoni knew well, since he had once lived there, and which he used in his 1762 play about quarrelling factions on the island.

In Venice his plays were performed in three of the 15 working theatres: San Samuele (which was pulled down in 1894), San Angelo (closed in 1803 and now gone) and San Luca, which survived, and which was renamed Teatro Goldoni when his name and works were revived after a long period of obscurity. Goldoni also fought a long battle to obtain rights for writers, who at that time had no legal or financial control over their works.

His attempts to transform the theatre were challenged by another very successful contemporary playwright, **Carlo Gozzi** (1720–1806), now almost forgotten. The bitter conflict which ensued might have contributed to Goldoni's decision to leave Venice. It is possible to follow these events by reading Goldoni's *Memoirs*, which he started in French in 1784. Carlo Gozzi similarly wrote his *Useless Memoirs*. Both writers give an interesting and detailed description of the city's cultural life, with their own petty literary skirmishes, observed wittily from the inside.

It is sad that Goldoni died poor and forgotten in exile. The Venetian playwright, a relentless traveller, was always happy, as in 1734, to be back in his city, marvelling afresh at its lovely sights: 'What cheerfulness, what liveliness in common people! Vendors sing while they sell their goods, apprentices sing on their way home from workshops, gondoliers sing while waiting for their masters, everybody sings in the streets and on the canals and the reason of their singing is not vanity, but pure joy.'

His judgement on Antonio Vivaldi, with whom he had some professional involvement, now seems surprising:

The drama which they were to give this year [1735] was not new; they had chosen La Griselda, an opera of Apostol Zeno and Pariati

[. . .] and the composer who was to set it to music was an Abbé Vivaldi called 'il Prete rosso' on account of his red hair [. . .] this ecclesiastic was an excellent performer on the violin but an indifferent composer.

In fact Goldoni considered Galuppi (Il Buranello), now hardly known, a much better composer.

The theme of love recurs in many of his plays, although Goldoni was not a libertine like Casanova or Lorenzo Da Ponte, and did not publicly boast of his affairs and amorous victories and adventures. His marriage to Nicoletta Conio in Genoa in 1736 is briefly mentioned in Chapter XXXIX of his *Memoirs*: 'There I was, the happiest and most contented man in the world; but could there be satisfaction without trouble soon to follow? The first night of my marriage I was struck by a fever and the smallpox I had suffered as a child in Rimini returned to attack me again.' If he had amorous dealings with other women, he seems to have been very discreet about it, although he may have been smitten with Casanova's mother, Zanetta Farussi, a beautiful actress, whom he referred to as 'a very pretty and skilled widow called Zanetta Casanova, who played young lovers on the stage'. She was then working for the theatre director Imer, who was probably her lover and whose jealousy inspired Goldoni to write a musical intermezzo in 1734, *The Ward* (*La pupilla*). 'My source for the play was the director's private life. I observed that he was much taken by the widow, his colleague, I saw that he was jealous, and I played him myself.'

Goldoni also admitted having borrowed from his observation of real-life arguments for *The Lovers* (*Gli innamorati*), a play about unhappy love, marred again by intense jealousy:

I began and finished in two weeks a play in three Acts, entitled The Lovers. [. . .] I felt I could make of it a scene to provoke some to laugh and the rest to be shocked [. . .] and I was right to paint thus the madness of love in a place where the climate heats the passions and the spirit more that anywhere else.

Goldoni knew that love would always be a very popular subject on the stage, whether it was unhappy, comic or tragic. The city of Venice later paid two tributes to Goldoni: first with the installation of a statue by Dal Zotto in 1883 on Campo San Bartolomeo near the Rialto, much used nowadays as a meeting place, and then with the opening of a Goldoni Museum in Palazzo Centani in 1953, his birthplace in the district of San Tomà.

Like Goldoni, Da Ponte and Casanova, writers and artists moved around a great deal in the eighteenth century, many forced into exile for political and financial reasons. One spirited Englishwoman, **Lady Mary Wortley Montagu** (1689–1762), deserves particularly to be remembered, as her original motive for exchanging London for Venice was love. Very few women in her time were free to make decisions, let alone to abandon their homeland. She was born in London in 1689, daughter of Evelyn Pierrepont and Lady Mary Fielding. An intelligent, well-read, wilful woman, she married against her parents' wishes Edward Wortley Montagu, whom she accompanied to Turkey when he was appointed ambassador in 1716. She was a cousin of Henry Fielding and was also friendly with other writers, including Alexander Pope (although it was a relationship which subsequently turned sour). She wrote poetry and was a keen letter-writer, sometimes compared to Madame de Sévigné, although she commented: 'The last pleasure that fell my way was Madame de Sévigné's letters; very pretty they are, but I assert without the least vanity that mine will be fully as entertaining forty years hence.' This remarkable woman was also a feminist before her time, as well as a philanthropist, and an early supporter of vaccination against smallpox.

In 1736 in London, approaching 50, she met the magnetic Venetian Francesco Algarotti, then 24, and this meeting changed her life for ever. She fell for him, as had many others, including her friend Lord Hervey. Ready to abandon everything to follow him, she left for Italy in 1739, ostensibly for health reasons, but really in the hope of finding happiness with Algarotti in Venice. She arrived with two servants and a library, but to her great disappointment she did not meet Algarotti again until two years later in Turin, where he was on a diplomatic mission. Their relationship was largely restricted to letter-writing. In spite of this turn of events, she nevertheless settled happily in Venice for a time, writing to her husband on her arrival in October 1739: 'I have nothing to complain of here.'

Quite well provided for financially by her husband, who did not seem to bear her a grudge for having left him, she took lodgings in Palazzo Mocenigo on the Grand Canal, and if she did not find the love she had been pursuing, she nevertheless found something as important: 'a universal liberty, that is certainly the greatest agreement in life'. Free from social conventions, she declared proudly in another letter: 'I have most philosophically torn off all the chains of customs and subjections.' Embarking on a busy social life, she boasted of having a salon in her lodgings at Palazzo Mocenigo: 'my house is properly a meeting of Literati.' She hosted young Englishmen on their Grand Tour and even offered the British prime minister, Robert Walpole, her services: 'If you would have me, I will inform you of all I hear amongst the Foreign Ministers.' She claimed that she could be of some use, as she entertained foreign ambassadors and powerful Venetian friends, including Doge Grimani, and could use her position as a single woman, despite her unconventional lifestyle: 'Here are foreign ministers from all parts of the world who, as they have no court to employ their hours, are overjoyed to enter into commerce with any stranger. As I am the only lady here at present I can assure you I am courted as if I was the only one in the world.' In copious correspondence sent to various friends and family (including her long-suffering husband), she described things in great detail, including the famous annual Ascension Day celebration of La Sensa.

Her vivid letters give a shrewd and entertaining description of eighteenth-century Venice, where she stayed until October 1740. Algarotti had failed to respond to her pleas for commitment: 'Do me the favour of letting me know your Intentions. I have left Venice and am ready to go where you wish. I await your orders to regulate my life.' She left Venice and spent many years wandering in France and Italy, but she was back in Padua and Venice from 1756, where she met Algarotti again for the last time. This second period in Venice was less of a success, as she was at odds with John Murray, the British Minister Resident, and his friend and brother-in-law, Consul Joseph Smith. Suffering from poor health, and pressed by her daughter, Lady Mary finally decided to return to England at the end of 1761, after 22 years of exile, embarking on a long and painful journey home via Rotterdam. She died in London a few months later. More would be known about her time in Venice and Italy if her daughter, to avoid public embarrassment, had not burned her diary and some of her letters.

The object of her passion, **Francesco Algarotti** (1712–64), was born in Venice, in the Calle larga dei Boteri, the son of a rich merchant. Although he came from a wealthy background, he did not belong to the nobility, which might partly explain why very little of his short life was spent in his home town. Algarotti was a prolific correspondent and polyglot, and his letters reveal a witty and astute view of contemporary society.

His travels took him throughout Europe as far as Russia. Many of his letters were addressed to his friends in London – Lord Chesterfield, Thomas Gray, George Lyttelton, Alexander Pope and Thomas Hollis, with whom he corresponded regularly – and in Paris, where he had stayed with Voltaire, who was clearly smitten by him, and referred to him as 'our Socrates' and his 'dear Swan of Padua'. Voltaire had introduced him to Lord Hervey, who in turn introduced him to Lady Mary Wortley Montagu, with whom Algarotti became embroiled in a bisexual love triangle. Often likened to Giacomo Casanova, Algarotti behaved disgracefully towards Lady Mary Wortley Montagu, who had fallen under his spell and made herself completely available to him: 'If your affairs do not permit your return to England, mine shall be arranged in such a manner as I may come to Italy.' Despite arranging to meet her in Venice, he travelled abroad instead, perhaps even seeking to avoid her. He was brilliant and charming, but a shamelessly fickle opportunist. He was also a true European before his time, as noted again by an admiring Voltaire: 'he belongs to Europe.' Later he settled for seven years in Saxony and Prussia, where Frederick II had ennobled him and his brother Bonomo in 1740. He was rumoured to have become Frederick's lover.

In 1750 he and Bonomo had bought a Venetian palace. Palazzo Corniani, built in 1550, stands behind Fondamente Nove and part of it is now a luxury hotel. It was packed with works of art in his lifetime, as Algarotti made purchases for his network of contacts, but also for his own private collection, which was very much admired by his contemporaries. It included about 200 paintings, among them works by Bellini, Dürer and Poussin. His interest in the neo-classical and love of landscapes with ruins gave him a preference for artists like Panini, Nogari, Bellotto and Canaletto, known for their *vedute* (cityscapes). He was also particularly keen on Tiepolo, whom he befriended and probably introduced to Karl Philipp von Wenceslaus, who commissioned him to paint exceptional frescoes for his palace in Würzburg. Algarotti wrote on his many artistic interests, in 1755 proposing a simplified model of *opera seria* which was to influence composers such as Christoph Willibald Glück, and including a 1756 essay on architecture and painting. He continued to travel after his return to Italy, dividing his time between Venice, Milan and Pisa, where he died of tuberculosis. Frederick II had a monument erected to him there in the Campo Santo (cemetery).

Love in Venice in the eighteenth century was not all libertinage. Some passionate love affairs developed into long-term friendship, as in the case of French artist **Dominique Vivant Denon** (1747–1825), who arrived in Venice in October 1788. Hardly had he settled in his hotel, Alla Regina d'Inghilterra, than he was introduced by his powerful Venetian friend Angelo Querini to a Venetian beauty, **Isabella Teotochi Albrizzi** (1760-1836), with whom he immediately fell in love. Her portrait painted in 1792 by Elizabeth Vigée le Brun shows an exotic-looking lively young woman. 'I needed love, I sought it, I found it,' wrote the love-struck French artist.

At the time Isabella had a famous salon in the area of San Cassiano, but through her marriage to Count Albrizzi she moved to the more impressive Palazzo Albrizzi, a sixteenth-century palace situated close to the Church of Sant'Aponal, fully equipped with a secret garden (not to be confused with the other Palazzo Albrizzi in Cannaregio, which hosts the busy Italo-German Association).

In the course of their long relationship Vivant Denon sent her at least 350 letters, later published as *Lettres à Bettine*. Vivant Denon thoroughly enjoyed his 'sixty months in Venice', drawing and meeting people. His activities and revolutionary ideas, however, aroused the suspicion of the authorities, who had him followed. In July 1793 he was expelled – probably unjustly – considered 'a dubious dangerous man' and officially accused of owning obscene engravings. Contessa Albrizzi's initial despair when he left Venice did not last long, and she became romantically involved with a 17-year-old Italian romantic, the poor but promising writer, **Ugo Foscolo** (1778–1827). Their mutual passion lasted several years, followed by a 30-year friendship. She managed to obtain a divorce from Count Albrizzi and invited Foscolo to move in with her. He wrote a partly autobiographic epistolary novel, *The Last Letters of Jacopo Ortis,* published in 1802, whose main female character, Teresa, was inspired by Isabella. He too was made unwelcome in Venice for his political activities and went into exile to Switzerland and thence to London, where he died almost forgotten and in poverty in the London suburb of Turnham Green in 1827. Although he was buried in St Nicholas Churchyard in Chiswick, there is now only a memorial referring to him as 'the wearied citizen poet', as his remains were taken to Florence at the request of the Italian king in 1871, one of many gestures to symbolise the unification of Italy.

A writer in her own right, Isabella Teotochi Albrizzi wrote pen portraits of her contemporaries and described her young lover as having 'a furrowed brow, flaming hair, hollow cheeks, an intense appearance, serious, humane, loyal, intelligent, true'. In an unfinished novel, *The Sixth Book of Me (Sesto tomo dell'io)*, Foscolo pays her this tribute: 'To this priestess of Venus I have consecrated the best of my youth. She loved the virtues of women and avoided [. . .] their vices [. . .] She lived and let live. Mystery drew open and closed the curtains of her bed [. . .] she was a lover for five days but a friend for life.'

In the meantime, Vivant Denon reappeared in Venice in 1805, commissioned by Bonaparte to select and requisition precious Venetian artworks. He had become a friend of Joséphine de Beauharnais in Paris after his expulsion from Venice, and she introduced him to her consort Bonaparte, who then invited him to join the Egyptian campaign of 1798. He had Bonaparte's complete trust and was appointed in 1798 as the first director of the Louvre in Paris, where he is now commemorated by the Vivant Denon Wing. During Napoleon's historic ten days in Venice in 1807, Vivant Denon was back in the city, and the lovers met again after a 12-year separation, and then met a final time in Paris in 1817. In 1826, one year before he died, Vivant Denon reminisced about their long affair: 'It is certain, my dear friend, that we love each other more than we say, it is a private secret shared with all of Europe, but nobody knows that we should reproach ourselves for it.'

It should not be forgotten that Vivant Denon and his compatriots systematically looted vast numbers of works of art on France's behalf, first in Venice and Italy, and elsewhere in continental Europe during the Napoleonic Wars. To the enduring concern of Venetians, many works remain in France's possession, including Veronese's *Last Supper*, which is still in the Louvre.

Like Countess Albrizzi, **Marina Querini Benzon** (1757–1839) also had a successful salon, which she held in the elegant Palazzo Benzon on the Grand Canal, visited by celebrities like the sculptor Canova, Lord Byron (whom it seems she tried unsuccessfully to seduce), Stendhal and others. She is remembered also for her numerous love affairs, and for the famous barcarolle she inspired the poet **Antonio Alberti** (1757–1832) to compose, *The Blonde Girl in the Gondola* (*La biondina in gondoletta*). It is so sexually explicit that it was banned by the Austrian occupiers. Nowadays every Venetian knows the song by heart, here in Laura Sarti's translation (there are several good recordings of it):

> As I gazed intently at my love's features,
> Her little face so smooth, that mouth, and that lovely breast;
> I felt in my heart a longing, a desire,
> A kind of bliss which I cannot describe.
> But at last I had enough of her long slumbers
> And so I acted cheekily, nor did I have to repent it;
> For, God what wonderful things I said, what lovely things I did!
> Never again was I to be so happy in all my life!'

Marina Benzon, a beautiful, original, intelligent and liberated woman, was not afraid to shock. Stendhal gives a vivid portrait of her in a letter:

> Her palace was on the Grand Canal on the corner of the Rio Michiel. A prominent person in the city, with an impressive physique: very tall, substantial, she had much shocked the Venetians – not usually much inclined to take offence, and who dubbed her 'the disembowelled mattress' – by dancing the Carmagnole, half-clad, in the company of Ugo Foscolo, around the Tree of Liberty, which had been erected on the Piazza San Marco at the fall of the Republic in 1797.

Benzon was celebrating the arrival of Bonaparte's invading troops. Many experienced an initial romantic enthusiasm for the changes Bonaparte and the French Revolution were promising to bring – hopes which were soon almost universally succeeded by profound disillusionment in Venice.

Thirty years later, the city became the stage for a much publicised semi-tragic love affair involving the French writer **George Sand** (1804–76) and the dissolute Romantic poet **Alfred de Musset** (1810–57), who met in Paris in July 1833 and were immediately swept up into a passionate affair. Having decided to go away together to Italy, but disagreeing on the destination, they tossed a coin to choose whether to go to Rome, which George Sand would have preferred, or to Venice, where Musset, a keen admirer of Lord Byron, had always dreamed of going. He had already written evocative poems about Venice in his 1829 *Tales of Spain and Italy* (*Contes d'Espagne et d'Italie*).

His first play, not a great success on the Parisian stage in 1830, was called *The Venetian Night* (*La nuit vénitienne*). In his narrative poem *Portia* (1829–35), he had conjured up a fanciful city with a grass-covered Piazza San Marco:

> An hour in Venice, the time of serenades,
> when around St Mark's under shaded arcades,
> feet in the dew and a mask in the hand,
> no sound disturbs in the ancient palaces
> the majesty of the saints beneath the porticos.

The couple's arrival by gondola on 31 December 1833 in the depth of a bitterly cold winter was hardly propitious, and anything but romantic. George Sand settled in a first-floor room with a view at the Hotel Danieli while Musset stayed the first night at the neighbouring Hotel de l'Europe before joining her there. She had been suffering from a severe case of dysentery during the whole journey from Paris and took to her bed immediately upon arrival: 'I was shivering, and sensed that there was something terribly sad in this boat. That black, narrow, low-lying, enclosed gondola seemed like a coffin. At last, I felt it glide over the water.' Thanks to the expert care of a local physician, **Pietro Pagello** (1807–98), she recovered after two weeks and started exploring the city. Now she was ready to love Venice, 'the city of my dreams'.

In the meantime, rather bored, Musset was reading Casanova's *The History of My Life* and following in his hero Byron's footsteps. He visited the island of San Lazzaro (where Byron had studied Armenian), Palazzo Mocenigo (where Byron had lived for a few

23   *View from Room 10,*
where George Sand and
Alfred de Musset stayed
(courtesy of the Hotel
Danieli)

years), Giudecca, Chioggia, and also explored local brothels and taverns, also no doubt visited by Lord Byron.

No sooner had George Sand recovered than Musset himself fell seriously ill with a high fever, culminating in what seemed to be frightening fits of madness. Naturally the compliant doctor Pagello was back to care for the sick poet, sharing the long days and nights at Musset's bedside with George Sand. Disillusioned and angry with the poet who had neglected her during her own illness, and perhaps taking some kind of revenge, one night she wrote a note to Pagello, which appeared to be a declaration of love. By March, however, Musset's health had improved, and he was now aware of the liaison between George Sand and the Venetian doctor, which had been developing behind his back.

For financial reasons, Musset and George Sand left the Danieli to take rooms round the corner in Calle delle Rasse. But the damage was done, and the affair seemed to be over. While he was drinking in the taverns, she was going to operas and concerts at the Fenice. Their visit together to the Jewish cemetery at the Lido left a lugubrious impression on them both, symptomatic of their mood:

> The dreadful Lido,
> Where on the grass of a grave
> The pale Adriatic comes to die.

Musset wrote, and also described their confrontation at the cemetery:

> I managed to throw myself next to her in the gondola and we left together. She said not a word throughout the crossing. Disembarking at the Lido, she began to run and jump from grave to grave in the Jewish cemetery, and I followed her, jumping behind her. Eventually she sat down on a tombstone and began to weep from anger and pique. If I were you, I said, I would give up the whole impossible idea. You will not succeed in getting Dr Pagello for yourself and having me locked up in an asylum. Why do you not admit you are a whore? I do admit it, she replied. And a miserable one, I added. And having won, I took her home.

The painful break was inevitable, and on 29 March she accompanied him to Mestre, her 'heart full of a sad sweet mystery', and from there he returned alone to Paris, never to see Venice again. George Sand moved to rooms on the floor above Pietro Pagello in Corte Minelli, near the Fenice theatre.

During the lovely spring months which followed, she enjoyed Venice to the full in the company of her Venetian lover, when he was not required in the hospital. As a socially concerned writer, she was not blind to people's misfortunes, noting her shock at glimpsing some of the sad inmates of the island of San Servolo, then in use as a psychiatric hospital, where she wrote:

> A pale thin old man sitting at a window, his elbows on the sill. His forehead rested on one hand; his empty eyes stared into the distance. For a moment he lifted his hand, revealing a narrow bald head, and fell immediately back into his original gaze. It held something so terrible that my eyes were involuntarily drawn to it.

San Servolo is now a much more cheerful place, hosting a conference centre and Venice International University, but it still recalls its grim past with a Museum of Madness.

On the whole, and despite her writing deadlines and their financial implications, George Sand enjoyed the relaxed pace and the famed quality of life in Venice:

> The Venetians share the laziness and fatalism of the Turks, with whom they have been mixed for centuries. Thanks to the generosity of Nature, who provides the fruits of the sea and the land at little cost, they are able to live without working, dedicating themselves to delightful indolence – very different to the frenetic life of Paris, where every day one must battle to survive.

She loved listening to the music on the Grand Canal from the gondola she shared with Pietro Pagello, who would serenade her on the water with the barcarolle he wrote for her, *On the Sleeping Waters* (*Sopra l'acqua addormentata*). The first two stanzas give some idea of it:

> Let not melancholy thoughts upset you:
> Come, let us get into our gondola,
> And head for the open sea.
> We will go past harbours and islands
> Which surround the city,
> And the sun will die in a cloudless sky
> And the moon will appear.
>
> Oh what a joy, what a sight
> The lagoon presents
> When all is silent
> And the moon climbs into the sky;
> And spreads its soft hair
> Over the sleeping waters,
> It looks at its reflection and caresses itself
> Like a woman in love.

Her enthusiasm is revealed in the detailed and sympathetic descriptions of Venice in many of her writings, especially in *Traveller's Letters*. Venice also appears in many of her novels, *Leone Leoni* (1834), *Consuelo* (1842), *Master Mosaicists* (*Les maîtres mosaïstes*) (1842) and *She and He* (*Elle et lui*) (1859). This last work is her fictionalised account of her relationship with Alfred de Musset and the doomed trip to Venice. Musset's own (and rather different) version is told in *Confessions of a Child of the Century* (*Les confessions d'un enfant du siècle*).

By the summer of 1834 George Sand had been called back to Paris for work and family reasons, but she was reluctant to leave the city where she had finally found love and happiness: 'but I will return, for having tasted this place, leaving for Paris is being chased out of Paradise [. . .] Venice is the loveliest thing in the world.'

She did not leave alone, however; Pietro Pagello accompanied her back to Paris, where they arrived on 14 August. At this stage she had probably tired of the romance, which could not survive outside Venice. She returned to the harsh realities of her family and professional responsibilities, and temporarily renewed the complicated relationship with Musset. Later she would move on to other lovers. Left alone in Paris, and somewhat out of his depth in the company of George Sand's friends, such as Eugène Delacroix, and French artists with whom he had little in common, poor Pietro Pagello returned alone to Venice on 24 October, never to see George Sand again.

Pagello continued to write and translate Italian poetry, and is also remembered for some specialist medical articles, as well as his own account of his affair with George Sand. In a letter to a friend, he fondly recalled that she would say to him, 'You are an angel', and he would answer self-deprecatingly, 'Yes but without the g' (which in its original French would portray him as a fool, *un âne*).

On 25 June 1834 George Sand had written to a friend in France, 'Life is the most beautiful thing in the world when one loves, and most hateful when ones ceases loving. In my opinion, love is everything [. . .] true love is when the heart, the spirit and the body understand each other and embrace.'

Years later in 1860, Louise Colet, Gustave Flaubert's mistress, went specifically to the Hotel Danieli to see 'the room where Alfred de Musset almost died'. She had herself had an affair with Musset, so George Sand is not surprisingly omitted from her account of the visit. The hotel is still proud of its famous guests in Room 10, 'les enfants du siècle'. This is also the title of a film shot by Diane Kurys in 1999, retelling their story and including the tragicomic Venetian episode.

Venice welcomed and tolerated embarrassing and eccentric visitors like the cigar-smoking George Sand, who went about the city wearing male clothes, signed the hotel register under a man's name and indulged openly in promiscuous behaviour. The kind of freedom foreigners were allowed in Venice attracted those who would have to conceal their sexuality in more repressive countries like England or Germany. The Serenissima had not always treated kindly those denounced or accused of transgressive behaviour. Documents from the city's archives and Sanudo's diaries suggest that in the past offenders were imprisoned, interrogated under torture and eventually condemned to an atrocious death, burned at the stake between the two columns in on the Piazzetta, or decapitated and then burned. Things eased in the seventeenth century, and from the beginning of the eighteenth century indigenous homosexuals, and particularly visitors, would not have necessarily been harassed or publicly condemned. In any case, foreigners were very rarely prosecuted, and their wealth allowed them to indulge.

Most of these foreign visitors were from Germany or England, where the 1885 Criminal Law Amendment Bill decreed two years of hard labour for consensual homosexual acts in private. The fate of Oscar Wilde served as a powerful deterrent in Britain, probably forcing many men (including Henry James) to adopt a life of solitude and secrecy. A hundred years earlier William Beckford had written, 'How tired I am of keeping a mask on my countenance. How tight it sticks – it makes me sore.' He had found it wise to leave England (or was encouraged to do so) following his involvement with a youth, William Courtenay, and not long afterwards Lord Byron had gone abroad for similar reasons.

At about the same time as Byron, the German poet and dramatist **August von Platen** (1796–1835), who had the means to spend most of his short life in Italy thanks to a pension he received from his friend and patron King Ludwig of Bavaria, became a regular visitor to Venice, probably finding life easier there than in less tolerant Germany. On his first trip in September 1824, von Platen arrived by boat and settled in the Locanda del Pellegrino, a well-established hotel, originally intended for pilgrims, situated near the Marciana Library in Piazza San Marco. The German poet, who had met Goethe and Giacomo Leopardi, kept a diary from the age of 17 and sent many letters home, describing, for example, how he adapted to this extraordinary place: 'Here, at least in the first few days, it is impossible to write anything, and I am still, you might say, so stupefied by everything I see, that I could not pull my wits together.'

A dedicated tourist, he was disappointed by the Church of San Giorgio, not sharing Goethe's passion for Palladio. Although he was staying in Piazza San Marco, he enjoyed exploring humbler parts of the city like Cannaregio, 'where there are lovely broad streets, perfectly straight, with canals full of clear water which are often paved on both sides, which is rare in Venice'. He was keen to meet Venetians from different social backgrounds and was so pleased with his first stay that he returned in October 1829, this time arriving via the Brenta on his birthday. It was an inauspicious start as it was raining, but he stayed for a whole month.

On his third visit (25 July–17 August 1832), von Platen stayed in Casa Calegari, enjoying a view onto Rio San Moisè. He was desperately lonely and, not interested in casual encounters, longed for someone whom he could love. It seems that this was not to be. At the time prostitution was rife in the city, in part a consequence of the deep poverty affecting much of its population. Temptation was everywhere. Going to Chioggia, he reported being pursued all the way by young boys: 'Escorted everywhere by dozens of little blond boys swimming ahead of us and crying "Padroni?".'

At some stage he reported meeting a young man after a visit to see a comedy at the theatre:

> The other day I went to the theatre where they were giving Il Berretto Nero and I saw there a flautist whose good looks struck me. Two days later I met him again at the theatre and had an opportunity to speak to him. His name is Angelo Salvetti, he is twenty-five years old, and is a most pleasant and debonair young man. Since then we have met almost every day and I have even begun to take flute lessons from him, partly to overcome my moments of solitude, partly also to support Angelo, who has a wife and children and a very modest income.

It was quite common for solitary foreigners like him to develop a relationship with impoverished Venetians, often gondoliers, and to support them and their whole families financially.

Von Platen also spent many studious hours reading in the Marciana Library or in the company of the erudite local historian Emanuele Antonio Cicogna, and enjoyed taking fellow countrymen sightseeing, since he knew the city well by now. He was back again in 1834 to stay in Locanda del Gallo on Campo San Paternian (now Campo Manin). It was his last visit, and he left Venice on 12 May 1834. In December 1835 he died in Syracuse in Sicily. He had said that, in order to know Italy well, one had to visit 'the country where the lemon trees flower', the very place where he died. There is some mystery over the nature of the illness – probably cholera – which caused his death, similar to that of Aschenbach, Thomas Mann's central character in *Death in Venice*.

Apart from his diaries (written in French), in which he wrote quite openly about his attraction to boys and young men, Venice inspired him to write some lovely poetry, including his *Venetian Sonnets*, published in 1825, which conjure up a melancholic city, reflecting his sense of loneliness, as in Sonnet XIV (here in the 1914 translation of Reginald B. Cooke):

Whenever deep sorrows on my spirit weigh,
I may disport round the Rialto's stalls,
To warrant that no vanity enthrals
The mind, I seek the calm which ends the day
[. . .]
And when I stand on these marbled piers
And lose my gaze abroad on the dark sea,
Whose sight henceforth no Doge's heart endears,
From time to time, in this mute reverie,
From far away canals the Gondoliers'
Resounding cry scarcely disquiets me.

Von Platen's 'gondoliers' resounding cry' was also one of the main reasons why the erudite English poet and art historian, **John Addington Symonds** (1840–93) spent so much time in Venice. He had become a keen visitor to Italy for health reasons, as he was suffering from tuberculosis. He was deeply attracted by the magical, cultural city:

Venice, thou Siren of sea-cities, wrought
By mirages, built on water, stair o'er stair.

As an art historian he was very sensitive to the dreamlike colours and quality of light, about which he rhapsodised in a letter:

Venice seems made to prove that La vita è un sogno [. . .] Motion that is almost imperceptible, colour too deep and gorgeous to strike the eye, gilding so massive and ancient as to wear a mist of amber brown upon its brightness, white cupolas that time has turned to pearls, marble that no longer looks like stone, but blocks cut from summer clouds [. . .] these are some of the ingredients of the dream which are too familiar for description.

He liked to come in spring and autumn, accompanied by his wife and children, borrowing or renting the mezzanine floor of Ca'

Torresella on the Zattere, where his friend Horatio Forbes Brown lived with his mother. Their lives remained closely intertwined: Symonds had been Brown's teacher in England; Brown himself had been a permanent resident in Venice since 1879. Together they would spend many hours in Brown's *sandolo* (a traditional Venetian boat), the *Fisole*.

There is no doubt that Symonds was, like others before him, attracted to the city by the relative tolerance shown to homosexuals in Venice, as well as the availability of attractive young men. Interestingly, Symonds did not attempt in any way to conceal his homosexuality, and was one of the first to try openly to bring about a change in attitudes, which so far had been met with incomprehension, hypocrisy and personal or official condemnation. In his work, *A Problem of Modern Ethics*, published at his own expense, he makes an open plea for the public recognition of love between men. He was a courageous and unusual advocate of 'male love', 'Greek love' or what he also called 'l'amour de l'impossible'.

In Venice he kept a diary, which was not published until 1984, a century after his death, as part of his *Memoirs*. It tells in great detail how he became besotted with the young gondolier Angelo Fusato (aged 24) whom he met in May 1899 in the Fighetti wine shop at Santa Maria Elisabetta at the Lido. He described him thus: 'Large, fiery grey eyes, an intense look, which emits powerful electricity. The wild look of a triton [. . .] Angelo's eyes as I met them had the flame and vitreous intensity of opals, as though the quintessential colour of Venetian waters were vitalized in them and fed from inner founts of passion [. . .] He fixed and fascinated me.' The strong emotional involvement inspired Symonds to write love sonnets, *Animi Figura, L'amour de l'Impossible*, and he tells in his *Memoirs* how the relationship lasted at least eight years, followed by 'a steady friendship'.

Symonds was fully aware of the problems, sense of guilt and dangers of entering into such a relationship: 'My good sense rebelled, and told me that I was morally a fool and legally a criminal. But the love of the impossible rises victorious after each fall given it by sober sense.' Nor was he fooled by Angelo's financial demands and the economic dependency on which the relationship was based:

> He was careless by nature, poor by circumstances, determined to have money, indifferent to how he got it. Besides, I know from what he has since told me that the gondoliers of Venice are so accustomed to these demands that they think little of gratifying the caprice of ephemeral lovers – within certain limits, accurately fixed according to a conventional but rigid code of honour in such matters.

In spite of this, the relationship developed: 'the more I knew him, the more I liked him.' 'He took hold of me by a hundred subtle threads of feeling, in which the powerful and radiant manhood of the splendid animal was intertwined with sentiment for Venice, a keen delight in the landscape of the lagoons, and something penetrative and pathetic in the man.' Following an established pattern, Symonds supported Angelo and employed him as his private gondolier, enabling Angelo to marry his mistress, who had borne him two sons.

Incidentally, the English poet and classicist **Alfred Edward Housman** (1859–1936) also befriended a 23-year-old gondolier, Andrea, when he visited Venice in 1900. He kept in touch with him for many years and even cared for him and his family when he fell ill. But the final parting eventually came in 1902, the year when the Campanile collapsed (it was rebuilt by 1912):

> Andrea, fare you well;
> Venice, farewell to thee.
> The tower that stood and fell
> Is not rebuilt in me.

Symonds was accompanied everywhere by his gondolier Angelo. On one occasion they arrived together at Poggio Gherardo at the home of an English aristocrat who had been told beforehand that Symonds would be with an essential companion, 'an old peasant'.

She was greatly surprised to see him appear with 'a lovely figure of a man, thirty-three years old, a Venetian gondolier'. Symonds found that Venice tolerated these arrangements, as long as they were considered to be permanent: 'I have been here [. . .] alone in my little house, with Angelo and his wife to look after me,' Symonds wrote at the end of his life in a letter to his friend and fellow author Edmund Gosse. Symonds finally died of tuberculosis in Rome, aged 53, Angelo at his side.

Hearing of his death, Horatio Forbes Brown, who was his literary executor, lost no time in destroying some 1,500 letters. With Edmund Gosse he collaborated on an expurgated version of Symonds's life, *John Addington Symonds, A Biography*, published in 1895, omitting all reference to his homosexuality. When Horatio Forbes Brown himself died in 1926, he bequeathed Symonds's memoirs to the London Library with the instruction that they were not to be published for 50 years. This was to respect the wishes of Symonds, who had written in a letter to Brown in December 1891: 'I want to save it from destruction after my death, and yet to reserve its publication for a period when it will not be injurious to my family.' His daughter Katharine had access in 1949, and the *Memoirs*, published in 1984, are now publicly available.

It is perhaps interesting here to note that Angelo Fusato was Constance Fenimore's gondolier at the time of her death, and might well have been the very gondolier who rowed Henry James into the lagoon on that nightmarish trip when the writer struggled to drown Constance's clothes (and perhaps with them his feelings of guilt).

Horatio Forbes Brown (1854–1926) maintained a close and long-lasting relationship with another gondolier, named Antonio Salin, whom he installed with his family on a floor of the house on the Zattere (and where Symonds had so often stayed). It was a convenient arrangement:

I found the door, and at the top of the little staircase there was Antonio, his head fresh from a basin of water, all his masses of hair tossed back and dripping, like Bacchus stepped from Tintoret's loveliest picture, or Saint George with never a dragon left to conquer, a black and white flannel shirt, a blue sash round his waist, a towel in both hands, and his eyes laughing out as he gives the last scrub on his face.

Brown, living thus in close proximity to the inhabitants of Venice, understanding their beliefs, traditions and superstitions, dedicated his 1884 book *Life on the Lagoons*: 'To my Gondolier, Antonio Salin, my constant companion in Venice and Venetia.' The frontispiece to the book bore the handsome portrait of a man, probably Antonio.

Brown's relationships within the local population were unusual for the time. He was also a central figure in the British community in Venice and a respected member of the Anglican Church, St George's. During his open house on Mondays Brown entertained various members of the English community or passing visitors, offering them refreshments, whisky and sandwiches. These events were described by his ungrateful guest **Frederick Rolfe**, a.k.a. **Baron Corvo** (1860–1913), in his novel *The Desire and Pursuit of the Whole*, published posthumously in 1934. In this *roman à clef* Rolfe refers to Horatio Forbes Brown as Mactavish: 'The Mactavish's palace of Incurabili on the Zattere [. . .] was dark. Crabbe thought himself rather a fool for neglecting to go there on the three Monday evenings. Sandwiches and biscuits sometimes circulated with drinks about 23 o'clock.' In spite of the attraction of free food and drink, Rolfe was often reluctant to attend, as he would be expected to make conversation with Brown's mother, having to listen to her 'interminable, incomprehensible reminiscences about her youthful exploits in swimming'.

Less tedious conversation might have been provided by his fellow guests, the visiting artists John Singer Sargent and **Walter Richard Sickert** (1860–1942); Sickert painted Horatio Forbes Brown in 1900. Apart from painting conventional portraits and scenes like the Salute, Sickert would also pick his models, many of them prostitutes, from Trattoria Giorgione in San Silvestro.

Rolfe's background before he reached Venice was unusual. He had been brought up in a rigidly Protestant lower-middle class home in Cheapside in London, and at the age of 14 had had a cross tattooed on his chest. He converted to Catholicism after leaving Oxford University and left England for Italy in December 1889 to attend Scots College in Rome. Owing to his eccentricities and perhaps also his homosexuality, he was expelled, and returned to England in 1890. Abandoning the idea of becoming a priest, he returned to Italy in 1908 and arrived in Venice (which he was never again to leave) fully equipped: 'With his belongings packed in a laundry basket, a massive crucifix on his chest and an enormous pen filled with red ink, Rolfe left England in the late Summer 1908,' wrote Cecil Woolf in his introduction to Rolfe's *The Venice Letters*, published in 1963. Rolfe had taken a 20-year vow of celibacy, which was coming to an end. He was now 48, and losing his hair, which he had started to dye red. He initially planned a six-week stay at Hotel Bellevue et de Russie in Piazza San Marco (now gone, but at the time next to the Campanile), in the company of a friend and benefactor, Professor Dawkins. He was completely enchanted: 'She is absolutely unique. I haven't the faintest notion when I shall be able to leave. They say that when a middle-aged man falls in love he gets it very seriously: I fancy that I have fallen in love with the City of Venice.'

Hoping to fulfil in Venice some of his wildest dreams and fantasies, he set out to become more Venetian than the Venetians. That meant acquiring a boat, a *barcheta*, equipped with two handsome young gondoliers, Baicolo and Caicio, who would give him rowing lessons, standing up Venetian style, as well as lessons in the local dialect and customs. He set out to explore the city extensively, particularly the lesser-known islands in the lagoon, Santa Cristina, La Paluda della Rosa and Sant'Ariano, where on one occasion he came across a macabre sight: 'As I found myself staring and glaring at a mass [. . .] of whole and broken human skeletons, male by the pelvis I judged at first glance [. . .] two black serpents wriggled through the life-holes of skulls within reach of my foot, and slid away into the bushes.' Sant'Ariano was the ossuary island near Torcello which was used by the Venetians to offload their overflowing cemeteries.

Passionate about boats and rowing, he also joined the well-established rowing club Reale Società Canottieri on Rio della Zecca, on which he was to rely for sustenance in his subsequent periods of hardship. Spending most of his time in the lagoon suited him:

> I went swimming half a dozen times a day, beginning at white dawn and ending after sunset which set the whole lagoon ablaze with amethyst and topaz [. . .] One day, I replenished my stock of provisions at Burano; and at sunset we rowed away to find a station for the night. Imagine a twilight world of cloudless sky and smoothest sea, all made of warm, liquid, limpid heliotrope and violet and lavender, with bands of burnished copper set with emeralds, melting, on the other hand, into the fathomless blue of the eyes of the prides of peacocks, where the moon rose, rosy as mother-of-pearl.

The six-week stay lasted five years until his death, as Venice turned out to be a good place for pursuing young men and scrounging from well-meaning people when the money which Dawkins had given him ran out. He frequented a very particular brothel in Fondamenta Osmarin, which he introduced to interested visitors, 'to initiate rich amateur foreigners into the contemplation of the city's natural beauties and to pay homage to the Creator's most noble works'. In other words, he was pimping, and claimed that he had firsthand knowledge of what he was offering to prospective clients. He became particularly attached to the young gondolier Ermenegildo Vianello (Gildo or Zildo), who became Gilda in his novel *The Desire and Pursuit of the Whole: A Romance of Modern Venice*, based on his life in the city. His obvious admiration of and physical attraction to boys, gondoliers and young male Venetians appears in his private correspondence, subsequently published as *Venice Letters*: 'The keen, prompt level eyes, the noble firm necks, the opulent shoulders, the stalwart arms, the utterly magnificent breasts, the lithely muscular bodies inserted in (and springing from) the well-compacted hips, the long, slim, sinewy-rounded legs'.

He also found various little jobs which allowed him to survive, when he was not living off some generous soul, particularly during the cold weather when he could not sleep in his boat, although he did boast: 'I lived and worked and slept in my barcheta almost always.'

An eccentric vegetarian, he would sometimes go without food for a whole week. He was relying heavily on the charity of members of the English community, but his increasingly unusual, difficult and embarrassing behaviour did not endear him to them, nor did his extravagant spending when he did have money. Having failed to pay his hotel bill at Hotel Bellevue, he was homeless, and was rescued by the Anglican Church chaplain, Canon Lonsdale Ragg, who offered him an unheated room in Palazzo Contarini and introduced him to some well-established members of the English community, including Horatio Forbes Brown and Lady Layard. Later he moved to a room above the Trattoria Alboretti, still standing near the Accademia. He could not afford the rent and was helped once again, this time by an English couple, the van Somerens, who put him up in Palazzo Corner Mocenigo, where they lived. They were very curious to read the novel their tenant was completing. Rolfe had planned to write a homosexual love story with a happy ending, but instead *The Desire and Pursuit of the Whole* is in great part a description of Rolfe's first 15 months in Venice in 1908–9. It cruelly satirises and ridicules various members of the English community who were permanently installed in Venice or just passing through, including his hosts, the very people who had attempted to help him by offering him board and lodging for nine months.

The names of the characters were barely altered, or all too easily guessable. One of the victims was **Lady Layard** (1843–1912), a pillar of the English community, called in the book Lady Pash or La Pash: 'Lady Pash was powerful, and Venice was her wash-pot.' With her husband Sir Henry, a passionate and successful wealthy art collector (he was the proud owner of Gentile Bellini's portrait of *Mahomet II*, bought in 1865), Lady Layard had been instrumental in securing the English church in Venice in 1888. The couple had found the money to buy a suitable site and carry out structural alterations to the building already standing in Campo San Vio. Reluctant to attend a Christmas party to which he had been invited in Palazzo Cappello-Layard, Rolfe described with some venom these well-meaning people: 'He did not know Lady Pash, excepting by sight as one of those gaunt but flocculent females with a horse's long face, which she (of course) prolonged by a tall thin bonnet perched aloft and set with rigid vertical bows resembling the ears of an obstinate mare.'

The novel also chronicled the author's quarrels and intrigues, and openly expressed his homosexuality. The title is based on Plato's *Symposium*: 'The desire and pursuit of the whole is called love.' The book also gave an unparalleled and special view of Venice – no 'Gondola Days' here, but local simple working people, among them the young men he pursued. It also unusually described life spent largely on water, exploring canals and bridges and the lagoon with its lost and forgotten islands, which he prided himself on knowing as well as a native, or occasionally even better.

As soon as they became acquainted with the content of the book, the shocked and offended van Somerens gave Rolfe the choice of deleting offensive passages or leaving the house immediately. He opted to return to his precarious life on the street and the water.

After leaving Palazzo Mocenigo he spent some nights on the beach at the Lido, but finally returned to the Bellevue Hotel, whose owner, Evaristo Barbieri, took pity on him. He was assured he would be paid one day. He never was, and during the cold month of January 1911, Rolfe was back in his boat, where he apparently (and incredibly) stayed for almost an entire year. But he conceded: 'the pupparin, being an old bark with a floor of movable planks was not a comfortable couch on wet nights.' He ended up spending three weeks in the English hospital, then on the Giudecca, recovering from such a severe case of pneumonia that he was given the last rites. Once recovered, and thanks to the ever-generous support of the chaplain of St George's, he moved to Hotel Cavaletto in spring 1912 on Bacino Orseolo, clearly not the luxury hotel it is now, as he claimed to have caught 61 rats in two months there. To everyone's horror, including the owner's, the 'Barone furioso' proceeded to paint his whole room in crimson, perhaps to tone with his hair. Yet again the money ran out, and yet again unable to pay his hotel bill, Rolfe moved in March 1913 to Palazzo Marcello in Cannaregio (next to Palazzo Vendramin-Calergi, now better known as Venice's Casino). Probably weakened by years of cold and near-starvation, he was found in the morning of 26 October 1913 dead – not as legend would have it in his boat, but in his room, fully dressed. The worried British consul, Gerald Campbell, describes his hasty visit to the hotel to remove and throw into the canal any embarrassing material:

when I discovered [. . .] not his will but a large collection of incriminating letters and photographs which more than confirmed the suspicions of scandalmongers as to his unnatural proclivities. I tried to push some of these and other objets d'art out of the window into the Grand Canal, but I was being closely watched by two police officers. In the end I got safely rid of most of it, but what a haul it would have been for a blackmailer!

Rolfe was buried in the Catholic section of San Michele Cemetery. A. J. A. Symons, Rolfe's biographer, was shocked when he came across the *Venice Letters* correspondence:

As I read my hair began to rise [. . .] What shocked me about these letters was not the confession they made of perverse sexual indulgence [. . .] but that a man of education, ideas, something near genius, should have enjoyed without remorse the destruction of the innocence of youth; that he should have been willing for a price to traffic in his knowledge of the dark byways of that Italian city; that he could have pursued the paths of lust with such frenzied tenacity; these things shocked me into anger and pity.

Embarrassing and often intolerable, Rolfe has, not surprisingly, been forgotten for a century, but is now being rediscovered and his literary merits recognised. Anyone looking for his tomb in San Michele Cemetery might find the endeavour frustrating, as his remains have been moved, which is the custom after ten years, and they are now in a remote tomb-terrace.

Among the other European writers who found Venice congenial for similar reasons was the French writer, poet, designer, painter and film director **Jean Cocteau** (1889–1963), who claimed to have seen Venice for the first time in 1904 after running away from school, but this might have been pure fantasy. He was certainly there with his mother in the autumn of 1908. The visit must have left an indelible impression, as one of his group of friends, the 22-year-old Raymond Laurent, tragically shot himself on the steps of the Salute on 24 September. The suicide was apparently provoked by Laurent's love for a young American, Langhorn H. Whistler, who was staying at the same hotel as Cocteau, the luxurious Hotel Europa & Regina. The three young men had spent a day together at the famous Giardino Eden on the Giudecca. By the time Raymond died at around 2 a.m., Langhorn had already hastily left the hotel. The notes of another young man suggest that Cocteau too failed his friend:

> The holiday friends, not desirous of entangling themselves in the affair, had fled, starting with Mr Langhorn Whistler, as if insensible of the tragedy. One only would, with his poetic instincts, have been capable of a funeral ceremony worthy of one who died at the same age as Shelley. But this one man, Mr Jean C, was obliged to leave, not without having acted to his best ability.

Cocteau recalled the tragic event rather flippantly in one of his earlier poems, 'Memory of an Autumn Evening in the Eden Garden', which he surprisingly dedicated to Langhorn H. Whistler:

> A gesture . . . a gun shot,
> Red blood on white steps,

> People flocking and leaning over,
> A gondola, a covered body.
> A gesture . . . a gun shot,
> Red blood on white steps.
> O exquisitely fatal garden!
> And that was all! Some fright,
> Some friendly words,
> And in the joyful gondolas,
> The boredom of being only three.

The incident also appeared in his 1923 novel *The Miscreant* (*Le grand écart*), translated by Margaret Crosland:

> One night when the journalist was going back with Jacques as far as his hotel, he said: 'I live a vile life in Paris. I am in love with this girl who has no inkling of it. When I go back, I can't possibly continue with my old relationships, and on the other hand I know I shall find it very hard to break them off'.
>
> 'But if Berthe is in love with you?'
>
> 'Oh she doesn't love me. You ought to know that. In any case, I intend to kill myself in two hours.'
>
> Jacques jokingly reminded him of the classic suicide of Venice and wished him good night.

No one, so far, knows the exact circumstances, although the event was carefully chronicled at the time by the Venetian newspaper, the *Gazzetino*. Cocteau and other witnesses mention that the body was found on the marble steps of the Salute, but the newspaper reported that Laurent's body was found under the columns supporting the golden globe at Punta della Dogana (the Customs House), a few metres away. Had anyone moved the body? Perhaps Laurent shot himself because Whistler preferred Cocteau. Cocteau nevertheless often returned to a city which fascinated him: 'Venice is the shattered pieces of an ornate shooting-range on a fairground. By night, she is an amorous Negress lying dead in her bath with her tawdry jewels.'

In 1948 he worked with the Italian director Luciano Emmer on two documentaries, *The Legend of St Ursula*, which was based on Vittore Carpaccio's eponymous paintings in the Accademia, and *Venise et ses amants*. He also regularly attended the film festivals at the Lido, particularly after receiving the International Critics' Prize there in 1950 for his film *Orphée*. In 1955 he started to design glass objects for the Fucina degli Angeli, the Forge of the Angels, a name he himself had chosen for the Venice-based studio for several master glassblowers. Always keen on comfort, and all his life mixing with fashionable people, Cocteau liked to stay in Venice in the best hotels, including Hotel Luna, Hotel Europa & Regina and Hotel Bauer, and was often also a guest of Peggy Guggenheim and of the rich eccentric Marchesa Luisa Casati, who used to throw wild parties in Venice, and who was reported to walk semi-clad in Piazza San Marco with her panther, drugged to ensure its compliance. Cocteau called her 'the lovely serpent of this earthly Paradise'. The Venice he described is a happy, carefree, lively city: 'They say Venice is an unhealthy city, strange, sorrowful, romantic, whereas it reveals itself from the very first as the healthiest and most joyous city in the world. I see nothing but flying lions, horses on the roofs and pigeons walking up and down, their hands behind their backs and their heads nodding.'

What had been legendary tolerance of homosexuals in the city came to a halt in 1953 when a famous trial exposed shocking events in the Casino degli Spiriti in Cannaregio, owned at the time by a rich Englishman, David Thomas Edge, one of whose regular guests was the British consul, Kendall. The trial resulted in Edge's expulsion from the city.

The city of love provided a vibrant but less difficult canvas for Italian writers such as **Gabriele D'Annunzio** (1863–1938), who felt entirely at home in Venice. This not entirely sympathetic writer, poet, military hero and political figure was born in Pescara and started coming to Venice in 1887, when he stayed at Hotel Beau Rivage (now the Londra Palace) on Riva degli Schiavoni.

Enchanted with the city, on receiving news of the birth of his third child, he immediately thought of a very Venetian name, Veniero: 'I am speechless before Venice. No more lucid dream can equal in magnificence this which rises from the sea and blooms in the sky.'

On one of his many visits D'Annunzio visited the beautiful garden of the Palazzo Soranzo-Cappello, in which he set a party in his Venetian novel, *The Fire*: 'The stars glittered, the trees waved behind Perdita's head in the depths of the garden. Gentle breezes cooled the people through the open balconies, stirring the candle flames and the blooms of the flowers, entering by the doors and making the curtains tremble, giving life to the whole of the ancient Cappello Palace.'

His *Notebooks* (*Taccuini*) are full of detailed descriptions of this garden, which he knew very well. They were used for the careful restoration completed in 2004, as were those of Henry James, who set his novella *The Aspern Papers* there. It is still occasionally possible to visit it and its loggia, an essential element in elegant Venetian gardens, where the orchestra played for musical soirées:

> A little open temple on eight marble columns. On the timpanum five statues of the Seasons and the Sun God. In the interior of the temple, the back wall covered with frescoes, partly destroyed. A central figure still retains the original freshness of the flesh; and it has before it a kind of basin on which it is pleasant to place flowers.
>
> (*Notebooks*)

Miraculously, the garden sculptures have also survived, though not always intact: 'they are powerful men bearing young women in their arms, reminiscent of the Rape of the Sabines.'

D'Annunzio, an unashamed womaniser, is especially remembered for the passionate and tragic love affair he shared with Chioggia-born actress **Eleonora Duse** (1858–1924). She was famous throughout Europe and beyond, as in her long career she worked in countries as far away as Russia and the United States. Chekhov, who saw her in 1882, wrote a review of her performance and marvelled at her acting. He wondered at the fact that, although he did not know Italian, he felt he could understand every single word she spoke. From 1893 she had been living on the top floor of the fifteenth-century Palazzo Barbaro-Volkoff in Dorsoduro, owned by the Russian painter Alexander Volkoff, an admirer and former lover, who had organised her tour of Russia. She wrote: 'I have found myself a little place to live, with whitewashed walls, on the top floor of an old palace in Venice, under the roof, with a big, big oval window from which you can see the whole city.'

In 1894 La Duse and Gabriele D'Annunzio met and embarked on their intense relationship. The affair, the subject of much interest and gossip throughout Europe, began at Hotel Danieli, where he was staying. At their first encounter, when they talked about art and theatre, she fell in love, and entranced, she wrote to him: 'I see the sun and thank all the powers in the world for having met you.'

The fascination this man exerted on women is difficult to understand, as he seemed to collect conquests like Don Juan. Very self-important, he was short, bald, moustachioed, with rotten teeth and bad breath. Captivated nevertheless, many praised the seductive power of his hypnotic voice: 'When he spoke to his beloved he became the very likeness of Apollo,' wrote the dancer Isadora Duncan, one of his multiple conquests.

La Duse was about five years older than the poet, and the affair, which remained the most important of many in her life, lasted a little longer than five years, ending around 1900. It was a professional as well as a sentimental relationship, fruitful for both, as he wrote several plays for her, the costs of which she usually bore. In 1897 Eleonora Duse acted in D'Annunzio's *Dream on a Spring Morning* (*Sogno di una mattina di primavera*) in Paris, followed by *The Dead City* (*La città morta*) and *Francesca da Rimini,* all written specially for her. The poet was constantly penniless and pursued by creditors, which forced him to live in self-imposed exile in Arcachon in France between 1910 and 1915. There he wrote in French *The Martyrdom of Saint Sebastian* (*Le martyre de Saint Sébastien*) in 1911, set to music by Claude Debussy for the Ballets Russes.

Initially their relationship was passionate: 'We lived from minute to minute over two days of secret life in the Danieli Hotel, two days of oblivion, of utter delirium, in which we seemed together to have dispelled any notion of the world, and almost every awareness of what we were before,' he wrote in his *Notebooks*. It was so stormy that it could not last, owing in great part to his constant infidelities. La Duse also made great demands on her lovers and friends, and lived her life as if it were a stage tragedy. She often said that an actor cannot act pain, grief, loss, jealousy or love without personal experience.

In 1897, after a performance of *La Gioconda* in Teatro Rossini (now a cinema), D'Annunzio wrote in his notebooks: 'I have spent some of the saddest and most tragic hours of my life. She is taken over by a kind of demon which will not release her [. . .] The sweet creature becomes cruel and unjust towards herself and me, with no remedy.' But the turning point happened when *The Fire* came out in 1900, and La Duse felt publicly snubbed by the way he had portrayed her in the female character Perdita/La Foscarina in this Venetian *roman à clef*: 'He has paraded me like an animal at market,' wrote the broken-hearted actress bitterly, smarting from the shock of seeing herself publicly depicted as an ageing and temperamental diva.

She had for years financed his theatrical productions and expensive tastes, and now found herself penniless. Many of the dramas he wrote for the stage required huge expense and were not always easily accessible to the average audience. The public was often attending only to see her extraordinary acting and stage presence. Once she had overcome her grief and bitterness, and after they went their separate ways, she forgave him: 'I forgave him for having taken advantage of me, ruining me and humiliating me. I forgave him everything, because I loved.' As for D'Annunzio, he commented when she died, 'That woman whom I did not deserve is dead.'

Their tempestuous life was the subject of constant interest by the press, very much as celebrities are pursued today. From 1900 La Duse's career went into decline, and she had given up acting by 1909. Her meeting with Rainer Maria Rilke in Venice in 1912 revived her hope of returning to the stage, but it came to nothing, as the German poet felt ensnared by her excessive demands: 'Venice has entrapped me in its net, is still holding me, I do not know for how long.'

In 1916 she acted in a silent film, *Ashes* (*Cenere*) but made an astonishing and successful return to the stage in 1922 with Henrik Ibsen's *The Lady from the Sea*, *Ghosts* and D'Annunzio's *The Dead City*. Eleonora Duse died in 1924 in Pittsburgh during a tour of the United States and was brought back to be buried in the Sant'Anna Cemetery in Asolo on the mainland, where she had acquired a house in the later stages of her life.

As for D'Annunzio, after returning from his self-imposed exile in October 1915, he rented La Casetta Rossa, which faces Palazzo Barbaro-Volkoff on the Grand Canal. Feeling at home there, he symbolically planted a pomegranate tree in the garden. It is still in the front garden facing the Grand Canal. The house actually belonged to Prince Fritz von Hohenlohe, brother of Princess Marie von Thurn und Taxis, who often came there with her protégé, the poet Rilke.

24   *Casetta Rossa, one of Gabriele D'Annunzio's Venetian homes*

As she recalled, 'Rilke had made friends with my brother, who lived in a charming little house on the Grand Canal.' D'Annunzio had rented the house from the Prince, who was expelled from Venice during the First World War, when D'Annunzio reinvented himself as an heroic soldier and pilot. In 1916, recovering from an injury to his right eye, he became a regular visitor at Palazzo Morosini da Mula, where he courted the owner, Principessa Morosini.

It would take too long to list all the women D'Annunzio pursued, wooed and conquered. One of the most fascinating, and perhaps his greatest love, was **Luisa Casati** (1881–1957), whom he called 'the only woman who has overwhelmed me'. Her androgynous beauty, very much in vogue today, made her a muse, the *femme fatale* of the belle époque. She was portrayed and sculpted by many artists and admirers, including the society painters Kees van Dongen and Augustus John (with whom she had an affair). Originally very wealthy, she rented Palazzo Venier dei Leoni from 1910. There this most eccentric woman (just like her successor Peggy Guggenheim, who bought the palace to house her art collection in 1948) hosted extravagant parties where she would receive her guests dressed in extraordinarily beautiful outfits designed for her by Bakst, Poiré, Schiaparelli and Fortuny. The whole dramatic effect was enhanced by a menagerie including crocodiles, cheetahs, snakes, monkeys and parrots, attended by semi-naked waiters painted with gold varnish (apparently even causing the death of one of them). It is not surprising that she accumulated debts and soon found herself broke. After she moved out of Palazzo Venier her lonely life took a sad turn, and she wandered from one capital to another before finally dying in poverty in London, where she is buried in Brompton Cemetery.

One of the most enduring and positive sides of D'Annunzio was his love for and promotion of avant-garde music. He had become a great admirer of Richard Wagner, and in *The Fire* he devotes many passages to music and to the German composer: 'In Venice it is impossible to feel in any way but musically, and similarly you cannot think but through images.' His *Nocturne*

(*Notturno*), published in 1921, recreates magical musical moments he experienced in the city:

> I recall one summer night, a night in August. We had gone out to Murano by gondola [. . .] the lagoon was so phosphorescent that each movement of the oar raised long flames of white light [. . .] moving beside the walls of the cemetery we stopped our laughter and banter. The splash of the oars was audible. And below the funereal walls the phosphoresence created rings and garlands of light. A luminous melody encircled the island of the dead.

He attended many concerts at Palazzo Giustinian-Lolin on the Grand Canal, not far from Casetta Rossa. His hosts were Ugo Levi and Olga Levi Brunner. The couple had dedicated most of their life and money to music. Ugo had wanted to be a professional musician and was an excellent pianist, encouraged by D'Annunzio, who organised concerts for him at Palazzo Pisani, the present Venice Conservatorio. Olga also played the piano and sang. Their elegant palace, almost opposite the Accademia on the other side of the Grand Canal, was at the beginning of the twentieth century a temple to music, with an extraordinary collection and a distinguished salon, where concerts were held almost daily. It is now the Ugo and Olga Levi Foundation, holding events, conferences and music courses and offering accommodation, grants and scholarships for promising musicians. Thanks to the generous bequest of the Levis when they died, it is still managed by the city.

It goes without saying that Olga Brunner Levi had also fallen under D'Annunzio's spell. He fondly called her Vidalita, because the palace stood close to the Church of San Vidal. From 1916 to 1919 letters, presents, books and invitations went daily back and forth between the palace on the Grand Canal and the Casetta Rossa. 'Little one, little one, come back, because I cannot stand it any longer. Desire is torturing me; my heart is consuming me. I hunger and thirst for you. Every moment torments me,' wrote the enamoured poet to Olga on 19 February 1917.

To Olga's dismay, in 1919 D'Annunzio met the young pianist Luisa Baccarà at one of the musical evenings in her drawing-room. Also smitten, Luisa accompanied him on his political mission to Fiume in 1921 and remained his faithful companion until his death. Yet another conquest, also a regular visitor to Venice, was French writer and poet, **Marie de Régnier** (1875–1963), daughter of the Parnassian poet José Marie de Hérédia. She wrote under the pseudonym of Gérard d'Houville, claiming that using a man's name (as had George Sand and George Eliot) helped her career. This extraordinarily beautiful woman, with an androgynous charm like that of La Divina Luisa Casati, was openly bisexual, which was not unusual in some circles at the time. Finding her husband tedious, she carried on a long-term affair with the writer Pierre Louys, with whom she had a son, and was D'Annunzio's lover between 1914 (when they first met in France) and 1921. One of her several lovers said of her: 'She is as dangerous as a rose is perfumed.' She wrote novels and evocative poems, many on Venice, in a style reflecting contemporary sentiment:

> Reflected in the muddy waters
> Which stagnate where canals cross,
> Your face marked by Death,
> Your finery sullied.

She was one of the very few women writers whose merits were recognised, and in France received many of the literary prizes generally granted to men.

With her husband **Henri de Régnier** (1864–1936), she rented Palazzo Dario, and when it was unavailable, Palazzo Venier. A plaque in the little square at the back of Palazzo Dario commemorates Henri de Régnier's stay there. He is remembered mostly as the author of poems on Venice, as well as for his description of life in the city, *The Roof Garden, or Venetian Life* (*L'Altana ou la vie vénitienne*), published in 1928. He was particularly struck by Palazzo Carminati, near the Church of San Stae (now an educational institution), to which he dedicated a whole chapter in his book *Crazy Days in the Carminati Palace* (*Les folles journées du palais Carminati*), but he also used it as a setting for one of his novellas, *The Voyage of Love, or the Venetian Initiation* (*Le voyage d'amour ou l'initiation vénitienne*), published in 1930. The story, set just before the French Revolution, centres on a young Frenchman sent by his father to discover love safely away from any local temptation, Venice being for the father the obvious location:

> Venice is marvellously made for intrigue and adventure, as much for the labyrinth of its canals as for the mysterious gliding of its gondolas. Indeed, Venice is the city of love. You must add to this the fascination of its women; be they patrician or courtesan, all are expert. And therefore to those women I intend to dedicate the task of educating of my son in the arts of love.

These belle époque and so-called 'decadent' writers clearly believed in the myth of the *cité galante*.

Henri de Régnier died in Paris in 1936 from an illness he had caught while staying in the Palazzo Dario, and Marie died tragically after suffering severe burns as she sat by the fire in a house in Arcachon, the French place of exile of her former lover D'Annunzio. Ironically, he used to sign his love letters to her 'Frate Fuoco' ('Brother Fire').

Venice, in the decades around the start of the twentieth century, was truly cosmopolitan: Italians, French, English, Americans all met and socialised in a way which would have not been possible a century earlier. It is worth returning here to the German poet **Rainer Maria Rilke** (1875–1926), who attracted the attention of Eleonora Duse in 1912. Rilke was a regular visitor to Venice from 1897. Although still an impoverished student on his first visit, the poet spent three days at the impressive Hotel Britannia (now Hotel Europa & Regina), thanks to the financial support of a rich American. The hotel was at the time one of the three most luxurious in the city, offering a lift, central heating and a view over the Grand Canal. Rilke must have visited the Ghetto during his visit, as in 1900 he wrote *A Scene in the Venice Ghetto*, set in the eighteenth century. The protagonist, old Melchisedec, wishes to live in the highest house there (the houses were the tallest in Venice), in order to have a view of the sea: 'He remained for whole days on the roof trying to see the sea. But however high the building was, all he could see was the façade of the Palazzo Foscari. Some bell-tower or other, the dome of some church or other, and another one further away.'

Between September 1902 and 1920 the poet never settled anywhere for long, travelling restlessly throughout Europe and beyond, even visiting Russia and Egypt. Venice remained a favourite, as Rilke considered it the capital of the arts, 'loaded with literature', and on his several visits would stay in hotels when he had money, otherwise in rented flats or as the guest of friends and acquaintances. He had married in 1901 the sculptor Clara Westhoff (a pupil of Rodin), with whom he had a daughter, Ruth, but he barely shared a regular family life with them. He became sentimentally involved with a succession of women in Venice and elsewhere, always retreating from commitment. Instead, his intense long-term relationships, including his marriage, were restricted mainly to an exchange of letters.

In November 1907 he stayed for ten days 'in a little blue house overlooking the Zattere' belonging to the art dealer Piero Romanelli, whom he had met in Paris. Rilke's wife Clara was told about this visit in some detail in a letter (in the Jane Bannard Greene and M. D. Herter Norton translation):

This Venice seems almost hard to admire; it has to be learned over and over again from the beginning. Its marbles stand ashen there, grey in the greyness, light as the ashy edge of a log that has just been aglow. And how unexplained in its selection is the red on walls, the green on window shutters; and this is not from a hotel: from a little house with old things, two sisters and a maid; before which the water now lies, black and gleaming, a couple of sail boats in which the hawsers creak; and in an hour the full moon is bound to come across [. . .] I am full of expectancy.

There he fell in love with Romanelli's beautiful sister Adelmina (Mimi). They then met again briefly in Paris, where she usually spent the winter. Thereafter he began a long series of letters written to her from 1907 to 1912 in French, published in 1941 as *Letters to a Venetian friend* (*Lettres à une amie vénitienne*).

One of his first letters was a declaration of love:

After everything of which we have spoken and which we have felt during this time, it is entirely natural that I love you. The word must be restored to its former greatness: that is why I say it; from a distance: because I have taken all my solitude upon myself.

But he very clearly established the boundaries: 'There is one fatal error which we could make, and that is to become dependent upon one another, for even a moment.' He vaguely promised from Paris (where he was staying) some possibility of a shared life together: 'Yes, I shall be coming to Venice to work. You will give me a room and you will protect my peace and my labours. You shall be my Angel at the Gate and the silence surrounding my heart [. . .] But

25   *Casa Romanelli, one of Rilke's Venetian homes*

first I must finish my book there.' The promise predictably came to nothing.

When in Venice Rilke tended to mix with writers, artists and Venetian aristocrats such as Count Donà delle Rose, who invited him to his sixteenth-century palace, Palazzo Michiel delle Colonne on the Grand Canal at Santi Apostoli. The poet, impressed by the wealth displayed there, sent a detailed description to his wife:

> You should have seen the light of a Venetian afternoon on these Flemish tapestries and on the tarnished mirrors [. . .] with carved wooden frames wreathed with flowers bursting with their own Baroque exuberance. And there are long galleries with tall portraits of cardinals in scarlet and procurators in purple and steely generals standing to attention, and in the centre a heavy white horse with one leg raised as if to walk.

Always fascinated by great artists, he had wanted for years to meet the Venetian actress and diva Eleonora Duse, having been struck by her extraordinary acting on the stage. Not knowing her personally, he wrote 'Bildnis' ('Portrait'), a portrait of her in verse in 1907, but also perhaps of the city of Venice, a fading, fascinating female beauty, often seen similarly by visiting poets:

> through the tragedies of her features
> she slowly bears a wilting bouquet, lovely,
> bunched carelessly, and almost loose again,
> sometimes like a tuberose
> the tired lost flower of a smile emerges.

In 1912 Rilke was staying on the mezzanine floor of Palazzo Caldagno-Valmarana on Rio San Vio Palazzo (now Fondazione Giorgio Cini), which belonged to a friend he had met in Paris in December 1909, Princess Marie von Thurn und Taxis-Hohenlohe, and who was to become his admirer and benefactress. Her brother Fritz had commissioned the architect Domenico Rupolo to build the small Casetta Rossa, immortalised by D'Annunzio who, as we have seen, lived in it from 1915, and which was used also by many other writers and artists. At the time La Duse was also staying on the Zattere with her then lover, the writer Lina Poletti, who was planning to write a new dramatic part for her. Introduced by a common friend, the meeting finally happened. Eleonora took to Rilke immediately and started to monopolise him, to the concern and annoyance of Princess Marie, who referred to the meeting as 'a real disaster'. The actress and the poet spent whole days together, and she took him to unknown parts of the city, using her gondola to explore secret canals and gardens. She requested his help in looking for a suitable apartment, as she was planning to settle in Venice. Initially Rilke was 'entranced' in the same way as he had been by the French sculptor Auguste Rodin in Paris, whose secretary he had been for many years. He was apprehensive but bewitched: 'I scarcely dare to look at her [. . .] I am so afraid of seeing her disfigurement, or something which is no longer there, that I can remember almost nothing except her mouth [. . .] and the smile, of course, surely one of the most famous which has ever been smiled.' But above all for a while he thought that he and La Duse were kindred spirits:

> We were like two basins and formed a fountain on top of each other, and showed one another only how much perpetually escapes us. And yet it was inevitable that we should somehow communicate to each other the glory of being so full, and perhaps we even thought in the same moment of the vertical living stream, which rose above us, fell again and filled us so completely.

He completely surrendered to her for a few months, and even planned to get her back on the stage, possibly writing something suitable for her repertoire, but this came to nothing, to her great disappointment. Most of this was related in detail in the letters Rilke was writing to Princess Marie, who was getting increasingly concerned, and who advised him to be careful, as the temperamental behaviour of the difficult and ageing actress was legendary. She described her as 'a wondrous, formidable being – but a hopeless one. A sick, ageing, deeply unhappy woman.' After a few months the relationship cooled, the exhausted and disenchanted Rilke finding it difficult to cope with the constant bickering of the actress and her lover Poletti. Once again he withdrew, keen to avoid a binding involvement, as he stated in a letter: 'God forbid that she should include me in her future [. . .] Let her become what she will, I take no responsibility.' The affair was over, and this time no letters followed. In 1920 he wrote to his long-term correspondent Lou Andres Salomé: 'I learnt that Duse was coming to Venice, ill, in order to find somewhere to live. I was so terrified that this was now repeating itself as well, that I left within twenty-four hours and returned to Switzerland!'

With Princess Marie things were different, as she was happily married, was generous and made no demands in return, although one senses in her memoir of her relationship with Rilke a strong attraction on her part. With this educated, shrewd and intelligent woman he felt safe and could confide in her and discuss his work. From the time they met in 1909 until his death, he wrote her at least 460 letters (some lost during the war). She immensely enjoyed his company and travelling with him: 'I've never enjoyed a journey more than when I've had the good fortune to be travelling with Rilke; he also absorbed everything in a different way, different from normal people. It almost took your breath away.' Thanks to this friendship, Rilke was always a welcome guest in her Venetian palace, Palazzo Caldagno-Valmarana, and also in her castle by the sea in Duino near Trieste, where he found for a while a sort of haven where he was inspired to write what was possibly his major poetical work, the philosophical and mystical *Duino Elegies* of 1912–22, dedicated to her.

In Venice he spent much time in libraries and archives, as he had considered writing the biography of the illustrious fourteenth-century Venetian Carlo Zeno, and was planning another biography on the poetess and courtesan Gaspara Stampa, famous for her poems on tragic unrequited love, mentioned in the *Duino Elegies*:

> Does Gaspara Stampa
> mean enough to you yet, and that any girl whose beloved
> has slipped away, might feel, from that intense
> example of loving: Could I become like her?

In fact, he wrote mainly poems, many in 1908, addressing himself
directly to the city, as in his 'Late Autumn in Venice':

> The crystal palaces return your gaze less brightly
> And from the gardens the summer hangs
> like a heap of puppets, heads down, limp, lifeless.

He compared the city to a courtesan in 'Venetian Morning':

> Each morning shows her first the opals
> she wore yesterday, and draws rows
> of mirror images up from the canal.

His trips to Venice had to stop during the First World War,
which he spent mainly in Munich, when he was fulfilling his
military duties despite poor health. Unable to travel and having
lost all his belongings in Paris, he saw the war, as did many others,
as a 'rupture' and the world could never be the same: 'You would
not believe, Princess, how different, how different the world has
become, the task is now to understand it.'

And Venice had indeed changed, as he found in 1920, on what
was to be his last visit: 'Venice is an act of faith; when I first saw
it in 1897 I was the guest of an American. It's different now, and
so that a little reality should enter into this insubstantial world
I was bitten by a particularly virulent flea and am now more or
less localized round the itch.' But he did manage to complete
the *Duino Elegies* in 1922, and some disillusionment had crept
into his relationship with Princess Marie, the most important of
his aristocratic patrons: 'She has a vague idea that on the whole
I get by with a minimum for my necessities [. . .] These people

have for centuries been quite accustomed to presuming that the requirements of practical existence are ultimately a matter for the domestics, with the result that they will always miss the fundamentals of any situation.'

Probably not aware of this, Marie von Thurn und Taxis saw in some lines of the fourth elegy an acknowledgement of his inability to commit to love:

> Am I not right? And all of you, who loved
> That tiny germ of love I had for you,
> From which I always turned aside again,
> Because the space I'd loved in all your eyes
> Dissolved in cosmic Space: and you were gone.

He died of leukaemia, aged 51, alone in the Val-Mont Sanatorium in Switzerland.

Like so many of the love affairs which took place in Venice, that of **Franz Kafka** (1883–1924) during his short stay in Venice was marked by sadness and frustration. He visited Italy with his friends Max and Otto Brod in 1909 and 1911. Two years later in autumn 1913 he returned to Italy alone. He was already a published author, but following a period of discouragement was unable to write. He arrived in Venice, having travelled from Trieste by boat, and stayed for three days at Hotel Sandwirth (now called Gabrielli Sandwirth) on Riva degli Schiavoni, where a plaque commemorates his brief stay. He wrote daily letters to Felice Bauer, his fiancée, whom he had met a year before. Theirs was an intense emotional involvement, conducted mainly through letters, but doomed, as he was already thinking of ending it.

On arrival he sent her a postcard: 'Finally I am in Venice! Now I will also have to throw myself into the city, although it is raining heavily (which should wash away the days I spent in Vienna) and my head is still trembling from a bit of seasickness I had from a ridiculously short crossing, admittedly very stormy.' A more

26 Plaque on Hotel Gabrielli Sandwirth, where Franz Kafka stayed

In questo albergo
soggiornava
nel settembre 1913
Franz Kafka
e scriveva le sue lettere
d'amore a Felice Bauer,
la sua fidanzata

personal letter written on the hotel writing paper was sent the next day, and it read:

> On my return we wanted [. . .] to meet somewhere in order maybe to find strength in one another. Can't you see what a state I am in, Felice? [. . .] A prisoner of the inhibitions you know about, I am absolutely, absolutely, incapable of overcoming my internal obstacles. This morning, when I got out of bed, as I was looking at the clear Venetian sky and such thoughts were going through my mind, I felt sufficiently ashamed and I suffered consequently. But what are we to do, Felice? We must leave each other.

Four days after writing this letter, which had seemed final, Kafka sent a postcard to Felice from Verona. The relationship survived until 1917. A recent short poem by Kate Ruse in *Corridors* expresses Kafka's emotional dilemma:

> He arrives by train from Venice
> Sodden with dark worries,
> Weakened by insomnia
> [. . .]

> Later he wakes mutating again.
> Does he love her? Does he feel?
> 'This has to end', he writes. 'It is no more.'

The turn of the century saw many further arrivals from Prague and Vienna, attracted by the busy social and cultural life. They included Alma Schindler, who later became **Alma Mahler** (1879–1964). This formidable *femme fatale* collected admirers, lovers and husbands. Venice was the setting for her first serious love affair, with the painter Gustav Klimt, who was a friend of her stepfather, Carl Moll. The family party went to Venice in 1897 to attend a Toscanini concert. At the time many claimed that Alma was 'the most beautiful girl in Vienna'. Klimt was already well known, which appealed to her, writing in her diary that: 'he was more talented than anyone else. At thirty-five he was in his prime, beautiful in every way and already famous.'

The group stayed at the Lido. Klimt was passionately in love with her. Alma was probably enthralled and flattered, but her mother did not look kindly on the affair: 'our love was cruelly challenged by my mother.' Nothing came of it, and a few years later in Vienna she was to meet Gustav Mahler, whom she subsequently married. This first affair remained nonetheless a most important experience for her: 'It was the first great love of my life, but then I was just a child, immersed in music and unworldly. Klimt is responsible for many tears and also for my awakening.'

Twenty years later, after two marriages (to Mahler, who died in 1911, and to Walter Gropius, father of her daughter Manon), difficult lovers like the painter Oscar Kokoschka, with whom she lived for a few years, and a series of other emotional involvements, Alma returned to Venice and fell in love with a house situated near Santa Maria dei Frari on the Fondamenta Contarini. She bought it in 1922 and visited it regularly, until it was sold in 1935. In her letters she wrote how delighted she was with it: 'A little garden. A real paradise. Everything has turned out as I wanted it. I have had the whole house renovated.'

Here she entertained her lovers and friends, Arnold Schoenberg, Max Brod, Arthur Schnitzler, and also the man who was to become her third husband in 1929, the Austrian writer, Franz Werfel: 'And I have been here for a whole month alone with Franz Werfel – alone with him at last, entirely. We have been very happy without any longing for the outside world, without seeing anyone else.' The house became a refuge for them in 1934 when they became concerned by events in Vienna. Tragically, Manon Gropius fell ill in Venice. She was sent to Vienna for treatment, but died soon afterwards. Heartbroken, Alma decided to sell the house the next year: 'We all left for Venice, in order to sell our house, where we have been so happy, perhaps too happy. But the end of our dream has been so terrible that we will not be able to laugh even if we want to.'

Worse times were to come, as life was becoming increasingly dangerous for them in Vienna, particularly for Werfel, who was Jewish. To ensure his safety, and after many difficulties and hardship, the couple emigrated to the United States, where Alma took American citizenship. She was widowed for the second time when Franz Werfel died in 1945, but continued to live in America until her death in 1964.

The end of the Second World War saw a new influx of American visitors to Venice. The writer **Ernest Hemingway** (1899–1961) arrived in 1948 to write a sad story combining passion and death which created some scandal in the city. As a young man he had gone through a traumatic experience in the Veneto at the end of the First Word War: 'No one is very old in Venice, but they grow up very fast. I grew up very rapidly in the Veneto myself, and I was never as old as I was at twenty-one.' On 2 July 1918 the young Hemingway, waiting impatiently for action as a driver for the American Red Cross at the Battle of Fossalta di Piave in the Veneto (65 miles from Venice), was seriously wounded by a mortar blast as he was distributing chocolate and cigarettes to other soldiers. He was treated for his injuries, and went to recuperate in Milan. Once discharged, he witnessed one of the final victories against the Austrians at Bassano del Grappa. These

27   *Hotel Gritti, formerly Casa Wetzlar, where Hemingway stayed*

war experiences inspired his 1929 novel *A Farewell to Arms*. He left Italy after his convalescence on 4 January 1919, but returned to Fossalta and Cortina a few years later.

He arrived in Venice in October 1948 in his Buick with his fourth wife Mary Welsh and his Italian translator, Fernanda Pivano. They stayed at the recently inaugurated Hotel Gritti, described by Graham Greene as his 'Venetian home'. Thanks to his friendship with restaurateur and hotelier Giuseppe Cipriani, Hemingway spent much of his time at Cipriani's Harry's Bar in Calle Valleresso, where he had his own table in the Concordia Room. The bar had been founded by Giuseppe Cipriani in 1931 and then offered wonderful cuisine. The writer's Venetian novel *Across the River and into the Trees* was written partly at this table, the setting for some episodes: 'Then he was pulling open the door of Harry's bar and was inside and he had made it again, and was at home.' Hemingway's patronage of the bar contributed to its fame among foreign visitors.

The great American film director **Orson Welles** (1915–85) was a regular patron of Harry's Bar. He adapted the two Venetian

28   Harry's Bar, most closely associated with Americans in Venice

Shakespeare plays, *Othello*, shot in black and white in Venice, Rome and Morocco between 1949 and 1951, and *The Merchant of Venice*, shot partly in Venice in 1969. Orson Welles himself had taken the main parts of Othello and Shylock. *The Merchant of Venice* was the less successful venture and was never finished, since two of the three reels disappeared mysteriously before editing was complete. Welles attended the Venice Film Festival on numerous occasions, receiving a personal tribute in 1970. Orson Welles was invited to the famous ball for 1,000 guests hosted by Charles de Beistegui at Palazzo Labia in 1951. At Harry's Bar guests remember him devouring huge plates of shrimp sandwiches washed down by Dom Perignon. The story goes that his bill was paid at the station as the train departed, with Cipriani himself in pursuit of the cash thrown from the window.

To return to Hemingway – a Venetian friend of his, Raimondo Franchetti, took him duck shooting in the Venetian lagoon, and the events and love story which ensued are told in *Across the River and into the Trees*. It was written, sustained by nightly fuel of six bottles of his favourite wine, Amarone, in one of the rooms at the

Locanda Cipriani in Torcello, where he and his wife spent 'one of the happiest periods of their life'. The Locanda still displays many photographs of the American writer.

In November 1948 during one hunting trip, Hemingway met the beautiful 19-year-old Adriana Ivancich. He made her the heroine of his Venetian novel, naming her Renata. The novel describes shooting parties in the lagoon and outings to the Rialto Market: 'it was so concentrated that it was difficult not to jostle people, unintentionally, and each time you stopped to look, to buy, or to admire, you formed an "îlot de résistance" against the flow of the morning attack of the purchasers.'

In January 1950, while Mary was conveniently recovering in Cortina from a fracture caused by a skiing accident, Hemingway had gone back to Venice, and there saw Adriana, spending many evenings with her and her mother in Calle del Rimedio. Fernanda Pivano, in her 1985 biography of Hemingway, described the besotted writer:

> He often saw Adriana Ivancich, especially at Harry's Bar with two of her friends, and he used to gaze dreamily into her large bewitching eyes, and take in her curvaceous bust and long, slim legs; she was aware and proud of the famous writer's admiration and sat in posed cinema-like positions on the sofa, so as to show herself off to best effect: she would exchange glances with the writer, placing a hand beneath her chin and leaning forwards a little and then giving in to adolescent giggles in an aside to her friends. Hemingway was quite literally lost in gazing at her.

Hemingway and Mary left for Paris on 16 March 1950. They left a painting of a Madonna as a parting present to the gondoliers. A damaged reproduction still hangs on the external wall of the Hotel Gritti, with the original allegedly in the neighbouring Church of Santa Maria del Giglio.

Adriana and her mother visited Hemingway at his Cuban farm La Finca in 1950–1, but the affair was soon over, and after two failed marriages and depression, possibly exacerbated by drinking,

Adriana committed suicide in 1983. She wrote her own novel, *The White Tower* (*La torre bianca*), telling her version of the love story: 'And then I appeared. I was so full of life, of enthusiasm, which I passed on to him. He had started writing again and suddenly everything seemed easy. He had completed the book and then had written another one for me, even better. Now he could write again, write well, and he thanked me for it.' This confirmed what everyone had guessed, that the aged protagonist of the novel, Colonel Cantwell, was Hemingway's alter ego.

Across the River and into the Trees encountered some difficulties, as Hemingway's affair was considered scandalous, and publication in Italy was postponed for two years until 1952. The novel was greatly admired by his biographer Anthony Burgess: 'I know of no modern novel [. . .] that pays such eloquent homage to Venice.' In spite of the gossip, Hemingway was back in Venice in late March 1954 and stayed again at the Hotel Gritti. He was now a sick man, recovering from a serious aeroplane accident in Africa, but said that he was hoping that the local scampi and Valpolicella would restore him. Although only 55, he had become prematurely old, diminished by his drinking: 'The manager of the Gritti Palace in Venice', recalled Antony Burgess, 'tells me that three bottles of Valpolicella first thing in the day were nothing to him, then there were the daiquiris, scotch, Tequila, bourbon, vermouthless martinis.' For Hemingway this last stay of four weeks in Venice was 'a pilgrimage on the site of lost happiness'.

The Italian poet Eugenio Montale, who visited him there, wrote an article entitled 'Scorched and Happy: Hemingway Returns to Venice' on the meeting for the newspaper *Corriere della Sera*: 'Without having read Benedetto Croce, the American writer has discovered that "vitality" is the biggest secret in life.' From photographs taken at the time, one can guess that he was probably already suffering from depression, and indeed he was to shoot himself in July 1961 at his home in Idaho.

The final tragic ending will be left to **Giuseppe Berto** (1914–78), an Italian writer and screenwriter. Born and educated in Mogliano Veneto, a small town between Venice and Treviso, Berto became a recognised writer after the publication of his first novel *The Sky is Red (Il cielo è rosso)* in 1948.

He wrote the script for the first film of director Enrico Maria Salerno, *The Anonymous Venetian* (*Anonimo veneziano*), a story of love and death, which enjoyed huge success when it came out in 1970. Both writer and director were themselves ill and died prematurely, Berto from depression and cancer, and Salerno from lung cancer. Their protagonist Enrico, an oboist at the Fenice, disappointed in his musical career, discovers that he is soon to die from a brain tumour and decides to see his estranged wife Valeria, whom he has not seen for seven years. She is now living with someone else in Ferrara, and when they meet at the railway station is unwilling to revive the relationship. She agrees that she will spend one day with him in Venice, which is seen mainly as a familiar but sad, decadent place. 'It's so beautiful you could die,' says one character. 'Is it true that it's sinking?' The city is deserted, dark and wet, very different from the lively and bright Venice of the couple's youth and first encounter. They spend their last hours together having lunch at the Locanda Montin, buying beautiful fabric in Luigi Bevilacqua's workshop and going for the afternoon together to Enrico's flat in the neo-gothic Casa dei Tre Oci on Giudecca. The few people they meet or talk to are modest working Venetians.

As with many successful films, the music is particularly important. Enrico is a musician, and joins a student orchestra in the deconsecrated church of San Vidal (used in the film as a recording studio), playing a concerto by an anonymous composer – hence the film's title, *Anonimo veneziano*. The concerto was, in fact, Concerto for Oboe, Strings and Continuo in D Minor by Alessandro Marcello, the elder but less well-known brother of Benedetto Marcello, an eighteenth-century Venetian composer, famous in his day.

After he has declared 'there's no other city I could die in', the final parting between Enrico and Valeria is heart-breaking. It is clear that their mutual love is still alive, in spite of everything. A tearful Valeria returns to the station to join her family, while Enrico, alone, attempts to conduct the moving concerto.

7

DEATH AND MYSTERY

Whoever has seen Beauty, is already delivered over to Death.
(August von Platen, *Tristan*)

'There is no other city I could die in,' Enrico had said poignantly to Valeria after having broken to her the news of his imminent death. 'This is a place to die in beautifully!' enthused **Virginia Woolf** (1882–1941) in a letter to a friend in 1904. After this first visit with her family, reporting in a letter that she found Venice 'such an amusing and beautiful place', she came back for her honeymoon with Leonard Woolf in 1912, experiencing this time a rather less enticing city, as the weather remained wet and cold. She waited 20 years before returning in 1932 during the rise of Fascism, not an ideal time to be anywhere in Italy.

Chateaubriand and Théophile Gautier said that they would choose to die in Venice. Wagner, Browning and Ezra Pound did die there. Wagner, as we have seen, spent the last year of his life in Palazzo Vendramin-Calergi and expired in his bedroom there. Just a few weeks earlier Wagner's father-in-law, the Hungarian composer Franz Liszt, staying with Wagner's family in Venice, had in December 1882 composed a piece for piano and violin, *La lugubre gondola*. It was possibly inspired by the sight of funeral gondolas heading towards San Michele Cemetery, but was also perhaps a premonition of Wagner's imminent death, and of the gondola which was to bear him from Palazzo Vendramin-Calergi to the railway station.

Byron and Shelley had found their time in Venice blighted by death and grief at the tragic loss of their young children. Shelley had described a gondola in a letter to Peacock on 8 October 1818: 'The gondolas themselves are things of a most romantic and picturesque appearance; I can only compare them to moths of which a coffin might have been the chrysalis.' Clara, the daughter of Shelley and Mary Godwin, died in 1818 in Venice, and Byron's daughter by Claire Clairmont, Allegra, died in 1819, aged only five, in Bagnascallo, where she had been sent from Venice.

The Serenissima has been the scene of many suicides, the most notable perhaps those of Henry James's friend Constance Fenimore Woolson, and of Jean Cocteau's young travelling companion Raymond Laurent, who shot himself so dramatically near the Salute. Another casualty was the nineteenth-century French painter Léopold Robert, who committed suicide in Palazzo Pisani, before his large uncompleted painting, *Departure of Chioggia Fishermen for the Adriatic*. He was short of inspiration, or perhaps it was as the result of an unhappy love affair. He had organised a performance of Mozart's Requiem just beforehand.

In her 1864 book *L'Italie des Italiens*, **Louise Colet** (1810–76), the writer and close friend of Gustave Flaubert, visited the very room where Robert had cut his throat with his razor, and she described the gory scene: 'He was found sitting on a trunk, having cut his throat. The blood was gushing from him in floods. He had shown the singular courtesy of wiping the blades and tidying them away.' Louise Colet's Venice is a funereal city, impatient to shake off the Austrian yoke which finally happened two years later: 'The Venice which surrounded me seemed dead [. . .] a chilling cold came over me [. . .] seeing death makes one consider it, I thought, and what if I were to die here?'

The sight of the gondola reinforced these gloomy notions: 'I would never enter the felze with its black cover, as a coffin is draped in black.' She even compared the Bridge of Sighs to a sarcophagus. But a high point of her stay was seeing Alfred de Musset's room in the Hotel Danieli, where, by some coincidence, she was staying: 'We found ourselves in the room where Alfred de Musset almost died in Venice. With tenderness I looked at the bed where he had suffered so greatly, and at the tilted looking-glass in which his pale noble face had been reflected.' Predictably, not a word is said about her rival George Sand.

A few years later, another female George was involved in a disastrous honeymoon which almost ended in tragedy. In the summer of 1880 George Eliot's young husband, John Cross, attempted pathetically to kill himself by throwing himself into the Grand Canal from his bedroom balcony at the Hotel de l'Europe during their honeymoon. 'Please do not save me!' he is reported to have pleaded to the gondoliers trying to rescue him. Eliot never mentioned the episode in her letters, but Lord Acton noted: 'At Venice she thought him mad, and she never recovered from the dreadful depression that followed. Sent for Ricchetti (the doctor), told him that Cross had a mad brother. Told her fears. Just then, heard that he had jumped into the Canal.'

The French writer **Louis Aragon** (1897–1982) also attempted suicide, in 1928 in Venice, at the end of a stormy and unhappy love affair with the capricious heiress Nancy Cunard, who had fallen in love with a jazz musician. He took an overdose of sleeping pills, but he was saved by an English friend. It remains a mystery why Aragon, a student of medicine, underestimated the lethal dose.

Some met violent deaths in Venice at the hands of others. The beautiful fifteenth-century Palazzo Dario on the Grand Canal, for instance, is associated with a succession of deaths.

Many others chose, as did Stravinsky and Brodsky, to be interred in the beautiful cemetery on the Venetian island of San Michele. It is claimed that the famous French couturier Pierre Cardin, born in 1922, is considering whether he should be buried in Paris or in the San Michele Cemetery. He was born in Treviso and has a home, Palazzo Bragadin, near the Rialto. The former Spanish football trainer 'Mago' Herrera chose to be cremated in Venice, and his ashes are in San Michele, in an urn designed to resemble a sporting trophy.

Fame may well secure a permanent resting place in Venice, but space is limited, even for Venetians, whose remains are allowed to rest in the actual cemetery ground for 10 to 12 years before being disinterred. They are then loaded into a barge and consigned to a municipal ossuary, or a small space may be obtained for those who wish to scatter ashes on dry land. The third option is for the remains to be transferred to small containers in the cemetery.

The city is, however, prepared to be accommodating. It is now practically impossible for a foreigner to find space in the existing cemetery, but cremation and dispersal of ashes are allowed, providing strict regulations are respected and an appropriate fee paid. An article published in 2010 in *Corriere del Veneto* specifies that it is possible to scatter ashes from the vaporetto stop of San Michele Cemetery, but only in the presence of an attendant. The alternative is to disperse ashes out in the lagoon, at a minimum distance of 700 metres from the shore, but again only in the presence of a specialised city employee. These measures were taken when things were found to have got out of hand in 2004, when an urn containing the ashes of a deceased Frenchwoman was found floating in the Grand Canal. The local administration has recently introduced and promoted to Venetians the use of a light biodegradable coffin, more economical and ecological. This is also available to outsiders, but at a higher price.

Venice is a city where the presence of death is never very far away: the many Campi dei Morti and Corte della Morte are reminders of the time when the dead were buried in the small areas adjoining parish churches, before Napoleon's decision to move the dead out of the city to the adjacent island of San Cristoforo, which was later extended to become the Cemetery of San Michele.

Some brotherhoods and confraternities dedicated themselves to those condemned to death, like the Scuola San Fantin (opposite the Fenice, and now the home of the Ateneo Veneto), or to looking after those who had died from drowning, like the Scuola della Buona Morte at San Marcuola. The bodies of the drowned used to be laid out on the Ponte della Paglia near the Doge's Palace for identification. The Scuola dell'Angelo Custode near Santi Apostoli in Cannaregio, now an Evangelical church, helped the dying and

29　*The Church of San Geremia. Its Scuola dei Morti specialised in relief for the dying*

the grieving families with prayers. The Scuola dei Morti or Scuola di Santa Veneranda, founded in 1618, attached to the Church of San Geremia, still bears a relief of skulls and bones on its Grand Canal façade.

Like many other cities, Venice has had its share of killings and murders. Walking from the Rialto towards the Fenice you might come across Calle Rio Terrà dei Assassini, the site of murders and suspicious deaths. The street, nowadays less sinister, is worth visiting for its trattoria (dei Assassini) and one of the remaining good bookshops with competitive prices. There are various stories and legends explaining the name of the street and its adjoining bridge. One claims that it used to be especially dark at night and situated close to brothels. Prospective visitors to the establishments carrying money in their pockets were attacked and murdered on the bridge in the darkness. As a result the government improved the lighting in the city at night.

Throughout the centuries people have wished to be buried in Venice because of its theatrical funerals. Many will recall the elegant funeral scene at the end of Nicholas Roeg's film *Don't Look Now*, and Venetians have not forgotten Stravinsky's memorable funeral procession, recorded by contemporary photographs. Diaghilev's death and subsequent funeral, full of drama and uncontained emotion, has been recounted by his handsome dancer Serge Lifar, who recalled in his 1940 biography *Diaghilev*, translated by Stuart

Gilbert, the scene at the dead man's bedside where he fought with Diaghilev's secretary Boris Kokhno:

> All my life I shall remember that dreadful night in which I sat there, supporting the dying man on one side, Kokhno on the other, with Misia (Sert) sitting at his feet and the doctor and nurse silent by the window. And then before the mind had even learned to realize this was death [. . .] an almost incredible scene took place. On one side I, on the other side Kokhno, he striving with me, and both struggling over the dead man's body. It was necessary to remove us forcibly from the room.

More drama followed at the cemetery:

> And I took some earth [. . .] but suddenly it was impossible to hold myself back. I was swept away by some unknown force which surged irresistibly up in me, which swept aside all restraint, and I hurled myself into the grave, whereupon a dozen hands seized me and with immense difficulty managed to drag me back, for my manic delirium had endowed me with Herculean strength. Then I was led from the cemetery.

Later Lifar and Kokhno overcame their differences.

Up to the seventeenth century, terrible outbreaks of the plague would take more than half of the population. It did not spare anyone, young or old, but the poor were more vulnerable. Titian died of plague at 88 with a part of his household, and Tintoretto's beloved daughter Marietta was 36 when she died in 1590. The painter Giorgione died in 1510 of the plague at only 33. Little is known about his short life, but some think that his death was caused by the fact that he could not tear himself away from the woman he loved, Cecilia, another victim of the raging disease.

The deaths of the famous are well known, but not everyone has heard of the young nineteenth-century Austrian pianist Carl Filtsch. He came to Venice aged 15 to recover from tuberculosis, but died soon after his arrival. Immensely gifted, he died too young to become famous and be remembered.

It is not surprising that death in Venice has been a recurrent theme in literature and cinema; the city has been repeatedly chosen as a sumptuous but also a threatening and sometimes deadly background by writers, including Henry James in the *Wings of the Dove* and *The Aspern Papers*, Thomas Mann in his novella *Death in Venice*, Hemingway in *Across the River and into the Trees* – all works dealing with ageing, mortality and death.

Writers belonging to the Decadent literary movement of the end of the nineteenth century, like D'Annunzio in his 1894 *Triumph of Death* (*Trionfo della morte*) (1894) and Maurice Barrès in *The Death of Venice* (1916), intensified this trend, which persisted into the early twentieth century. Some of these literary works have been made into successful films, including Visconti's stunning adaptation of *Death in Venice*, and Giuseppe Berto's *Anonimo veneziano*.

The Belgian master of thrillers, **Georges Simenon** (1903–89), did write a thriller entitled *Le train de Venise* in 1965. The story starts in the night train departing from Venice. The main protagonist of *The Venice Train* remembers 'the days of the Lido' as being 'amongst the most luminous and pleasant in his life'. The story then follows the train route to Lausanne and on to Paris. Simenon had visited Venice with his wife at the end of August 1958, and returned twice with his children. His stays at Hotel Excelsior on the Lido in 1960 and at the Gritti in 1965 are mentioned in his *Intimate Memoirs*.

Many other writers who visited Venice around the turn of the twentieth century were part of this literary movement, described by French critics as *écrivains crépusculaires*. They shared this mournful, melancholic or morbid view of the city, recalling Charles Dickens's initial impressions of the city.

D'Annunzio was at their centre, and his description of the city in *The Fire* is representative of them all: 'A vision of Hades: a country of shadows, mists and waters. Everything evaporated and vanished like spirits.' One of his French friends was the French novelist **Maurice Barrès** (1862–1923), who wrote fictional and political works with a strong nationalistic bent. A keen traveller, his first love was Greece, but from 1887 he became a regular visitor to Venice, which he loved perversely as a city doomed: 'This prolonged agony, that is the greatest charm of Venice, which draws me.'

In 1892 he wrote, 'My whole life was determined at Venice.' He used his travel notebooks to publish *The Death of Venice*, in which he describes how he came to Venice as a young man, identifying strangely with Marcantonio Bragadin, a Venetian officer taken captive and used as a deterrent example by the Turks, who flayed him alive in macabre circumstances during the Siege of Cyprus in 1571: 'In my youth I spent a long period in Venice [. . .] I lived on the Fondamenta Bragadin, which pleased me, since the noble Bragadin was flayed alive, and sometimes it seemed to me as if, relatively speaking, I had received a similar fate.' When it was recovered in 1580, Bragadin's skin was stuffed with straw and stored in the mausoleum of the Church of Santi Giovanni e Paolo, where it is still on display.

Barrès liked to retrace the footsteps of painters like Turner, whom he admired, as well as writers including Hippolyte Taine, who had written enthusiastically about Venice during his own time there. Barrès wrote: 'One day I stretched out on a marble bench on the Schiavoni, by the water; it was Taine's bench, the bench on which he took his ease during his journey to Venice, from 20 April to 2 May 1864.'

But the book's most important aspect is the morbid pleasure Barrès seemed to take in what he called 'the decomposition of the city' whose demise he welcomed: 'I lament the loss of Venice at the moment time abandoned her, but I do not want her to be revived because of my lament.' Themes of disintegration and death were frequent in the Decadents' work. Barrès focuses especially on the many visitors who died or committed suicide in the city. Goethe, Chateaubriand, Mickiewicz, George Sand, Musset and Byron were for Barrès: 'the rootless people who frequent Venice [. . .] melancholic figures by nature or through grief, passionate disappointed souls'. He also included Shelley, whom he sees in a rather exaggerated way as depressed and sick in the city: 'He ruined his health in Venice. He was so weak that he could no longer digest any food at all, and he was consumed by fever.'

When he recalls the various love affairs unfolding in the city, they are bound to be doomed, like that of Alfred de Musset and George Sand, as he prefers to concentrate on unhappy events, scandals and sickness. He counted Wagner among this group, 'made miserable by his inability to gain public acknowledgement of his great artistic potential, and miserable because of an impossible love, he set off for Venice to compose the second Act of *Tristan* [. . .] Let us recognise in the crest of the waves to which Tristan takes us the nocturnal miasma rising from the lagoon.'

The doomed, rotting city is perceived as a foetid, unhealthy place: 'This city has always made me agitated [. . .] the feverish air from the lagoon confuses my judgement [. . .] I have taken quinine in vain, I feel as if millions of bacteria are multiplying within me. A dormant poison is renewing its virulence.' Barrès is attracted by the poor, deserted or abandoned islands: Murano, Mazzorbo, Burano, Torcello and San Francesco del Deserto, where there is 'no theme on which to dwell here save preparation for death'. As for San Michele, 'This is the island of death: a church of white marble, and a low red house, its windows facing the flat green water, while the gondoliers bringing the bodies here to the cemetery, stacked in the rocking boat, laugh and joke, caressing their flagons of wine.'

In Venice itself he prefers areas neglected by the average tourist, like Cannaregio with its remote, almost unknown church, Sant'Alvise: 'this abandoned part of the city, silence, weeds, and the constant presence of [. . .] this small church [. . .] the sun and the damp will be the destruction of Saint Alvise.' He is not indifferent to the deep poverty he witnesses in Cannaregio, Castello and Giudecca, but welcomes it as a blessing, contributing to the city's salvation: 'So thank God for its poverty! An administration with too much money to spend would certainly open wide corridors in order to run trains right up to the Dogana, and throw a bridge across the Giudecca Canal.'

The book ends with a lyrical evocation of the moribund city: 'Lie down beneath your lagoon, Venice. The lament still sings forth, but the lovely mouth is dead. The Ocean rolls through the night. And its waves, as they unfurl, orchestrate the eternal theme of death caused by too great a love of life.'

In Venice with his wife in April 1905, Barrès read *La Domination*, a Venetian novel by French poet **Anna de Noailles** (1876–1933), whom he had met in 1899, and with whom he subsequently had an affair. He enjoyed taking her round the less well-trodden parts of the city. She wrote many poems on Venice, published in 1907 in the collection *Eblouissements*.

> Arpeggio of sobbing, light and ecstasy,
> Venice, hollow watery vessel of a city.

Images of death, enticingly poetical, also recur in her verse, as in 'the black-painted shutters of the Palazzo Manzoni [. . .] the dark shawls of the Venetian women' which evoke 'black poppies in a sublime vase'.

In 1919 Barrès went to the Casetta Rossa to visit D'Annunzio, who dedicated his *The Martyrdom of Saint Sebastian* to him. At this later stage of his life Barrès was famous, a member of the French National Assembly and an Academician. He could afford to stay in style at the prestigious Hotel Danieli and dine at Caffè Florian, and perhaps by this time he could enjoy a less gloomy view of the city.

In *The Fire* D'Annunzio also dealt with these themes of decay and death. He describes gloomy abandoned palaces, gardens with broken statues and the famous funeral procession leaving Palazzo Vendramin-Calergi. Although he did not know Venice before 1897, his alter ego in the novel, Stelio Effrena, is one of the six young Italians carrying Wagner's coffin. He is the author of the lines on the plaque which commemorates Wagner, on the garden wall of the palace facing the Grand Canal, and which may be read from the vaporetto by an attentive passenger:

> In questo palagio
> L'ultimo spiro di Riccardo Wagner
> O dono le anime
> Perpetuarsi come la marea
> Che lambe i marmi.

> In this palace
> Richard Wagner took his last breath
> O let his soul be
> As eternal as the sea
> That laps at the marble.

D'Annunzio's novel also describes an outing to Villa Pisani by the Brenta where the two lovers Stelio Effrena and La Foscarina, surrounded by decomposition, discuss the end of their affair and their deaths: 'We are moribund; you and I are moribund: We are dreaming and dying.' There 'the slow honeyed savour hovered above a vast rotting vegetation which seemed also to touch stones, walls and buildings.' The death of La Foscarina, the *femme fatale*, is essential to liberate Stelio the poet, the Nietzschean superhero who will then be able to find inspiration without hindrance.

When **Oscar Wilde** (1854–1900) arrived in Venice in 1875 for the summer vacation with his former tutor and mentor from Trinity College Dublin, John Pentland Mahaffy, one of the first things he described to his mother was the gondola bearing their luggage, a funereal vision to him as to so many other foreign visitors, 'a black hearse-like barge, such as King Arthur was taken away in after the fatal battle'. Wilde also recounted that they 'visited some of the islands off Venice; on one an Armenian monastery where Byron used to live [. . .] another, the Lido, a favourite place on Sundays.' There they had a feast of oysters and shrimps before returning to the city 'in the flood of a great sunset. Venice as a city just risen from the sea; a long line of crowded churches and palaces; everywhere white or gilded domes and tall campaniles [. . .] a great pink sunset with a long line of purple thunder clouds behind the city.' Wilde was enchanted by the 'wonderful moon', shining at night after an outing to the theatre and the circus. 'Believe me,' he wrote, 'Venice in beauty of architecture and colour is beyond description. It is the meeting-place of the Byzantine and Italian art – a city belonging to the East as much as the West.' The two men then proceeded to Padua, where the Giotto frescoes filled Wilde 'with wonder and reverence'.

This stay was brief but not forgotten, as the dichotomy of Venice to which he referred in his first letter home was not driven out by the beauty of the sunsets, but was evoked in the more macabre section in Chapter 14 of his 1891 novel, *The Picture of Dorian Gray*. Having killed Basil Hallward, the painter responsible for the fatal portrait, whose body is still lying in an upstairs room of his house, Dorian Gray is plunged into a deep poetical reverie and comes by chance upon Théophile Gautier's 'lovely stanzas upon Venice' in his library.

> How exquisite they were! As one read them, one seemed to be floating down the green waterways of the pink and pearl city, seated in a black gondola with silver prow and trailing curtains. The mere lines looked to him like those straight lines of turquoise-blue that follow one as one pushes out to the Lido. The sudden flashes of colour reminded him of the gleam of the opal-and-iris-throated birds that flutter round the tall, honey-combed Campanile, or stalk, with such stately grace, through the dim, dust-stained arcades [. . .] He remembered the autumn that he had passed there, and a wonderful love that had stirred him to mad, delightful follies. There was romance in every place [. . .]
>
> Basil had been with him part of the time, and had gone wild over Tintoret. Poor Basil! What a horrible way for a man to die!

The other main character in Wilde's novel is intriguingly named Lord Henry Wotton, a manipulative self-indulging aristocrat.

Théophile Gautier (1811–72), author of those 'lovely stanzas', had visited Italy in 1850 and stayed for two months in Venice; for him too it was a city of melancholy. His *Voyage in Italy* (*Voyage d'Italie*), published in 1852, gives us a detailed poetic record of what he saw, praising the wonderful light, and describing a long nocturnal walk from Hotel Europa, where he was staying, towards 'the other side of the city'. His romantic imagination was so much aware of the Gothic atmosphere that 'We were all surprised not to hear a body fall from a balcony or a half-open door.'

The ultimate piece of writing on the subject of death was produced 20 years later by the German writer, **Thomas Mann** (1875–1955). He became a regular visitor to Venice from his second trip to Italy in October 1896. During the three weeks he stayed in the city he was inspired to write a short story, 'Disillusionment', recounting a meeting between a narrator and an enigmatic character in Piazza San Marco, 'sumptuous marvel of colour and line which stood out with luminous enchantment against a tender pale-blue sky'. The straightforward story concludes with 'the worst disillusionment of all', death.

Mann's personal experience of the city became the source for his writing. In 1905, while he was staying on an island outside Venice, there was an outbreak of cholera. Returning with his wife in May 1907, he spent three weeks at the Grand Hotel des Bains, which had just opened. They were there again the next year with his brother **Heinrich Mann** (1871–1950). The war interrupted his visits to Venice, but he was back in March 1925 and July 1935. After a period of exile during and after the Second World War, he made his final trip to the Serenissima in 1952, invited for a UNESCO conference.

His most notable visit had taken place in 1911. It was then that he wrote *Death in Venice*, published in 1912, 'a story of an ageing artist who falls in love with a boy'. Mann's sister Carla had taken her own life in July 1910, aged 29. This traumatic event was followed by an important meeting in Munich with the Viennese composer

Gustav Mahler, who himself died soon after, in May 1911. When Mann went to Venice on 26 June of the same year he had just learned of Mahler's death. He gave the main character of his story, Aschenbach, many of Mahler's physical characteristics (as well as his first name Gustav, and his family name was derived from Ansbach, von Platen's place of birth).

It was during that visit of 1911 that he met a young handsome Polish boy, Baron Wladyslaw Moes, the inspiration for the character of Tadzio. In Aschenbach the 'ageing artist' we recognise not only Mahler, but Mann himself, who acknowledged that his writings were closely connected with his personal life: 'I regard my life work as the result of an extremely personal and very precarious coming to terms with art.' Moreover his wife Katia rather disingenuously recalls in her *Unwritten Memories* (translated by Hunter and Hildegarde Hannum) that:

All the details of the story, beginning with the man at the cemetery, are taken from experience [. . .] In the dining room, on the very first day, we saw the Polish family, which looked exactly the way my husband described them; the girls were dressed rather stiffly and severely, and the very charming beautiful boy of about 13 was wearing a sailor suit with an open collar and very pretty lacings. He caught my husband's attention immediately. This boy was tremendously attractive, and my husband was always watching him with his companions on the beach. He didn't pursue him through all of Venice – that he did not do – but the boy did fascinate him, and he thought of him often.

Death appears at the very beginning of the novella, as Aschenbach, still in his home town of Munich, goes for a walk to the North Cemetery. The writer is dissatisfied with his life, which has turned out to be a kind of living death. In Joachim Neugroschel's translation:

Too busy with the tasks imposed upon him by his own ego and the European soul, too laden with the care and duty to create, too preoccupied to be an amateur of the gay outer world, he had been content to know as much of the earth's surface as he could without stirring far outside his own sphere [. . .] Now more than ever his life was on the wane.

Like von Platen before him, Aschenbach arrives in Venice by boat; 'he thought that to come to Venice by the station is like entering a palace by the back door,' and he is stirred by its beauty: 'He saw it once more, that landing place that takes the breath away.' The gondola taking him to his hotel at the Lido immediately evokes death: 'That singular conveyance [. . .] black as nothing else on earth except a coffin [. . .] what pictures it calls up of lawless, silent adventures in the splashing-light; or even more, what visions of death itself, the bier and solemn rites and last soundless voyage' (H. T. Lowe-Porter's 1928 translation for Secker and Warburg). It seems to be taking him on his final journey: 'the trip will be short, he thought, and wished it might last forever.' It is particularly acute as he feels powerless in the hands of the ill-tempered old gondolier taking him directly to the Lido against his will: 'Even if you hit me in the back with your oar and send me down to the kingdom of Hades, even then you will have rowed me well.'

His morbid thoughts are dispelled once he is installed in the brand-new Hotel des Bains, where he catches a glimpse of 'a long-haired boy of fourteen'. He is bewitched by 'the lad's perfect beauty [. . .] His face recalled the noblest moment of Greek sculpture [. . .] the sight of this living figure, virginally pure and austere, with dripping locks, beautiful as a tender young god, emerging from the depths of sea and sky. It conjured up mythologies.' But thoughts of sickness and death return, this time relating to the child: 'He is delicate, he is sickly. He will most likely not live to grow old.' The fatal attraction he feels keeps him entrapped in a city which has now lost its fascination, finding it now abhorrent with its 'foul-smelling lagoon' and 'the hateful sultriness in the narrow streets' as well as 'the predatory commercial spirit of the fallen queen of the seas'. And 'the city proved in certain weathers rather inimical to his health.'

Still he stays, as if under some kind of spell, and is stirred into writing, inspired by the presence of the boy: 'He would write, and moreover he would write in Tadzio's presence. This lad should be in a sense his model; his style should follow the lines of this figure that seemed to him divine.' Although Aschenbach is living largely on the island of the Lido, Venice itself is ever-present in the novella, as Aschenbach follows the young boy and his family sightseeing around the city. He seeks him out in alleyways, gets lost and finds him unexpectedly in the Basilica: 'He passed from the glare of the piazza into the golden twilight of the holy place, and found him he sought bowed in worship over a *prie-dieu* [. . .] But through all the glamour and glitter he saw the exquisite creature there in front turn his head, seek out and meet his lover's eye.'

But Venice is now hit by a serious outbreak of cholera of the worst type, 'the most malignant form of the contagion. In this form the victim's body loses power to expel the water secreted by the blood vessels, it shrivels up, he passes with hoarse cries from convulsion to convulsion, his blood grows thick like pitch and he suffocates in a few hours.' And the inevitable happens. Aschenbach himself dies on the beach at the Lido, in the presence of the boy now personified as Hermes, the god guiding dead souls to the Underworld:

> He paused to look: with a sudden recollection, or by an impulse, he turned from the waist up, in an exquisite movement, one hand resting on his hip, and looked over his shoulder at the shore. It looked as if the pale and lovely Summoner out there smiled at him and beckoned [. . .] Some minutes passed before anyone hastened to the aid of the elderly man sitting there collapsed in his chair.

Death is here described 'as a seductive anti-moral force' and its powerful lure is closely connected to Aschenbach's homoerotic desires, shared by Thomas Mann, who confided as much in his diaries.

The film of *Death in Venice* by Luchino Visconti was shot at the Lido in 1971. The Italian director had the lobby of the Grand Hotel des Bains lavishly refurbished. The once-magnificent building (a favourite of Diaghilev, who had died there in 1929) has lately become a casualty of property development at the Lido and is closed. Most of the stunning beach scenes in the film were not shot on the hotel's own private beach, but on the less crowded and more expansive neighbouring Alberoni beaches. The soundtrack made use of Mahler's Adagietto from his Fifth Symphony.

Thomas Mann's unforgettable novella was adapted two years later by the English composer **Benjamin Britten** (1913–76). He was careful not to see the film, in order to avoid accusations of plagiarism. *Death in Venice* is his last opera, premiered in 1973 at the Fenice in Venice. Britten had been suffering from heart disease since at least 1968, and was too ill to attend. His partner Peter Pears sang the role of Aschenbach, written for him, with the wordless role of Tadzio given to the Royal Ballet dancer Robert Huguenin. The English artist John Piper was responsible for the sets, his wife Myfanwy Piper for the libretto and Frederick Ashton for the choreography. After various further productions it returned successfully to the Fenice in June 2008.

Britten's Aschenbach on arrival first sees his beloved Serenissima as a welcome haven:

> Ah, Serenissima!
> Where should I come but to you
> To soothe and revive me,
> Where else live that magical life
> Between the warm sea and the city?
> Ambiguous Venice,
> Where water and stone interchange
> And passion confuses the senses?
> Ambiguous Venice.

But delusion follows. As Mann's novella was a reflection on art and death, so Britten's work, composed in the final years of his life, is a reflection on youthful beauty, old age and imminent death in a

Venice of funeral gondolas, 'black, coffin black, a vision of death itself', in the pestilential lagoon and a corrupt city struck by cholera: 'Crime, drunkenness, murder, organized vice – evil forces are rife.'

Few writers treat death with cheerful humour, but the French writer **Jean Giono** (1895–1970) is one of the few. Claiming not to enjoy travel, he set out from his beloved Manosque in Provence in 1951 in the company of his wife and two friends, to embark on a trip to Italy, home of his paternal grandfather. In his *Journey in Italy* of 1954 he describes how they arrived by car, to spend a few days in Venice, a place he was not initially even particularly keen to visit: 'When we left France, I did not want to come to Venice: honeymoons, gondolas, Wagner, D'Annunzio repelled me along with the thousands of postcard and film scenes. Despite Byron, Stendhal and Casanova, despite Proust, I wanted to bypass Venice.' But he was immediately won over by the city, staying in a hotel near the Church of San Zaccaria and giving a poetic description of the city, seen at times unusually through a barman he befriended in Caffè Florian, who also provided him with recipes for local dishes. Part-Italian himself, Giono enjoyed the Venetian food, which reminded him of childhood meals, and describes the fried fish, a particular favourite. He viewed the funerals he witnessed as colourful and theatrical affairs: 'The dead set off in red boats, along streets hung with purple, propelled by boatmen in black singing the Lamentations of Jeremiah.' Unlike other visitors, who inevitably compared the black gondola to a floating coffin, he finds the colour black cheerful: 'this is the only place in the world where black can be worn and the black remains pure. Trousers, shirt and sandals in purest black: an admirable costume. There is nothing brighter.' Giono's approach is almost unique.

Most foreign visitors see threat and danger in the city once they get off the beaten track, as do the protagonists in Daphne du Maurier's short story 'Don't Look Now', written in 1970. During a visit to Venice she mistook an adult with dwarfism for a child and met elderly twins on the island of Torcello. Both incidents are used in the disturbing story, in which the young English couple John and Laura Baxter, attempting to recover from the tragic death of their child, visit the city and initially enjoy its magical charm: 'They went out laughing in the warm soft night, and the magic was about them everywhere.'

The unpleasant combination of approaching darkness, rain and getting lost in unfamiliar surroundings near the Church of San Martino in Castello has a sobering effect: 'Now, ill-lit, almost in darkness, the windows of the houses shuttered, the water dank, the scene appeared altogether different, neglected, poor, and the long narrow boats moored to the slippery steps of cellar entrances looked like coffins [. . .] The soft humidity of the evening, so pleasant to walk about in earlier, had turned to rain.'

Not only has the city, seen now as 'a bright façade put on for show, glittering by sunlight', become menacing, but the dwarf, wearing a red raincoat – an echo of their dead child – is in fact a dangerous serial killer, and the story ends with an horrific, unexpected killing: 'The creature fumbled in her sleeve, drawing a knife, and as she threw it at him with hideous strength, piercing his throat, he stumbled and felt the sticky mess covering his protecting hands [. . .] Oh God, he thought, what a bloody silly way to die.'

The brilliant cinematic adaptation was made by Nicholas Roeg in 1973 and became a cult film. Although the city is one of the safest in the world and the crime rate is low, the simple sight of a red raincoat in a narrow alleyway on a rainy day in Venice is enough to make shivers run down the spine.

Numerous thrillers were set in Venice but perhaps one of the best is *Dead Lagoon* by **Michael Dibdin** (1947–2007), published in 1994, a story of corruption, political intrigue, corpses and skeletons. One location is an island of the dead. Dibdin's saturnine Venetian detective Aurelio Zen – who appears in many other novels set elsewhere, such as *Blood Rain*, *And Then You Die* and *Medusa* – appears only once in his native city, to investigate the disappearance of a rich American who had been living in Venice. His inquiries take him on an unpleasant journey in an icily cold city shrouded continuously in fog. Although he is the last descendant of the great Venetian Zen family, he feels uncomfortable and alienated in a city which he left a long time ago to work in Rome, as do so many young Venetians today:

> It was absurd to think that he could make a life for himself here at this late stage. There was nothing here for him now. He had used the place up, converted to experiences and memories that made up the person he was. To return would be to condemn himself to a form of spiritual incest. Nothing could happen to him here, nothing real.

Inspector Zen would not dream of returning to live in Venice, but many outsiders do. **Salley Vickers** (b. 1948) had her character Miss Garnet choose to settle there for her retirement after the loss of a friend, intending never again to leave: 'Death is outside life but it alters it: leaves a hole in the fabric of things which those who are left behind try to repair.' These are the opening words of her novel, *Miss Garnet's Angel*, which was tremendously successful when it was published in 2000, with a possible film adaptation to come. The novel is about Venice, angels, self-discovery, a failed love affair and death. Miss Garnet requests that her body 'be cremated, the ashes to be scattered in the lagoon of Venice'.

The novel attracted visitors to a hitherto overlooked part of Dorsoduro, unfairly neglected, as it offers three outstanding churches: San Sebastian, known principally for its decoration by Paolo Veronese; the charming twelfth-century San Nicolo dei Mendicoli; and Angelo Raffaele, the church at the centre of the novel, in which the panels of its organ case, painted by Guardi in the eighteenth century, tell the biblical story of Tobias and the Angel. This story is retold in the novel in parallel with that of Miss Garnet, who has started a new phase of her life in her apartment close to the church. Salley Vickers spoke in an interview on her website of having used her own discoveries and experience of this city packed with angels for her character:

I gave to my heroine the experience I had on first encountering St Mark's [. . .] I remember stopping, as Miss Garnet does, on the wooden Accademia bridge, and seeing the dome of S. Maria della Salute, like a vast soap bubble breasting the Grand Canal, and when I [. . .] saw the basilica, like a great pearl adorned with gilded waves of angels mounting to the sky, I fell in love and, happily, have never recovered.

Many visitors go to Venice to retrace Miss Garnet's footsteps, and many do the same after reading the Venetian thrillers of **Donna Leon** (b. 1942). She is an American writer, born in New Jersey, who has made her home near the Church of the Miracoli in Venice for more than 30 years. Her love for the city has been transmitted to the chief protagonist of her hugely successful detective novels, the Venetian policeman Commissario Guido Brunetti: 'These were the hours when, for Brunetti, the city became most beautiful, just as they were the same hours when he, Venetian to the bone, could sense some of her past glory [. . .] Like many women of a certain age, the city needed the help of deceptive light to recapture her vanished beauty.' And like his creator, Brunetti is also annoyed by 'the worst tourist junk' invading the city.

Before settling in Venice, Donna Leon worked as a university lecturer, as does Brunetti's wife Paula, a specialist in American Literature, and in Henry James in particular. The first Brunetti book, *Death at La Fenice*, published in 1991, was, the author claims, almost written as a joke. But it was a huge success, particularly in Germany, as the victim Wellauer, a famous German conductor, was associated by many with Herbert von Karajan. Other novels followed at the rate of one a year, and most have been translated into many languages, but not into Italian, as the author said in an interview that she wished to remain incognito in the city: 'I do not take any pleasure whatsoever in being a famous person. The tenor of my life would change if these books were translated into Italian, because I'm completely anonymous here.'

Indeed, some people in the city would perhaps not be happy with the way they are depicted in these books, read by millions of people. For example, Professor Rezzonico, a character in *Death at La Fenice*, talks rather disparagingly about Venetian concert-goers: 'The most complimentary thing that can be said of them is that they are dogs. They don't go to the theatre to listen to music or hear beautiful singing: they go to wear their new clothes and be seen by their friends, and those friends are there for the same reasons.' However attractive their local police inspector, Venetians are doubtless none too keen to read stories dealing with scandal and corruption in their city.

The books' titles, including *Death at La Fenice*, *Death in a Strange Country*, *Fatal Remedies*, *Death of Faith*, highlight the fact that death is ever present; even if it is kept in the wings, unpleasant events certainly happen in the stories. An admirer of Agatha Christie, Leon says that she used to read murder mysteries to relax from her university teaching. Her books, full of references to classical authors and classical music, tend to appeal to those with knowledge of the city. They seem to give an authentic view of Venetian life and atmosphere, as well as a good sense of topography. Brunetti often walks, allowing the reader to travel with him across the city, and the routes from his home in Campo San Polo to his work at the Questura by Campo San Lorenzo become familiar. The places where he stops for a coffee, an ice cream or lunch can easily be tracked down (Brunetti guided walks are on offer to visitors in Venice). This gives the reader the impression of having acquired insider knowledge of Venice. In *Death at La Fenice*, Brunetti and his wife go a party given by his wife's parents in their palace, of the kind to which many would love to be invited:

The light that filled the room came from two immense chandeliers, covered with playful angels and Cupids, which hung from the frescoed ceiling, and from candle-filled stanchions that lined the walls. The music came from a discreet trio in the corner, who played Vivaldi in one of his most repetitive moods. And the scent emanated from the flock of brightly coloured and even more brightly chattering women who decorated the room.

Guido Brunetti's appeal is based on the fact that he is an intellectual, interested in history. He likes his food and appreciates classical music. He is a family man, and his wife and two children frequently come up with useful suggestions or ideas to help to solve a case. He is often cynical and, although his main task is to fight wrongdoing, he knows perfectly well that evil cannot be defeated.

Each novel treats a socially or politically challenging issue. Sensitive subjects like lesbianism and paedophilia are touched upon in *Death at La Fenice*. Corruption is a recurring subject in Donna Leon's books; the murderer is not always brought to justice. Her popularity has spurred her into writing a cookery book based on Paola Brunetti's recipes, *Brunetti's Cookbook* (2010), but Donna Leon is also closely involved with research into and promotion of Baroque music in the city, as well as with the ensemble Il Complesso Barocco.

Her books can be found in local bookshops along with a variety of other Venetian-based thrillers such as *The Lizard's Bite* (2006) by a British journalist, **David Hewson** (b. 1953). In his novel his Roman detectives Nick Costa and Gianni Peroni have been kicked out of their city and exiled for indiscipline to Venice, which they consider a 'beautiful graveyard of a city', where they are to investigate two deaths which have occurred on a small island attached to Murano, owned by the Arcangeli glassmaker family. Uriel, one of the three Arcangeli brothers, has been found dead, as has his wife Bella.

The book exposes some familiar aspects of the Venice myth as it continues into our time: 'This is what remains of Venice in the last years. It is not a real city anymore.' The less well-off as well as people in power are prepared to sell the city to the highest bidder; rich foreigners such as property developer Hugo Massiter are planning to transform the city into some kind of theme park.

The city is in danger of losing its identity and uniqueness. It does not have much of a chance, as the local police and politicians are corrupt. Traditional activities which have been the pride of Venice in the past, like lacemaking in Burano and glassmaking in Murano, are now critically endangered, threatened by cheap competition, mainly from the Chinese.

David Hewson turned to Venice again in 2012 to write *Carnival for the Dead*. Here Teresa Lupo, the pathologist who appeared in previous novels, arrives to be welcomed by a masked man, ominously dressed as a plague doctor. She has come to investigate the disappearance of her Aunt Sofia during the February Carnival, when the city is usually freezing and overcrowded, providing a typical setting for a thriller.

The bestselling author **Dan Brown** (b. 1964) has more recently turned his attention to Venice for his 2013 thriller *Inferno*, a Dante-inspired title. The 'symbologist' Robert Langdon, already well-known to readers of *The Da Vinci Code* (2003), finds himself trapped in the crypt of the Basilica in the course of his attempt to decipher the mysterious poem printed on Dante's death mask. A film adaptation might well follow here too, making the most of the photogenic Venetian locations.

The immense popularity enjoyed by these novels perhaps explains the extraordinary quantity and variety of art and historical Venice-based thrillers, largely from writers in England, the USA, Spain, France and Italy. The historical thriller by **Iain Pears** (b. 1955), *Stone's Fall*, published in 2009, falls into this category. It is set first in London where John Stone, a wealthy financier and armaments manufacturer, mysteriously falls to his death from the first-floor window of his study. Iain Pears sends the investigation into his death chronologically backwards from Edwardian London to Paris in 1890 and finally to Venice in 1867. The Venice of this novel is a city of double-dealing, hidden secrets and espionage, but in profound decline – 'a corpse whose soul has departed'. It is a melancholic and rotting place with crumbling palazzi and a stranded community of English expatriates.

Iain Pears was also the author of *The Titian Committee* (1991), where the victim this time is an American art historian, Louise Masterson, a member of the committee cataloguing Titian's paintings. She has been stabbed to death in a public garden, and pictures have been stolen from the Marchesa di Molino's palace. The investigator sent by the art theft squad in Rome is Flavia di Stefano. She and English art historian Jonathan Argyll try to solve the case, hindered by the corrupt local politicians and the inefficient Venetian police.

In art-based thrillers, Venice is not a safe place for art historians. Corruption, greed, inefficiency, theft, forgery and violence are recurring themes, as in *The Tempest*, written in 1997 by Spanish author **Juan Manuel Prada** (b. 1970), where yet another unsuspecting young art historian, Alessandro Ballesteros, arrives in the middle of winter in Venice for some research, staying at the fictional Albergo Cusmano. The buildings are blanketed with snow, the streets are impenetrable because of the dense fog and the canals are flooded. The city and the truth are shrouded. 'The Giudecca, marinaded in a milky mist, was the mirror of decrepitude in which Venice's image was reflected.' Ballesteros's original plans to research Giorgione's mysterious masterpiece *La Tempesta* (1508–10) are immediately thwarted by a series of disasters. In the matter of a few days an art forger is assassinated, Alessandro falls in love with Chiara, the daughter of a museum director, and he meets a succession of shady characters. The book is gripping and was very successful, selling nearly half a million copies in Spanish and in translation. It also won the prestigious Premio Planeta in Spain. It was translated into English in 2003, and a film adaptation *The Tempest* quickly followed in 2005, directed by English director Paul Tickell. It is shot in Venice but also in Luxembourg, as Venetian locations are expensive. The result disappointed the author.

Adrien Goetz (b. 1966), a French art historian, has followed the trend with his 2012 *Intrigue à Venise*. Here the main protagonist and investigator, Penelope, another art historian, arrives reluctantly on her first trip to Venice to attend a conference dealing with the esoteric topic of 'Gondolas, galleys and galleasses, the instruments of conquest'. On her first day she discovers a decapitated cat by Colleoni's statue on Campo Santi Giovanni e Paolo, and a respected French author is killed, with the prospect of other deaths to follow. The amateur detective Penelope investigates, assisted by her fiancé Wandrille. The case is connected to a Rembrandt painting hidden somewhere in the city. The plot centres on the famous celebrity ball given in 1951 by the then owner of Palazzo Labia, Charles de Beistegui (which Orson Welles had attended). The thriller, which sold 22,000 copies, is amusingly irreverent, making gentle fun of academics and writers.

The Bellini Card, written by English author **Jason Goodwin** (b. 1964) in 2008, was also very popular, and has been translated into various languages, including Italian. It starts in 1840 in Istanbul, a city the author knows very well. In this case the detective sent to Venice is Yashim, an Ottoman eunuch, who is asked by his master the sultan to find a missing masterpiece by Gentile Bellini, the *Portrait of Mehmet the Conqueror* (now in the National Gallery in London). It is 'somewhere in Venice'. Yashim enlists the help of a friend, the Polish ambassador Palewski, and the two collaborate in the search as a kind of Sherlock Holmes and Dr Watson double act. We are exposed again to the dangerous world of art dealers and high society in a city portrayed in its nineteenth-century decaying splendour with neglected palaces and impoverished owners.

The reader should not be put off visiting the city, as violent deaths happen rarely in Venice and art theft only occasionally. The most notable theft occurred when the priceless Giovanni Bellini *Madonna with Child* (1478) was stolen from the Church of Madonna dell'Orto in Cannaregio on the night of 1 March 1993 – some say this was the third time. This real-life mystery remains unsolved, and the church has now put a copy in its place. It probably goes without saying that security has been greatly reinforced since then in all churches.

'The palaces of the Grand Canal seemed to be buildings closed since time immemorial, their facades corroded like the bodies of lepers scarred by sores. Like a leper, Venice insisted on remaining on her feet despite the death sentence meted out to her.' The moribund city thus described by Prada in *The Tempest* has been a recurrent theme since the beginning of the twentieth century. It has persisted throughout the century, not only in the innumerable mystery and crime novels filling the shelves of the remaining Venetian bookshops, but also in travel writings such as *Venises* by French writer and diplomat **Paul Morand** (1888–1976), a diplomat, writer and aesthete. He first knew Venice when he was 16, when his father, an amateur painter, rented a flat next to Traghetto San Maurizio near the Accademia: 'With a canvas under one arm, his box of paints under the other and his easel on his back, in the tradition of Monsieur Courbet, my father crossed the waters and installed himself on the steps of the Salute, opposite the Abbey of San Gregorio.'

Morand was privileged to know personally a number of the writers associated with the Serenissima at the turn of the twentieth century. Among them were Marcel Proust, Henri de Régnier, Gabriele D'Annunzio and Jean Cocteau, as well as painters, all referred to in *Venises*, which was published towards the end of his life in 1970 by Gallimard, and in English in 2002 in Euan Cameron's translation. Morand's book contains his impressions of Venice throughout his life, from youth to old age, covering both wars (mainly as a diplomat). The city had already been portrayed in his earlier novel *Les Extravagants*, written in 1910, alongside other cities he loved and knew well, including Oxford and London. He was spellbound by Venice and returned regularly, witnessing the damage inflicted by Austrian bombardment during the First World War:

> In Venice, through the shattered dome of Santa Maria, one could see the blue sky; the Arsenal was damaged, the wall of the Doge's Palace was cracked, St Mark's was choking beneath fifteen feet of sandbags held in place by beams and wire netting; the horses of the Quadriga had vanished! The Titians had been wrapped up; the canals had been emptied of gondolas, the pigeons had been eaten.

He is here referring to Santa Maria di Nazareth, the seventeenth-century church close to Santa Lucia railway station in Cannaregio and better known now as Scalzi, hit by an Austrian bomb in 1915. The beautiful angel-packed ceiling completed by Tiepolo in 1745 was almost entirely destroyed; some rescued fragments can be seen in the Accademia. Another witness of First World War damage to the city was D'Annunzio, who noted in December 1917 in his *Taccuini* (*Notebooks*) that Verrocchio's famous statue of Condottiere Colleoni had been removed for safety. It is fortunately now back *in situ* in Campo Santi Giovanni e Paolo.

Morand wrote of his own book in his diary: 'There is something of everything in *Venises*: frivolity, memories, meditations, serious themes, portraits, politics (without bias). It's a form that is hard to define. I believe its success is a result of this.' But he was also aware of the more sombre side of the city and its contrasts: 'Along the same canal passed both the Wagner of the duet from *Tristan* and the man of the funeral gondola, singing his own *Non nobis, Domine.*'

In one of the later chapters of the book, 'September 1970', he speculates on the possible demise of Venice, giving an apocalyptic view of a town finally submerged by water:

Sometimes I attempt to drain the lifeblood out of myself by imagining Venice dying before I do, imagining her being swallowed up without revealing her features upon the water before she disappears. Being submerged not to the depths, but a few feet beneath the water; her cone-shaped chimneys would emerge, like miradors, from which the fishermen would cast their lines, and her campanile a refuge for the last cats from St Mark's. The vaporetti, tilting under the weight of visitors, would survey the surface of the waters where they coalesce with the mire of the past; tourists would point out to each other the gold from the mosaic, held afloat by five water-polo balls: the domes of St Mark's; the Salute would be used as a mooring buoy by cargo ships; bubbles would float up from above the Grand Canal, released by frogmen groping around for American ladies' jewels in the submerged Grand Hotel.

Like Barrès, Morand seems almost to welcome this dreadful scenario, concluding: 'Venice is drowning; it may well be the best thing that could happen to her.'

In the same vein, the Arezzo-born **Pierfrancesco Prosperi** (b. 1945), an architect and novelist, wrote an intriguing short story, 'The City Which Never Was' ('La città che non c'era'), included in a 1989 anthology of Venetian-based science fiction, portraying a father and son on their way by train to see Venice. The father had been there on a conventional honeymoon some time before, when his son was still a baby. Once in Mestre station they find, to the child's great disappointment and the father's dismay, that the following stop is not Venice but Portogruaro. Venice has gone and is practically forgotten, as if it had never existed, or had possibly been just a dream or a mirage:

> And sometimes, he was not very sure, so many years had passed, and then memory is not often reliable, he had dreamed of seeing from his window [. . .] the lights of a hundred bell-towers, a hundred golden domes, the magical profile of a city-mirage immediately before him, in the middle of the lagoon . . . such a city could only exist in dreams.

The last word on the subject, however, should perhaps be left to the Spanish writer and columnist **Javier Marías** (b. 1951). Born in Madrid, he has lived and worked in cities such as London, Oxford and Venice, which he visits regularly. His 1988 *Venice, a Living Space* (*Venecia, un interior*) is a collection of articles he wrote in the city between 1984 and 1990. The book is a tribute to what he calls 'the city par excellence or the city of cities'. For him Venice is *un interior*, a 'living space', as 'beyond it nothing is needed'. This gives a strong sense of superiority to its inhabitants, who consider themselves in the centre of the world. The drawback is that, according to Marías, they are constantly and obsessively worried about possible threats to their beloved city:

Since I came to Venice the first time in 1984, I have always come back a couple of times or more a year. I may be wrong, but I have always had the feeling that the threat of catastrophe, irrevocable calamity, total annihilation is, more than a real fear of its inhabitants, a real necessity. This conscious apprehension, in my opinion provoked, immediately affects visitors, probably even the most transient, who as soon as they set foot on a bridge have the feeling that this could be the city's last day.

A doomed Venice is not entirely impossible. It almost happened in 1966 when the city was hit by its worst floods to date, and other threats have followed: the vast cruise ships allowed to move down the Giudecca Canal could so easily permanently damage the priceless buildings on either side which they wash past several times a day. They also disturb the foundations of the buildings and the islands as well as causing serious pollution, a constant worry for Venetians and the international community. An earthquake is always possible. The Veneto has had its share of earthquakes in the past, one in 1233 causing great damage to Venice, and another reported in Marino Sanudo's diaries. Tornadoes, which are quite frequent, always leave a trail of serious damage.

Scenarios of destruction have been explored in American cinema: in Steven Spielberg's 1989 film *Indiana Jones and the Last Crusade*, for example, which stages an explosion in the eighteenth-century Church of San Barnaba in Dorsoduro. Venice in this case is considered to be the ideal stop on the quest for the Holy Grail. Various action-packed James Bond films have been shot in the city, starting in 1963 with *From Russia with Love*. *Moonraker* (1979) features a lethal funeral gondola packed with guns spreading death and havoc on the Grand Canal, and many will remember in the same film the famous chase in the canals involving a motor-powered gondola landing precariously on Piazza San Marco, missing the Doge's Palace by a whisker. More recently, *Casino Royale* (2006) lit the Grand Canal with fireworks and reduced a whole palace to ashes after a huge explosion.

*

In recent years, and since the advent of mass tourism, the number of visitors to Venice has become a flood of unmanageable proportions. Many great cities – Barcelona, Paris, London, Oxford and New York, for example – have had to deal with growing numbers of short-term visitors who erode the fabric of these popular tourist destinations, but the fragility of Venice means that it is surely the worst affected. A great number of Venetian houses and palaces have been converted by their owners into accommodation for the 25 million or more visitors who arrive each year, and at the same time it is being abandoned by its inhabitants: 1,000 Venetians have moved out each year since 2005. In the last 60 years their numbers have fallen by two-thirds, while the number of visitors has increased by over 500 per cent. If this frightening process continues, and it seems set to do so, one wonders how much can survive of the Venice of the Venetians. Outlets for fast food, cheap masks and souvenirs have spread all over the city, and nowadays the fewer than 57,000 inhabitants remaining (the falling numbers are recorded in Campo San Bartolomeo) are losing their local services as a result. Discouraged by the practical difficulties of living in what is inevitably sometimes an uncomfortable urban space in the twenty-first century, they continue gradually to abandon the city, which in the eighteenth century was, along with Paris, one of the most populated in the world.

The main threats (as cited by *La Nova*) are corruption scandals involving a former mayor, and including others at all levels of admin-stration; the damage caused by the huge cruise ships and by motor boats on the Grand Canal; the city being abandoned by its inhabit-ants; and the scourge of cheap tourism with all its consequences.

Venice is in danger of disappearing, but the film industry seems not to be at risk, as at least 500 films have been shot there so far. As for the book industry, it is positively booming, despite Henry James's claim that there was nothing left to say. Each year at least 500 books are published covering every Venetian subject in various languages, including comic strips and children's books.

Contemporary writers, local or not, are not all gloomy, or dealing exclusively with crime, destruction and death. For example, Venetian-born **Tiziano Scarpa** (b. 1963) in his *Venezia è un pesce* (2000), translated into English in 2008 as *Venice is a Fish*, gives an up-to-date, positive and lively view of the city. His 'sensual guide of the city' is a reflection, a meditation, but above all a tribute to a place which admittedly is 'falling to bits' but where 'every angle radiates beauty'. Legends, nostalgic memories, love of the robust Venetian vernacular, ghosts from the past, literary and otherwise, are all jumbled together. It is a rare but refreshing reminder that the city is alive and well, but that it is in urgent need of care and commitment. This message is endorsed by the national and international organisations whose purpose is to attempt to save Venice; the number of these organisations has multiplied since the great floods of 1966.

30   *Putto beneath the Fondamenta at the Salute – powerless in the face of the constant wave of tourists*

Centuries of artistic and literary legacy have given us such rich insights into this remarkable city, apparently so fragile and yet resilient. If Titian were to cross the centuries and meet Casanova and Henry James today, they would see that the waves of historical events might well have altered the political character of the city, but not its physical presence or magic. They would recognise not only the buildings they frequented but many of the traditions of the city they knew. This is the lasting power of La Serenissima. Its bold foundation in the lagoon ensured the survival of its early population. It flourished because of its strategic and commercial power, which drew so many of the visitors whose testimony is reported here. Invasion and occupation left it scarred, but it rose up again. The myth of Venice endures.

Let the Italian music critic and writer **Bruno Barilli** (1880–1952) have the last word as he pleads here for the city to be handled with care: 'Far from the world and time, detached, immobile and imperishable, Venice should be respected as long as possible.'

Venetian Words and Phrases

acqua alta	high water, when the high tide floods the city
apparati	theatrical set designs, intended for temporary outdoor use
Arsenale	the fortified centre for construction and repair of warships in Castello (Arzanà in Venetian)
Ateneo Veneto	the Centre for Venetian Historical Studies
bàcaro	small Venetian bar or restaurant where traditional cicheti are served
Bacino San Marco	the basin; area of water at the end of the Grand Canal
baùta	mask to cover the whole face, worn with a black hood or cape
bocca di leone	a stone lion's head, through the mouth of which denunciations were posted
bravi	private bodyguards, alternatively thugs
Brenta	the mainland waterway linking Padua to the lagoon
Bucintoro	the great ceremonial vessel of the doges
Burchiello	the historical boat service on the Brenta, still in use
ca'	abbreviation of *casa* in Venetian dialect – house or residence
Caffè Florian	famous café on Piazza San Marco, formerly Caffè alla Veneziana Triunfante
calle	street

campanile	bell tower
campiello	small square
campo	square (*piazza*); St Mark's Square is the only square in the city given the name piazza
Carbonari	the resistance supporters who fought for Italian independence
casino	private building, sometimes within a palace garden, used for intimate meetings, socialising and entertainment. Origin of establishments now used for gambling
castrato	man castrated in order to preserve his high singing voice
cicerone	escort or male chaperone (also known as *sigisbée*)
Compagnia della Calza	association of young nobles, linked to festivities and pageants in the Renaissance. Recognisable by their distinctive patterned or particoloured hose
condottieri	mercenaries drawn from higher social order
confraternità	lay association usually of charitable or religious nature
consorteria	lesser element of the *scuola*, set up to support individual families before and during bereavement (also known as *scuole minori*)
conterie	small glass beads made from the fourteenth century, used for necklaces and rosaries
conversazione	social and cultural meeting in a salon
Council of Ten	the core power group managing state affairs, chosen from the great Venetian families
darsena	Venetian word for dock
Dogana del Mar	customs offices where goods arriving from the sea were unloaded and duty paid
doge	highest authority and figurehead in Venice until the fall of the Republic

felze	removable cabin on a gondola, in use until the twentieth century. Originally provided privacy as well as shelter, with louvred (Venetian) blinds or curtains
fondaco	depot or warehouse (*fontego* in Venetian)
fondamenta	pathway or street alongside a canal, also an embankment
Ghetto	the separate area housing Jews in Cannaregio
gondola	traditional Venetian boat, steered in a standing position by a gondolier using a long oar
Lazzaretto	an island used to isolate the sick or quarantine travellers
maestro di cappella	master of music
Molo	the broad quayside at the entrance to the Piazzetta, used for greeting visitors
ospedale	institution taking in the weak, sick or orphaned
Piazzetta	the section of Piazza San Marco between the Marciana Library and the Doge's Palace, site of the two columns between which public executions took place
Piombi	(Lit. The Leads) – the prison cells beneath the lead roof of the Doge's Palace
Procuratie Nuove	further quarters (built by 1583 by Scamozzi) for nine procurators of St Mark's
Procuratie Vecchie	the earliest procurators' offices and residence (rebuilt partly by Mauro Codussi in the early sixteenth century) on Piazza San Marco. Procurators were high-level magistrates or administrators
ridotto	an establishment used exclusively for gambling
rio terrà	(also *terà*), an old canal, filled in, and now a paved street
riva	a street flanking a canal
Schiavoni	the name given to people originally from Dalmatia (Slavs)

scuola	the great building of a lay brotherhood or confraternity, which played a central role in charity and patronage of the arts. Fifteenth-century Venice had six *scuole grandi* (great schools) – San Marco, San Rocco, San Teodoro, San Giovanni Evangelista, Misericordia, Santa Maria della Carità (now the Accademia) – and about 400 *scuole minori* or *consorterie*
Serenissima	name given by the Venetians to Venice, the Most Serene Republic
sestieri	the six districts of Venice: San Marco, Cannaregio, Castello, Dorsoduro, San Polo, Santa Croce
sigisbée	public formal escort and sometimes acknowledged extramarital lover of a noble lady (also known as *cicerone*)
Sposalizio del Mare	the ceremonial marriage of the doge of Venice to the sea, still performed annually by the mayor of Venice at the feast of the Ascension (generally known as La Sensa)
squero	gondola and small boat repair workshop
strapado	one of the most unpleasant public punishments, a type of torture
traghetto	gondola adapted for public use, steered by two gondoliers, ferrying passengers across the Grand Canal
vaporetto	water bus
veduta	view, name given to painting of cityscapes or street scenes
zoccoli	chopines, shoes with often extravagantly raised soles

PEOPLE AND THEIR
VENETIAN LOCATIONS

The numbering system in the six *sestieri* allows visitors to find the building.

Pedro Antonio de Alarcón y Ariza (1833–91): Hotel de l'Europe, Palazzo Giustinian, San Marco 1364 Calle del Ridotto

Isabella Teotochi Albrizzi (1760–1836): Palazzo Albrizzi, San Polo 1940 Campiello Albrizzi

Francesco Algarotti (1712–64): Palazzo Algarotti-Corniani, Cannaregio 5356 Calle larga dei Boteri

Dante Alighieri (1265–1321): Guest of Doge Giovanni Soranzo at Palazzo Soranzo, San Polo 2169–2171 Campo San Polo

Hans Christian Andersen (1805–75): Albergo Luna (now Baglioni Hotel Luna), San Marco 1243 Calle Larga dell'Ascensione; Hotel Danieli, Castello 4196 Riva degli Schiavoni

Gabriele D'Annunzio (1863–1938): Casetta Rossa, San Marco 2709 Calle del Tagliapietra

Louis Aragon (1897–1982): Palazzo Vendramin ai Carmini, Dorsoduro 3462 Fondamenta Foscarini

Pietro Aretino (1492–1556): Palazzo Bollani, Cannaregio 5662 Campiello Riccardo Selvatico; Ca' Dandolo, San Marco 4168 Riva del Carbon

Giorgio Baffo (1694–1768): Palazzo Bellavite-Soranzo, San Marco 2760 Campo San Maurizio

Maurice Barrès (1862–1923): Hotel de l'Europe, Palazzo Giustinian, San Marco 1364 Calle del Ridotto; Hotel Danieli, Castello 4196 Riva degli Schiavoni

William Beckford (1760–1844): Al Leone Bianco (Ca' da Mosto), Cannaregio 5637 Corte del Leone Bianco

Pietro Bembo (1470–1547): Palazzo Bembo, San Marco 4785 Riva del Carbon; Palazzo Camerini, 59 via Altinate Padova (Museo della Terza Armata)

Marina Querini Benzon (1757–1839): Palazzo Benzon, San Marco 3927 Calle Pesaro

François Joachim de Bernis (1715–94): Palazzo Surian-Bellotto, Cannaregio 967–975 Fondamenta di Cannaregio

Alexander Blok (1880–1921): Lido (address not identified)

Giovanni Boccaccio (1313–75): probably a guest of Petrarch

Napoleon Bonaparte (1769–1821): Villa Manin, (Passariano in Friuli); Palazzo Pisani-Moretta, San Polo 2766; Villa Pisani, (Stra in the Veneto); Procuratie Nuove (during construction of Palazzo Reale), San Marco 52 Ala Napoleonica (now Correr Museum)

Josef Brodsky (1940–96): Fondamenta degli Incurabili, Dorsoduro 417 Zattere; Pensione Accademia, Dorsoduro 1058; Fondamenta Bollani Palazzo Marcello, San Marco 3666 Fondamenta della Verona

Charles de Brosses (1709–77): probably Al Leone Bianco (Ca' da Mosto), Cannaregio 5637 Corte del Leone Bianco; possibly Lo Scudo di Francia (now gone), San Marco 4168 Riva del Carbon

Horatio Forbes Brown (1854–1926): Ca' Torresella, Dorsoduro 560 Campiello drio degli Incurabili

Rawdon Brown (1806–83): Ca' Dario, Dorsoduro 352–353 Ramo Barbaro; Ca' Giustinian-Businello, San Polo 1207 Fondamente Businello; Ca' Gussoni-Grimani della Vida, Cannaregio 2277 Calle Minio

Robert Browning (1812–89): Ca' Alvisi (now Palazzo Michiel Alvisi), next to Hotel Europa & Regina, San Marco 2159; Corte Barozzi Ca' Rezzonico, Dorsoduro 1336 Fondamenta Rezzonico

Commissario Brunetti (Donna Leon's fictional detective): Palazzo Ziani (Commissariato), Castello 5053 Fondamenta San Lorenzo; San Polo Calle Tiepolo

Olga Levi Brunner (1885–1961): see **Ugo Levi**.

Valeri Bryusov (1873–1924): unidentified hotel in Calle Valleresso

Charles Burney (1726–1814): Lo Scudo di Francia, San Marco 4168 Riva del Carbon

George Gordon, Lord Byron (1788–1824): Casa Segati, San Marco 1676 Frezzeria; Palazzo Mocenigo, San Marco 3348 Calle Mocenigo; Palazzo Priuli-Venier-Manfrin, Cannaregio 342–343 Fondamenta Savorgnan

Bianca Cappello (1548–87): Palazzo Cappello, Castello 6391 Ponte Storto

Giacomo Casanova, Chevalier de Seingalt (1725–98): San Marco 3282 Calle Malipiero; Palazzo Bragadin, Castello 6050 Ramo Bragadin; Piombi, the prison in the Doge's Palace

Luisa Casati (1881–1957): Palazzo Venier dei Leoni, Dorsoduro 701 Calle San Cristoforo

François-René de Chateaubriand (1768–1848): Al Leone Bianco (Ca' da Mosto), Cannaregio 5637 Corte del Leone Bianco; Hotel de l'Europe, Palazzo Giustinian, San Marco 1364 Calle del Ridotto

Anton Pavlovich Chekhov (1860–1904): Hotel Bauer, San Marco 1459 Campo San Moisè

Jean Cocteau (1889–1963): Baglioni Hotel Luna, San Marco 1243 Calle larga dell'Ascensione; Hotel Westin Europa & Regina, San Marco 2159 Corte Barozzi; Hotel de l'Europe, Palazzo Giustinian, San Marco 1364 Calle del Ridotto; Hotel Bauer Grunwald, San Marco 1459 Campo San Moisè

Louise Colet (1810–76): Hotel Danieli, Castello 4196 Riva degli Schiavoni

Philippe de Commynes (1447–1511): San Giorgio Monastery

Thomas Coryat (1577–1617): unidentified building on Fondamenta San Girolamo, Cannaregio

Lorenzo Da Ponte (1749–1838): Campo San Luca (exact location uncertain); Palazzo Zaguri, San Marco 2631 Campo San Maurizio. Met Casanova at Palazzo Memmo-Martinengo, Cannaregio 1756 Fondamenta Martinengo

Dominique Vivant Denon (1747–1825): Locanda alla Regina d'Inghilterra (now gone), San Marco 1812 Ramo dei Fuseri

Sergei Diaghilev (1872–1929): Hotel des Bains, Lido Lungomare Marconi 17

Charles Dickens (1812–70): Hotel Danieli, Castello 4196 Riva degli Schiavoni

Albrecht Dürer (1471–1528): Fondaco dei Tedeschi, San Marco 5562 Salizada del Fondaco dei Tedeschi, Calle del Fontego

Eleonora Duse (1858–1924): Palazzo Barbaro-Volkoff, Dorsoduro 351 Ramo Barbaro

Sergei Esenin (1895–1925): Hotel Excelsior, Lido Lungomare Marconi 41

John Evelyn (1620–1706): Black Eagle Inn, Rialto (now gone)

Mariano Fortuny y Madrazo (1871–1949): Palazzo Martinengo, Dorsoduro 178 Calle del Traghetto San Gregorio; Ca' Pesaro degli Orfei, San Marco 3858 Campo San Beneto (now Fortuny Museum)

Ugo Foscolo (1778–1827): Castello 3224 Campo de le Gate

Théophile Gautier (1811–72): Hotel de l'Europe, Palazzo Giustinian, San Marco 1364 Calle del Ridotto

Johann Wolfgang von Goethe (1749–1832): Locanda alla Regina d'Inghilterra (now gone), San Marco 1812 Ramo dei Fuseri; Al Leone Bianco (Ca' da Mosto), Cannaregio 5637 Corte del Leone Bianco

Carlo Goldoni (1707–93): Palazzo Centani, San Polo 2793 Calle dei Nomboli (now Goldoni Museum)

Peggy Guggenheim (1898–1979): Palazzo Venier dei Leoni, Dorsoduro 701 Calle San Cristoforo (Guggenheim Museum)

Ernest Hemingway (1899–1961): Hotel Gritti, San Marco 2467 Campo Santa Maria del Giglio; Locanda Cipriani, Piazza Santa Fosca 29, Torcello

Henri III of France (1551–89): Ca' Foscari, Dorsoduro 3246 Calle Foscari; Palazzo Michiel, Cannaregio 2536 Fondamenta della Misericordia

Alexander Ivanovich Herzen (1812–70): Hotel Danieli, Castello 4196 Riva degli Schiavoni

Nicolas Amelot de La Houssaye (1634–1706): French Embassy, probably Palazzo della Vecchia (now gone), Cannaregio Fondamenta della Misericordia

William Dean Howells (1837–1920): Palazzo Falier-Canossa, San Marco 2904 Calle Falier; Palazzo Brandolini-Giustinian, Dorsoduro 3228–3232 Calle Giustinian

Henry James (1843–1916): Ca' Alvisi, now Palazzo Michiel Alvisi, San Marco 2207 Calle del Traghetto; Palazzo Barbaro, San Marco 2840 Fondamenta Barbaro (*The Wings of the Dove*); Palazzo Soranzo-Cappello, Santa Croce 770 Fondamenta Gradenigo (*The Aspern Papers*)

Franz Kafka (1883–1924): Hotel Sandwirth (now Gabrielli Sandwirth), Castello 4110 Riva degli Schiavoni

D. H. Lawrence (1885–1951): Ponte delle Maravegie, Dorsoduro 1061 Fondamenta Nani

Edward Lear (1812–88): Hotel de l'Europe, Palazzo Giustinian, San Marco 1364 Calle del Ridotto; Hotel Danieli, Castello 4196, Riva degli Schiavoni

Ugo Levi (1878–1971) and **Olga Levi Brunner** (1885–1961): Palazzo Giustinian-Lolin, San Marco 2893 Calle Giustinian (now Levi Foundation)

Ignatius of Loyola (1491–1556): Ospedale degli Incurabili di San Biagio, Giudecca (site of Molino Stucky)

Mary McCarthy (1912–89): Castello 5063 Campo San Lorenzo

Alma Mahler (1879–1964): Oltre il Giardino, San Polo 2542 Fondamenta Contarini

Thomas Mann (1875–1955): Hotel des Bains, Lido Lungomare Marconi 17

Tommaso Marinetti (1876–1944): Palazzo Bollani-Erizzo, Cannaregio 5662 Campiello Riccardo Selvatico

John Milton (1608–74): probably Palazzo Gussoni-Grimani della Vida, Cannaregio 2277 Calle Minio (formerly English Embassy)

Lady Mary Wortley Montagu (1689–1762): Palazzo Mocenigo, San Marco 3348 Calle Mocenigo

Michel Eyquem de Montaigne (1533–92): Palazzo Michiel (French Embassy), Cannaregio 2536 Fondamenta della Misericordia

José Joaquín Guzman de Montealegre (1698–1771): Palazzo Sceriman, Cannaregio 168–170 Lista di Spagna

Paul Morand (1888–1976): San Marco 2725 Fondamenta del Traghetto di San Maurizio; Hotel Bauer Grunwald, San Marco 1459 Campo San Moisè

Wolfgang Amadeus Mozart (1756–91): Ca' Falletti, San Marco 1864, next to Ponte dei Barcaroli

Alfred de Musset (1810–57): Hotel Danieli, Castello 4196 Riva degli Schiavoni

Friedrich Nietzsche (1844–1900): Palazzo Berlendis, Cannaregio 6296 Corte Berlendis

Anna de Noailles (1876–1933): Hotel Danieli, Castello 4196 Riva degli Schiavoni; Palazzo Contarini dal Zaffo (now Palazzo Contarini-Polignac), Dorsoduro 875 Calle Rota

Pietro Pagello (1807–98): Palazzo Minelli, San Marco 1878 Ramo Minelli Corte Minelli

Francesco Petrarca, Petrarch (1304–74): Palazzo Molino, Castello 4145 Riva degli Schiavoni

August von Platen (1796–1835): Locanda del Gallo (now gone), San Marco Campo San Paternian (now Campo Manin)

Ezra Pound (1885–1972): Dorsoduro 252 Calle Querini

Marcel Proust (1871–1922): Hotel Danieli, Castello 4196 Riva degli Schiavoni; Hotel de l'Europe, Palazzo Giustinian, San Marco 1364 Calle del Ridotto

Henri de Régnier (1864–1936) and **Marie de Régnier** (1875–1963): Ca' Dario, Dorsoduro 352 Campiello Barbaro; Palazzo Carminati, Santa Croce 1882 Salizzada Carminati

Rainer Maria Rilke (1875–1926): Grand Hotel Britannia (now Hotel Westin Europa & Regina), San Marco 2159 Corte Barozzi; Palazzo

Valmarana, Dorsoduro 864 San Vio (now Giorgio Cini Foundation); Casa Romanelli, Dorsoduro 1471–1472 Zattere

Léopold Robert (1794–1835): Palazzo Pisani, San Marco 2809 Campo Santo Stefano (now Venice Conservatoire)

Frederick Rolfe (Baron Corvo) (1860– 1913): Hotel Bellevue et de Russie (now gone), San Marco 289 Piazzetta dei Leoncini; Trattoria Alboretti, Dorsoduro 884 Rio Terrà Antonio Foscarini; Palazzo Corner-Mocenigo, San Polo 2128 Campo San Polo; Hotel Cavaletto e Doge Orseolo, San Marco 1107 Bacino Orseolo; Palazzo Marcello, Cannaregio 2137 Corte Erizzo

Jean-Jacques Rousseau (1712–78): Palazzo Surian-Bellotto, Cannaregio 967–975 Fondamenta di Cannaregio

John Ruskin (1819–1900): Hotel Danieli, Castello 4196 Riva degli Schiavoni; Casa Welzlar (now Gritti Palace Hotel), San Marco 2466 Campo Santa Maria del Giglio; Palazzo Ferro Fini (then Grand Hotel, now HQ of Regione del Veneto), San Marco 2322 Ramo Secondo Minotto; Pensione La Calcina, Dorsoduro 781 Zattere ai Gesuati; Hotel de l'Europe, Palazzo Giustinian, San Marco 1364 Calle del Ridotto

George Sand (1804–76): Hotel Danieli, Castello 4196 Riva degli Schiavoni; Palazzo Minelli, San Marco 1878 Ramo Minelli Corte Minelli

Francesco Sansovino (1521–86): Procuratie Vecchie, San Marco (next to the Clock Tower)

Marino Sanudo (Sanuto) (1466–1536): Palazzo Sanudo, San Polo 1758 Fondamenta del Megio

John Singer Sargent (1856–1925): Palazzo Barbaro, San Marco 2840 Fondamenta Barbaro; Ca' Rezzonico, Dorsoduro 1336 Fondamenta Rezzonico

William Shakespeare (?1564–1616): (Desdemona's house) Palazzo Contarini-Fasan, San Marco 2307 Campiello Contarini

Percy Bysshe Shelley (1792–1822): Hotel de l'Europe, Palazzo Giustinian, San Marco 1364 Calle del Ridotto; Palazzo Mocenigo, San Marco 3348 Calle Mocenigo

Walter Richard Sickert (1860–1942): Dorsoduro 770 Calle dei Frati

Georges Simenon (1903–89): Grand Hotel Excelsior, Lido Lungomare Marconi 41; Gritti Palace Hotel, San Marco 2466 Campo Santa Maria del Giglio

Joseph Smith (1682–1770): Palazzo Mangili-Valmarana, Cannaregio 4392 Strada Nova

Anne-Louise Germain de Staël (1766–1817): Al Leone Bianco, (Ca' da Mosto), Cannaregio 5367 Campo Leone Bianco

Marie-Henri Beyle, better known as **Stendhal** (1783–1842): Hotel de l'Europe, Palazzo Giustinian, San Marco 1364 Calle del Ridotto; Locanda alla Regina d'Inghilterra, San Marco 1812 Ramo dei Fuseri

Igor Stravinsky (1882–1971): Hotel des Bains, Lido Lungomare Marconi 17; Hotel Bauer, San Marco 1459 Campo San Moisè; Palazzo Contarini-Polignac (formerly Palazzo Contarini dal Zaffo), Dorsoduro 875 Calle Rota

John Addington Symonds (1840–93): Ca' Torresella, Dorsoduro 560 Zattere Rio San Vio

Torquato Tasso (1554–95): Rio di Ca' Dolce, Cannaregio

Pyotr Ilyich Tchaikovsky (1840–93): Hotel Londra Palace, Castello 4171 Riva degli Schiavoni

Ivan Turgenev (1818–83): Hotel Danieli, Castello 4196 Riva degli Schiavoni

Joseph Mallord William Turner (1775–1851): Al Leone Bianco, (Ca' da Mosto), Cannaregio 5367 Campo Leone Bianco; Hotel de l'Europe, Palazzo Giustinian, San Marco 1364 Calle del Ridotto

Giuseppe Verdi (1813–1901): Hotel de l'Europe, Palazzo Giustinian, San Marco 1364 Calle del Ridotto; Palazzo Badoer-Tiepolo (Albergo Europa), San Marco 2161 Corte Barozzi

Antonio Vivaldi (1678–1741): Castello 3805 or 3809 Campo Bandiera e Moro; Castello 5879 Fondamenta del Dose; San Marco 4644 Calle Bembo

Richard Wagner (1813–83): Palazzo Giustinian-Brandolin, San Marco 3228 Calle Giustinian; Hotel de l'Europe, Palazzo Giustinian, San Marco 1364 Calle del Ridotto; Palazzo Contarini delle Figure, San Marco 3327 Calle Mocenigo; Palazzo Vendramin-Calergi, Cannaregio 2040 Campiello Vendramin

Horace Walpole (1717–97): unidentified hotel in San Marco, probably Al Leone Bianco, (Ca' da Mosto), Cannaregio 5367 Campo Leone Bianco

Oscar Wilde (1854–1900): Hotel San Marco (now gone), Piazza San Marco Corte Ca' Maruzzi

Virginia Woolf (1882–1941): Palazzo Ferro-Fini (then Grand Hotel, now Regional Council of Venice), San Marco 2322 Ramo Secondo Minotto

Henry Wotton (1568–1639): Palazzo da Silva, Cannaregio 1469 Calle del Porton, Ponte dei Ormesini; Palazzo Gussoni-Grimani della Vida, Cannaregio 2277 Calle Minio

CHRONOLOGY

	Literary and Cultural Events	*Political Events*
421		Supposed foundation of Venice.
639		First settlement on Torcello.
727		Election of first doge.
810		Venice prevails against attack by Pepin, son of Charles the Great.
812–14		Doge's Palace moves to Rialto (Rivo Alto).
828		Body of Mark brought to Venice.
1000	First celebration of La Sensa.	Venice extends territory into Dalmatia.
1003	Church built to house remains of St Mark.	
1202–4		Fourth Crusade; Four Horses brought to Venice after sacking of Constantinople.
1222–4	St Francis in Venice on return from Crusades.	
1278		Adriatic shaken by major earthquake.
1297		Great Council determines that Venice becomes aristocratic.

	Literary and Cultural Events	Political Events
1310		Baiamonte Tiepolo attempts to topple the government, leading to formation of Council of Ten.
1321	Dante in Venice.	
1355		Doge Marin Falier deposed and beheaded.
1362	Petrarch settles in Venice.	
1363	Boccacio visits Petrarch in Venice.	
1364		Cypriot (Candian) rebellion put down; Petrarch attends celebratory feast in Venice.
1430	Presumed date of birth of Giovanni Bellini.	
1453		Constantinople falls to the Turks; Venice no longer dominant in the Levant.
1456		Jacopo Foscari (son of Doge) exiled to Cyprus; father subsequently deposed.
1472	First Venetian printing press set up by Filippo di Pietro.	
1477	Giorgione born.	
1489		Caterina Cornaro, widow of James II of Cyprus abdicates; Venice formally annexes the island.
1490	Presumed date of birth of Titian; Manutius founds Aldine Press.	
1492		Columbus reaches America.
1494		France sends Philippe de Commynes as ambassador to Venice.

	Literary and Cultural Events	Political Events
1505	First documented visit of Albrecht Dürer to Venice.	
1508		League of Cambrai formed; much of Europe against Venice.
1516		First ever Ghetto created in Venice for Jews.
1519	Presumed date of birth of Tintoretto.	Charles V becomes Holy Roman Emperor.
1523	Ignatius of Loyola arrives in Venice.	
1525	Bembo proposes that poetry be written in Italian.	
1527	Jacopo Sansovino starts work in Venice.	Sack of Rome by armies of Charles V.
1550	Vasari's *Lives of the Artists* published.	
1570	Palladio's *Four Books of Architecture* published.	
1571		Battle of Lepanto.
1576	Doge Alvise Mocenigo authorises building of Redentore.	
1578	Bernardo and Torquato Tasso arrive in Venice.	
1580	Montaigne arrives in Venice.	
1588	Construction of Rialto Bridge starts; completed in three years.	
1596	Shakespeare writes *The Merchant of Venice*.	
1603	Shakespeare writes *Othello*.	James I succeeds Elizabeth I of England.

	Literary and Cultural Events	Political Events
1604		Henry Wotton's first diplomatic mission; papal condemnation of Protestant prayerbook in Venice.
1606		Jesuits expelled from Venice until 1657.
1608	Thomas Coryat in Venice.	
1612	Prince Henry of England dies.	
1618		Bedmar Plot in Venice.
1629	First visit of Velázquez to Venice.	
1639	John Milton in Venice.	
1645	John Evelyn visits Venice.	
1685		Revocation of the Edict of Nantes.
1687	F. M. Misson in Venice.	
1688	*Journey to Italy* published.	
1703	Vivaldi appointed to teach at the Pietà.	
1728	Montesquieu in Venice.	
1729	Disgraced banker John Law dies in Venice.	
1739	Charles de Brosses in Venice.	
1739	Lady Mary Wortley Montagu arrives in Venice.	
1741	Horace Walpole's Grand Tour.	
1743		Rousseau in Venice as secretary to the French ambassador.

	Literary and Cultural Events	*Political Events*
1744		Joseph Smith appointed consul in Venice.
1749		Spanish ambassador Montealegre starts lifetime service in Venice.
1755		Casanova imprisoned; escapes nine months later.
1762	Goldoni leaves Venice for Paris.	
1769	Lalande's *Voyage d'un Français en Italie* published.	
1770	Charles Burney in Venice.	
1771	Mozart in Venice.	
1780, 1782	William Beckford's visits to Venice.	
1786	Goethe's first visit to Venice; Mozart writes *Marriage of Figaro*.	
1787	Mozart writes *Don Giovanni*.	
1789–93		French Revolution.
1797	*Marriage at Cana* by Veronese plundered and taken to Paris.	Venetian Republic falls to Bonaparte's French army.
1805–14	Vivant Denon appointed by Napoleon to select artworks.	Venice occupied by Napoleon.
1807		Napoleon enters Venice as emperor; 'Ten Days' in December.
1815–66		Venice under Austrian rule.
1816	Byron arrives in Venice.	
1818	Shelley joins Byron in Venice.	

	Literary and Cultural Events	*Political Events*
1824	First of von Platen's visits to Venice.	
1833	Alfred de Musset and George Sand at the Danieli.	
1844	Dickens in Venice in November.	
1846		Railway link to mainland completed.
1848		Manin leads unsuccessful attempt to expel Austrians.
1849	First visit to Venice of John and Effie Ruskin.	
1851–3	Ruskin publishes *Stones of Venice* in three volumes.	
1858	Richard Wagner first travels to Venice.	
1866–7		Unification of Venice with Kingdom of Italy.
1869	Henry James's first visit to Venice.	
1883	Statue of Goldoni erected in Campo San Bartolomeo.	
1887	Verdi's *Otello* completed; D'Annunzio comes to Venice.	
1888	Browning's son Pen buys Ca' Rezzonico.	
1895	First Art Biennale opened in April.	
1897	Rilke arrives in Venice.	
1900	Grand Hotel des Bains on Lido completed; Marcel Proust in Venice.	

	Literary and Cultural Events	*Political Events*
1902	Collapse of Campanile on Piazza San Marco.	
1910	Marinetti writes his manifesto.	
1912	Thomas Mann writes *Death in Venice*.	
1914–18		First World War.
1915		Bombardment of Santa Maria di Nazareth (Scalzi).
1920	D. H. Lawrence in Venice.	
1922	Alma Mahler resident in Venice to 1935.	Mussolini comes to power.
1931	Harry's Bar opened by Cipriani.	
1939–45		Second World War.
1945		Venice liberated from German occupation by Allied troops.
1948	Peggy Guggenheim buys Palazzo Venier dei Leoni; Hemingway in Venice.	
1966		Greatest flood in Italian history; Venice submerged by Adriatic.
1973	Benjamin Britten's *Death in Venice* performed at La Fenice.	
2007	Restored 1895 Molino Stucky opens as hotel.	
2008	Calatrava Bridge opens.	

FURTHER READING

The reader is directed in the text to primary sources or original works of fiction. The list here does not seek to be comprehensive, but to suggest works used as sources or for wider interest. Works of specific local interest published in Italian or French are included.

Aretino, Pietro, *Aretino, Selected Letters*, trans. George Bull, London, Penguin Books, 1976.

Baffo, Giorgio, *Poesie*, Milan, Mondadori, 1991.

Barker, John, *Wagner and Venice*, Rochester, NY, University of Rochester Press, 2008.

Barrès, Maurice, *Amori e dolori sacrum*, Paris, Juven, 1903.

Bassi, Shaul and Alberto Toso Fei, *Shakespeare in Venice*, Treviso, Elzeviro, 2007.

Beckford, William, *Italy with Sketches of Spain and Portugal*, London, Richard Bentley, 1834.

Berendt, John, *The City of Falling Angels*, New York, Penguin Press, 2005.

Bernis, Cardinal de, *Memoirs and Letters of Cardinal de Bernis*, Katherine Prescott Wormeley, Cambridge, MA, Hardy, Pratt, 1902.

Brodsky, Josef, *Watermark*, New York, Farrar, Straus & Giroux, 1992.

Brosses, Charles de, *Selections from the Letters of de Brosses*, London, Kegan Paul & Co., 1897.

Brown, Horatio F., *Venice, an Historical Sketch of the Republic*, London, Putnam, 1893.

—— *Symonds, John Addington, A Biography, Compiled from his Papers by Horatio Forbes Brown*, London, Smith, Elder & Co., 1903.

Burney, Charles, *Present State of Music in France and Italy*, London, Folio Society, 1969.

Calvino, Italo, *Invisible Cities*, trans. William Weaver, London, Vintage Classics, 2009.

Casanova, Jacques, Chevalier de Seingalt, *My Life and Adventures*, trans. Arthur Machen, London, Joiner & Steele, 1932.

Chambers, D. and B. Pullan, *Venice: A Documentary History 1450–1630*, Toronto, University of Toronto Press, 2001.

Clegg, Jeanne, *Ruskin and Venice*, London, Junction Books, 1981.

Colet, Louise, *L'Italie des italiens*, Paris, E. Dentu Libraire, 1863.

Collier, Peter, *Proust and Venice*, Cambridge, Cambridge University Press, 2005.

Comisso, Giovanni, *Agenti segreti di Venezia (1705–1797)*, Milan, Longanesi & Co., 1984.

—— *Les ambassadeurs vénitiens*, Paris, Gallimard, 2002.

Cook, E. T. and A. Wedderburn (eds), *The Works of John Ruskin*, London, George Allen, 1903–12.

Cooper, James Fenimore, *The Bravo*, New York, W. A. Townsend and Company, 1859.

Coryat, Thomas, *Coryat's Crudities: Hastily Gobbled Up in Five Months Travels*, Glasgow, James MacLehose and Sons, 1905.

Curzon, Gerald, *Wotton and his World: Spying, Science and Venetian Intrigues*, xlibris, 2004.

Debray, Régis, *Against Venice*, trans. John Howe, London, Pushkin Press, 1998.

Dickens, Charles, *The Letters of Charles Dickens*, London, Chapman & Hall, 1880.

Dowling, G., *In Venice and the Veneto with Lord Byron*, Venice, Supernova, 2008.

Dürer, Albrecht, *Lettere da Venezia*, Venice, Electa, 2007.

Foscolo, Ugo, *Last Letters of Jacopo Ortis*, trans. J. G. Nichols, London, Hesperus, 2002.

Fournoux, Amable de, *Napoléon et Venise 1797–1814*, Paris, Editions de Fallois, 2002.

Gemmett, Robert J. (ed.), *Dreams, Waking Thoughts and Incidents*, Stroud, Nonsuch, 2006.

Giono, Jean, *Voyage en Italie*, Paris, Gallimard, 1984.

Goethe, J. W. von, *Italian Journey, 1786–1788*, trans. W. H. Auden and E. Mayer, London, Penguin, 1982.

Haskell, Francis, *Patrons and Painters*, London, Harper & Row, 1963.

Herzen, Alexander, *My Past and Thoughts*, trans. Constance Garnett, London, Chatto & Windus, 1924.

Hewison, R., *Ruskin and Venice*, London, Thames and Hudson, 1978.

Howells, William Dean, *Italian Journeys*, London, I.B.Tauris & Co. Ltd, 2011.

—— *Vita veneziana*, Treviso, Elzeviro, 2005.

Ivancich, Adriana, *La torre bianca*, Milan, Mondadori, 1980.

Levey, Michael, *Painting in Eighteenth-Century Venice*, London, Phaidon, 1980.

Lovric, Michelle, *Venice: Tales of the City*, London, Abacus, 2005.

Loyola, Ignatius de, *A Pilgrim's Journey*, trans. Joseph N. Tylenda, San Francisco, Ignatius Press, 2001.

Lutyens, Mary (ed.), *Effie in Venice*, London, John Murray, 1965.

McBrien, William, *Cole Porter*, New York, Vintage, 2011.

McCarthy, Mary, *Venice Observed*, London, Penguin, 1956.

Massine, Leonid, *My Life in Ballet*, London, St Martin's Press, 1968.

Meneghetti, N., *Lord Byron a Venezia*, Venice, G. Fabbris di S., 1910.

Molmenti, Pompeo, *Venice: An Individual Growth from the Earliest Beginnings to the Fall of the Republic*, trans. Horatio F. Brown, London, J. Murray, 1906.

Montgomery, Michael, *Lear's Italy: In the Footsteps of Edward Lear*, London, Cadogan Guides, 2005.

Moore, Thomas, *Letters and Journals of Lord Byron*, London, Murray, 1931.

Morand, Paul, *Venices*, trans. Euan Cameron, London, Pushkin Press, 2012.

Morris, James, *Venice*, London, Faber & Faber, 1983.

Newett, Margaret, *Canon Pietro Casola's Pilgrimage to Jerusalem in the Year 1494*, Manchester, Manchester University Press, 1907.

Patanè, Vincenzo, *Il mito di Lord Byron*, Venice, Cicero Editore, 2013.

Pearsall Smith, Logan, *Life and Letters of Henry Wotton*, Oxford, Clarendon Press, 1907.

Pivano, Fernanda, *Hemingway*, Milan, Rusconi, 1985.

Plant, Margaret, *Venice: Fragile City 1797–1997*, New Haven, CT, Yale University Press, 2002.

Ponte, Lorenzo Da, *Memoirs of Lorenzo Da Ponte, Mozart's Librettist*, trans. Elizabeth Abbott, New York, J. B. Lippincott, 1929.

Pound, Ezra, *A Lume Spento and Other Early Poems*, London, Faber & Faber, 1965.

Quill, Sarah, *Ruskin's Venice*, Aldershot, Ashgate, 2000

Redford, Bruce, *Venice and the Grand Tour*, New Haven, CT, Yale University Press, 1996.

Rilke, Rainer Maria, *Duino Elegies*, trans. Stephen Cohn, Manchester, Carcanet Press, 1989.

Rolfe, Frederick (Baron Corvo), *The Desire and the Pursuit of the Whole*, London, Cassell, 1934.

Ruskin, John, *The Diaries of John Ruskin*, ed. J. Evans and J. H. Whitehouse, Oxford, Clarendon Press, 1956.

—— *The Stones of Venice*, ed. J. G. Links, London, Da Capo Press, 2003.

Saikia, Robin, *The Venice Lido*, London, Somerset Books, 2011.

Sanudo, Marino, *I diarii di Marino Sanuto*, ed. R. Fulin et al., Venice, F. Visentini, 1903.

Smith, Francis Hopkinson, *Gondola Days*, London, Bruce Rogers, 1897.

Stendhal, Marie Henri Beyle, *Rome, Naples and Florence*, trans. Richard N. Coe, London, John Calder, 1959.

Stokes, Adrian, *Venice, An Aspect of Art*, London, Faber & Faber, 1945.

Symonds, John Addington, *Letters,* ed. H. M.Schneller and R. L. Peters, Detroit, Wayne State University Press, 1967.

Symons, A. J. A., *The Quest for Corvo*, London, Cassell, 1934.

Tassini, Giuseppe, *Curiosità veneziane*, Venice, Filippi Editore, 1990.

Vasari, Giorgio, *Lives of the Artists*, Oxford, Oxford University Press, 1991.

Vivian, Frances, *Il Console Smith,* Vicenza, Neri Pozza Editore, 1971.

Volkov-Mouromtzoff, Alexander, *Memoirs*, London, John Murray, 1928.

Wagner, Richard, *My Life*, trans. Andrew Gray, ed. Mary Whittall, Cambridge, Cambridge University Press, 1983.

Walpole, Horace, *The Letters of Horace Walpole*, ed. W. S. Lewis, London, Yale University Press, 1937–81.

Wharton, Edith, *Italian Backgrounds*, London, Macmillan, 1905.

Whittaker, David (ed.), *Most Glorious and Peerless Venice: Observation of Thomas Coryat (1608)*, Charlbury, Wavestone Press, 2013.

Wilde, Oscar, *Complete Works of O.W.*, London, Collins, 1948.

Winterson, Jeanette, *The Passion*, London, Vintage, 2001.

Wortley Montagu, Lady Mary, *The Letters and Works of Lady Mary Wortley Montagu*, London, Bickers, 1861.

Wotton, Sir Henry, *Letters and Dispatches from Sir Henry Wotton to James the First*, London, W. Nicol, Shakespeare Press, 1850.

Wu Ming, *Altai*, London, Verso, 2013.

Zorzi, Rosella Mamoli, (ed.), *Letters from Palazzo Barbaro*, trans. Shaun Whiteside, London, Pushkin Press, 1998.

—— *Gondola Days*, Venice, Edizioni della Laguna, 2004.

—— (ed.), *In Venice and in the Veneto with Henry James*, Venice, Supernova, 2005.

Zorzi, Rosella Mamoli and Gianni Moriani, *Il Veneto di Hemingway* (bilingual exhibition catalogue), Venice, Antiga Edizioni, 2011.

Some Walking Guides

Douglas, Hugh A, *Venice on Foot*, London, Methuen & Co., 1907.

Freely, John, *Strolling Through Venice*, London, Tauris Parke Paperbacks, 2008.

Goy, Richard J., *Venice: An Architectural Guide*, New Haven, CT, Yale University Press, 2010.

Honour, Hugh, *The Companion Guide to Venice*, Woodbridge, Boydell & Brewer Ltd, 2001.

Jonglez, Thomas, *Secret Venice*, Versailles, Editions Jonglez, 2010.

Links, Joseph G., *Venice for Pleasure*, London, Bodley Head, 1979.

Lorenzetti, Giulio, *Venice and its Lagoon*, trans. John Guthrie, Trieste, Lint, 1975.

Norwich, John Julius, *Venice: A Traveller's Companion*, London, Constable & Robinson, 1990.

Suggested Further Reading on Venetian History

Ackroyd, Peter, *Venice, Pure City*, London, Vintage, 2010.

Fenlon, Iain, *Piazza San Marco*, London, Profile Books, 2009.

Horodowich, Elizabeth, *A Brief History of Venice*, London, Constable & Robinson, 2009.

Lane, Frederic C., *Venice, a Maritime Republic*, Baltimore, MD, Johns Hopkins University Press, 1973.

Morris, Jan, *Venice*, London, Faber & Faber, 1960.

—— *The Venetian Empire: A Sea Voyage*, London, Penguin, 1990.

Norwich, John Julius, *Venice, the Rise to Empire*, London, Allen Lane, 1977.

—— *History of Venice*, New York, Random House, 1989.

—— *A Traveller's Companion to Venice*, London, Constable & Co., 1990.

—— *Paradise of Cities*, London, Penguin, 2004.

Zorzi, Alvise, *Venice, 697–1797: A City, a Republic, an Empire*, Woodstock, NY, Overlook Press, 2001.

INDEX